ELEMENTS OF URBAN FORM

OF URBAN FORM George Banz

McGRAW-HILL BOOK COMPANY

New York   St. Louis   San Francisco
Dusseldorf   London
Mexico   Panama
Sydney   Toronto

Sponsoring Editor   William G. Salo
Director of Production   Stephen J. Boldish
Designer   Naomi Auerbach
Editing Supervisors   Susan Aiken/Laura Adler
Editing and Production Staff   Gretlyn Blau,
   Carol Ferrari, Teresa F. Leaden, George E. Oechsner

ELEMENTS OF URBAN FORM

03637

1234567890   HDBP   7543210

PREFACE

Powerful indeed is the empire of habit. Guided by habit, we continue to visualize our cities as embedded in nature long after nature has been in fact surrounded by the urban environment. We persist in thinking in terms of local communities and neighborhoods even while our families, our friends, and acquaintances live miles and often continents apart. We begin to realize that, in expanding the cities, the scale of our intervention in the natural environment has led to gradual changes in the climate; but we have yet to draw the logical conclusion that we could exercise a measure of local climate control through urban design. In locating highways, bridges, and buildings, we create boundaries of urban space, but we fail to relate these directly to human needs.

In short, the controls that are meant to guide urban development are tied to obsolete facts and obsolete concepts and are inadequate to cope either with the forces that shape urban growth or with the problems created in their wake. But to arrive at new concepts, our thinking about familiar phenomena must be redirected along new paths. Treasured bits of conventional wisdom may have to be discarded in the process, convenient thought categories sacrificed, and accustomed planning and design tools scrapped. This book represents an attempt to restructure the set of problems that relate to urban development and to help rechannel the thought processes responsible for the direction of such development.

However, the restructuring of a problem moves its elements out of focus. When we shift our point of view and examine familiar aspects of urban development in terms of basic human needs instead of the needs of the industrial production apparatus, in terms of constraints imposed by the limits of global resources instead of those imposed by conventional wisdom, and in terms of inherent contradictions and conflicts instead of isolated problems to be solved one by one, we find that conditions and relationships which appeared clear become obscure and confused.

Much of the book is thus devoted to placing familiar fragments of urban planning and design theory in a new focus and to relating them in the process both to man's individual and collective needs and to the limitations nature imposes on his quests. But needs and constraints prove not to be neat categories. Collective needs may constrain the freedom to satisfy individual needs, just as individual acts may obstruct collective aims. This conflict becomes pronounced when the concept of form determinants is expanded to admit the notion of an individual will to form that may, and often does, dominate functional considerations, and again when the time factor and its role in transforming needs into constraints are examined.

The analysis of urban form determinants in terms of individual and collective human needs on the one hand and natural constraints and conflicts between needs on the other is but one of many possible approaches to a closer understanding of urban phenomena. Any number of ordering principles might serve the purpose of analysis equally well. Analysis, however, is only a preliminary step in any program that envisages actual urban renewal. The conceptual structure presented in the early parts of the book thus finds its justification in the final chapter. What was conceived as an analytical tool proves to be applicable as an urban planning and design method. Moreover, the method that results is essentially a systems approach to urban problems that permits the application of computers to planning as well as to design tasks, and at every scale of the urban habitat.

When computers are applied to the determination of the physical features of the human environment, formerly creative functions may have to be delegated to artificial intelligence. And the myths that surround computers have made it necessary to clearly delineate their usefulness in the urban design and planning processes. Throughout the book, therefore, references are made to the new potential which computers introduce into such processes. Yet, now as always, the quality of the urban environment is defined essentially by the people that bring it to life, the structures they build and inhabit, the artifacts they create and use, and the elements of nature that animate their habitat. By itself, the application of the systems approach and computers contributes nothing to the enrichment of urban life. In the wrong hands these tools can indeed spell disaster for the human habitat. But the scale of urban problems has become such that any one individual's sensibilities can no longer cope with the dynamics inherent in urban growth, with the result that large-scale construction everywhere has become inhuman in conception regardless of the good intention and the undoubted ability of the planners and architects involved. Unless one is prepared to accept the deliberate demise of technology and a universal return to preindustrial conditions as a real possibility, the prospect of mastering the machine in all its manifestations with the help of computers remains the only hope of retaining human values in an urban environment that gradually envelops the globe. Technology may have become simply too strong to be brought back under direct human control. But by investing technology with artificial intelligence, its progress may be redirected if its "brain" is kept accessible to human manipulation. The method proposed to maintain such "thought control" is the submitting of planning and design processes to the systems approach.

Problems of urban planning and design have traditionally been treated as isolated incidents. By contrast, the systems approach promises an opportunity to see every such problem in terms of the whole urban environment. Urban growth, for example, will thus no longer appear to pose problems of simple addition, but will have to be faced as a phenomenon that inevitably causes the quality of every aspect of the existing habitat to change.

The modern city emerged from traditional containment with the advent of heavy industry. Industry, then transportation, and now communications, have been the functions that in turn dominated the urban environment. Yet in contrast to industry and transportation, communications functions are not directly tied to specific urban artifacts. Neither face-to-face contact nor communication over electronic media is closely related to any one place in the urban habitat; the functional links that used to tie individuals to specific places are disappearing.

There can be no question that the release of man from local bonds is having profound effects on his relations to the environment. Unfortunately, up-to-date psychological and sociological research into many of the questions touched on in the book's discourse is at best fragmentary and often nonexistent. Lying entirely outside or between established academic disciplines, urban development and urban form probably represent some of the largest unresearched areas of knowledge. Rather than take the safe course and ignore realms uncharted by science, I have chosen to present informed conjecture where compelling scientific evidence is lacking. Many parts thus rely heavily on the work of Marshall McLuhan, Jacques Ellul, Norman O. Brown, and others in assessing contemporary trends and their effects on the urban environment. To the extent that they can be considered a science at all, urban planning and design are an empirical science and must be, to quote Freud, "gladly content with nebulous, scarcely imaginable conceptions, which it hopes to apprehend more clearly in the course of its development, or which it is even prepared to replace with others."[1]

Sigfried Giedion has compared the pattern of human life to a weave whose threads, leading from the past, are interwoven with others in the present and continue unseen into the future. This analogy, suitably expanded and elaborated, could represent the pattern of urban life. The present book attempts to offer an overview of this pattern. Threads that appear on the surface are related to each other before they disappear again into the maze of the infinitely complex fabric of life. Patterns become discernible in the process, and the temptation to assume their future recurrence is sometimes irrepressible. But it is well to remember that the fabric has been seen from a single point of view. Other glimpses may yield different patterns, and those who pick up the individual threads and patiently follow them into the depths of the fabric will in turn have to explore to what extent the surface reflects the underlying pattern.

George Banz

---

[1] Sigmund Freud, *Collected Papers*, 5 vols. International Psycho-analytical Press, New York, 1924–1950, vol. IV, p. 34.

ACKNOWLEDGMENTS

This book grew out of a study of the applicability of computers to the design of multiple housing, undertaken in 1965 and made possible through a Research Grant by the Central Mortgage and Housing Corporation in Ottawa. This corporation again supported the completion of this book by awarding me a Study Grant, which freed me from the day-to-day demands of my practice during a crucial period. My first thanks thus go to the CMHC and its Advisory Board, in particular to Mr. Humphrey Carver and to Mr. Andrew Hazeland. I also am grateful to Mr. Alan Armstrong, the Executive Officer of the Canadian Council on Urban and Regional Research, who from the very start encouraged me to follow the direction of research I had chosen.

In addition, I am greatly indebted to Mr. Hans Blumenfeld who kindly agreed to read the manuscript and whose comments proved invaluable in completing subsequent drafts. Many of the ideas developed in the book originated in discussions with Mr. Hans Elte as well as with staff and students at the University of Toronto, in particular Prof. Ronald Whiteley of the Department of Architecture and Prof. Leslie Mezei of the Department of Computer Science.

Last but by no means least, I wish to express my thanks to my wife, both for encouraging me to write the book and for her help in editing the manuscript, and to Mrs. Marilynn Forbes who competently and efficiently typed one draft of the book after another.

George Banz

CONTENTS

Preface   v

CHAPTER ONE   COMMUNITY AND HABITAT   2

COMMUNITY AND ENVIRONMENT 3
The City in Nature 3
  Artifact in Nature—The Traditional City   3
  Artificial Habitat—The Modern City   5
Man and City   7
  The Traditional Urban Community   7
  The Urban Multicommunity   8
COMMUNITY AND TECHNOLOGY   10
Basic Communities and Basic Communications 10
  Community and Communication   10
  Community and Space   11
  Natural Limits of Communities   12
The Extended Community   13
  Transportation: Extended Physical Space   13
  Electronic Media: Global Space Awareness   14
The Extended Environment   16
  Plug-in Communities   16
  Man Lost in Space   18

URBAN CYBERNETICS   19
Environmental Feedback   19
  Channels of Urban Communications   19
  Jumbled Channels and Clashing Media   20
  Checks and Balances   21
  Control through Design   23

CHAPTER TWO   # INDIVIDUAL AND COLLECTIVE NEEDS   24

BASIC SHELTER NEEDS   25
The Concept of Minimum Shelter   25
  Individual Survival   25
  Survival of the Family   26
  Survival of the Community   27
The Conditions for Cultural Evolution   30
  Beyond the Hive   30
  Technology and Society   31
THE NEED FOR OPTIMUM SHELTER   31
Housing Unit, House, and Home   31
  The Optimum Dwelling   31
  Optimum Relations between Dwellings   33
Space Needs   35
  The Hierarchy of Urban Space   35
  Private Space   36
From Need to Demand   38
  Art and the Need for Stimulation   38
  Status and Its Symbols   40

CHAPTER THREE   # THE SOCIAL CONSTRAINTS   42

NEEDS AND CONSTRAINTS   43
Needs in Conflict   43
  The Conflicting Needs of Individuals   43
  Individual versus Society   45
  Conflicting Social Needs   46
Built-in Constraints   48
  Time and the Value Bias   48
  Establishments as Constraints   50
  Artifacts as Constraints   51
THE FORMS OF SOCIAL CONSTRAINTS   53
Traditions and Habits   53
  The Pall of Traditions   53
  The Price of Togetherness   54
  Problems of Mixed Urban Populations   55
Conventional Wisdom Codified   56
  Constraints as Stabilizers   56
  The Forms of Codification   58
  Guides and Straitjackets   60

CHAPTER FOUR THE PHYSICAL AND
ECONOMIC CONSTRAINTS 62

LAND AND ITS USES 63
Urban Land Resources 63
  The Uses of Land 63
  Population Densities 65
  Urban Land Values 66
Trends in the Uses of Land 69
  Trends and Their Extrapolation 69
  Variations and Alternatives 70
MATERIALS, ENERGY, AND TECHNIQUES 73
Stages of Production 73
  Basic Urban Shelter 73
  The Craft Stage of Building Production 74
  The Industrialization of Building 76
  The Prospect of Automation 78
Resources and Processes 78
  Raw Materials and Production 78
  Transportation 79
  Organization and Communication 80
The Human Element 81
  Aptitude and Labor 81
  Intelligence and Expertise 83
  Enterprise and Capital 84

CHAPTER FIVE FORM AND HABITAT 86

FROM FUNCTION TO FORM 87
The Evolution of Form 87
  The Sum of Functions 87
  Form as Function 88
The Determination of Form 91
  Form-determining Forces 91
  The Fit of Form 92
The Function of Form 95
  Communication through Form 95
  Feedback through Form 96
THE HIERARCHY OF FORM ELEMENTS 99
The Hierarchy of Scale 99
  Megascale 99
  Human Scale 101
The Hierarchy of Values 102
  Unit Form 102
  Collective Form 104

CHAPTER SIX   URBAN FORM, TIME,
                THE HUMAN WILL   110

THE GRIP OF THE PAST 111
Habitat and Tradition 111
    Roots and Ruts 111
    The Urban Mix 113
The Urban Time Continuum 114
    Rural Traditions in Urban Life 114
    Sense of Time and Sense of Place 117
CONSTRAINING THE FUTURE 118
The Future's Predictable Features 118
    Concurrent Stages of Urban Development 118
    Predictable Obsolescence 120
    Paths Blocked to Change 122
The Future beyond Prognosis 124
    Facing the Unknown 124
    Dreams, Visions, and Utopias 125

CHAPTER SEVEN   BEYOND THE STATUS QUO   128

SHIFTING CONSTRAINTS 129
Symptoms and Trends 129
    Glimpses of the Invisible 129
    The Urban Potential 130
Emerging Tools 132
    Communication and Transportation 132
    Methods and Materials 133
CHANGING NEEDS 136
The New Awareness 136
    Global Expectations 136
    Housing Urban Nomads 138
    Dissolving Boundaries and Dying Centers 140
Objectives and Integrities 141
    The Nature of Urban Activities 141
    Integrated Concepts 144

CHAPTER EIGHT   SYSTEMS APPROACH AND
                  COMPUTER APPLICATION   148

THE PROBLEM STRUCTURE 149
Coping with Urban Problems 149
    The Growth of Complexity 149
    Real and Conceptual Structures 151
    Dynamic Structures, Processes, and Systems 152
Urban Systems and the Systems Approach 154
    The Hierarchy of Systems 154

The Conceptual Macrosystem   155
The Systems Approach   156
From Systems to Form   159
THE SCOPE OF COMPUTER APPLICATION   159
Computer Uses   159
The Total Problem and Its Solution   159
Computers and Compartments   161
Process, Form, and Automation   162
The Computer's Terms   162
The Automated Design Process   166
The Limits of Design Automation   170
Beauty and the Brain   170
Aims and Priorities   173

References   177

Bibliography   183

Illustrations   189

Index   193

ELEMENTS OF URBAN FORM

CHAPTER ONE

COMMUNITY AND

HABITAT

COMMUNITY AND ENVIRONMENT
The City in Nature

*Sometimes when reading about nature's terrible visitations and
her massacre of the innocents, it seems to me that we are
surrounded by devouring, pitiless forces, that the earth was
full of anger, the sky dark with wrath, and that man had built
the city as a refuge from a hostile, nonhuman cosmos.*
Eric Hoffer, *The Temper of Our Time*

Artifact in Nature—The Traditional City. The urban habitat has traditionally been conceived for the privileged. To live in the early city was to be in the visible presence of the gods, was to be a member of a supercommunity. The walls of the city gave spiritual protection and at the same time sheltered the lives and possessions of its inhabitants. The resulting urban habitat, however, came to mean more than safety from enemy attack. It signified protection from extremes of climate; detachment from the soil; controlled continuity and predictability of daily life; and often maximum comfort for ruling elites, burghers, and merchants. To wrest a living from nature became increasingly a task performed exclusively by peasants and farmers, physically and mentally removed from the maturing urban centers. Thanks to trade or

figure 1 *The traditional city was a closed artifact beleaguered by untamed forces of nature that completely encircled it.*

extortion, the city's dependence on nature became indirect only; the direct link between community and nature was broken.

Where urban communities emerged, they did so in a distinctly hostile environment. This fact found its natural expression in the city's traditional image: a compact complex of buildings, spatially defined by walls and towers. The traditional city was an artifact in nature and in deliberate contrast to it. Its walls kept buildings in and nature out. (Figure 1.)

Nature threatening the early city was untamed. The weapons with which the individual could fight back were entirely inadequate even though man had mastered fire by this time and had learned to domesticate animals and plants. But mastery over nature could only be achieved through communal effort, and the early city was a primitive communal tool to control the natural environment. In times of peace and stability, it could be refined to include elaborate comfort control elements, such as the central heating systems and baths of Imperial Rome. In unsettled times the same tool was shaped to serve the needs of military defense. Always, however, one of the functions of the early city was to serve as a tool with whose help its inhabitants kept nature at bay.

What environmental control could be exercised was very much communal; even so, it was minimal by today's standards. For a long time urban life remained dominated by the forces and cycles of nature. Communal life was possible only during daylight; at night streets and squares were abandoned. The changing seasons similarly affected urban life, forcing on it, in many regions, periods of communal hibernation of varying duration in winter. Floods or drought might even spell the end for urban life in particularly hard-hit areas.

The proud citadels of traditional cities belied their almost complete dependence on the products of the surrounding countryside. It was this dependence which limited urban expansion to an overall size which could still be perceived as a physical entity. This same limitation, however, ensured accessibility of the open country to all city dwellers, permitting occasional relief from what must have been at times an oppressive crowding within the walls. If life within the walls had its drawbacks, they were, however, more than balanced by the feeling of security the city offered the enfolded community. In this respect today's megalopolis has little in common with the city of the past. Perhaps the closest modern man can come to experiencing this aspect of traditional urban life is on board an ocean liner, where a closed community is sheltered by a human artifact from the surrounding hostile nature.

Artificial Habitat—The Modern City.   One recurrent theme of all history is man's assumption of control over his natural environment. Only where nature was extremely hostile, as in the tropics, the deserts, or the arctic, has eventual human control ever been in doubt. If the basic outcome of man's fight for survival varied little, there were, however, great differences in the forms human control over nature took with different peoples, in different regions of the globe, and at different times in history. They ranged from techniques of adaptation to the forces of nature as perfected by Bushmen and Eskimo to attempts at their domination by man, typical of urban civilizations.

Again, among the urban civilizations, human attitudes toward nature differed greatly. The Maya, Aztecs, and ancient Chinese developed controls no more than adequate to secure the bases for their great cultures. It remained for our Western civilization to push the development of tools of domination over natural forces far beyond any conceivable communal needs.

In the process, nature has been made largely subservient not only to mankind's collective will, but also to that of every single individual who is increasingly in a position to personally control his immediate natural environment. Ceasing to be a threat, nature has been domesticated and, in docile form, introduced into the city. It has become a plaything, something to be enjoyed. To the urbanite, nature is lawns and parks and trees and golf courses and beaches. Acre by acre and region by region nature is being tamed and absorbed into the urban habitat. The parts which are not immediately suitable for enjoyment are used in other ways: waterways as sewage systems, lakes as waste depositories, ravines as garbage dumps. Highways prepare the land for urban consumption: first in the form of visual appreciation, and in later stages for the "extraction" of its real estate values.

It is easy to overlook the fact that there is no longer any adventure in the domination of natural forces. Urban expansion is part of bureaucratic routine; the submission of nature has become a technique. Mountains, for example, which can be viewed comfortably from above or scaled by cable car by today's traveler, were to Renaissance man objects to be sought and climbed "for the exaltation that comes from the conquest of distance and the attainment of a birdseye view."[1] (Figure 2.) By contrast, during the Middle Ages mountains were as a matter of course avoided "as mere terrifying obstacles that increase the hardship of travel."[2]

But then medieval man had unconquered nature at his doorstep, while today's urbanite must travel to even make contact with raw nature. That few take the trouble suggests that present attitudes toward nature are, in a way, closer to the attitudes of the Middle Ages than to those of later periods. The main difference is that nature, no longer feared, is allowed within the city to a greater extent than before. In the process the urban fabric has had to be loosened, but with the power and technique to cope with natural forces now in the hands of individuals, the tightly woven defense structures of earlier times have become obsolete in more than military terms.

The techniques which permitted this development were the same that led to the increasing interlinkage of cities on a global scale. Today it is possible to circle the globe, stopping over in urban centers located in every possible climatic zone, without regard for the day-night cycle and without ever leaving the climate-controlled, artificial environments of airplanes, trains, limousines, hotels, and restaurants for more than minutes at a time. The prospect of an urbanized globe has become real. The transition from the stage where the urban habitat fitted into an all-embracing natural habitat

figure 2 *Even remote mountaintops, reached in modern comfort, become a part of the urban environment.*

to one where fragments of nature must fit into an all-pervading urban habitat appears complete. Unfortunately, this trend has not been preceded by a clear understanding of man's psychological relation to nature. Nature continues to be treated as a resource that can be extracted in the name of technological progress, without regard for the possible danger that man's deliberate loss of contact with nature may lead to his eventual dehumanization.

Man and City

The Traditional Urban Community.   An environment that is made up solely of artifacts is dead. Adding elements of tamed nature does not substantially change this fact. However, as the urban shell becomes populated and a human environment is superimposed on the purely physical one, the concept of the urban environment emerges. It is both communal container and human content.

The assembly of artifacts such as houses, streets, canals, and fortifications to produce the physical form of a city depends on the mobilization of organized human effort, which in turn requires central direction and control. The nature of such control becomes a major determinant of the character of the particular urban environment. What Mumford calls the *megamachine*—"an invisible structure composed of living, but rigid, human parts, each assigned his special office, role or task"[3]—obviously cannot be expected to produce an environment easily adaptable to the expression of individual freedom. Equally, the crooked streets of medieval cities did not fit the aspirations of later emperors and dictators. The plans of cities cannot help but betray the aims and values of the communities for which they were conceived.

Before the advent of high-speed transportation and instant communication, first on a continental and then on a global scale, society was made up of relatively autonomous local communities. The basis for a community was physical proximity, and links between communities were loose. The traditional community was thus entirely place-related. This relation was expressed most clearly in the agricultural village where the obtainable yield from arable land limited the size and number of the family groups which added up to the community. The village bound its community to the soil, as the traditional house tied together the members of families over generations. The homogeneous village was primarily a community of physical life, "like one individual household in its necessary relation to the land."[4]

The urban community evolved from the loosening of man's direct ties to the soil, made possible through the organization and direct collaboration of large numbers of individuals with common aspirations and goals who thus formed a community of the mind. Proximity, however, necessarily increased with urbanization, and mutual contacts multiplied, resulting in a community of physical life with a vastly more complex structure than that of the agricultural village. It was only natural that this new complexity would find its eventual expression in the spatial arrangement of the urban shells. The dominant physical characteristic became the city wall, embracing the whole community. What better way to symbolize the closed community? (Figure 3.)

The successful expression of functions and aspirations within the urban community must have strengthened the very forces which resulted in urban forms in the first place. The act of building represents in itself an effort by an individual or a community to establish and preserve values. Thus, as the urban community found its fitting form, it became an institution. Form itself, particularly monumental form, became a dominant force in the stabilization and eventual ossification of the traditional urban social structure.

The Urban Multicommunity. In the traditional city, community of the mind and community of physical life were largely synonymous. As urban life spilled over its enclosing walls, however, this unity was lost. The organic whole of the traditional urban community became restructured into contractual relationships between members, and the concept of the urban society emerged. The citizen ceased to be a part of one all-embracing total community and became instead a unit in an abstract social system. Communities were reduced to the status of "recognizable sub-networks within the society," to use Toynbee's words.[5] It is as such subnetworks that communities have survived in the "underground" of the urban social system, while secondary, functional contacts, such as those of buyer-seller or reader-writer, have come to dominate urban communications.

Subcommunities have remained the framework within which urban man can find his personal identity. They have, however, little in common with the traditional community of the past into which the individual was born and to which he belonged for the rest of his life. Even in his immediate environment he now has the option of simultaneously joining any one of a vast number of potential communities, be they the neighborhood he chooses to live in, his place of work, his school, club, or church, or his circle of personal friends and acquaintances.

Urban subcommunities may be open or closed, organized formally or spontaneously; they may be place-related, or held together by any number of common interests. But the one thing they all have in common is that by their very nature they are specialized. Thus, any individual will belong to various subcommunities which he interlinks through his simultaneous membership. If this relationship is applied to a whole population, we arrive at the concept of the urban multicommunity, a multiple overlay of interlinked subcommunities. The dynamic multidimensional pattern of the interlinkage, how even and close it is, and the rate and characteristics of changes in the pattern, determine the nature of the multicommunity. The linkage

figure 3 *The traditional urban community tended to turn inward behind its protective walls.*

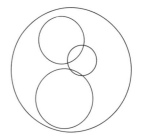

pattern reflects class structures and trends within society, the degree of centralization or diffusion of power, and the nature of the power structure, as well as the place of any one individual in the multicommunity. (Figure 4.)

While traditional communities found their appropriate expression in urban form, the modern multicommunity has so far evaded such positive definition. What formal structure there is reflects, in McLuhan's words, "literate man's analytic technology of fragmentation."[6] Suburban subdivisions and apartment blocks constitute the residential component of the urban environment. Central business districts and industrial zones form separate productive components, while minor functions are accommodated in "centers" of their own: shopping centers, cultural centers, health centers, etc. These physically separate fragments make up megalopolis. In contrast to earlier cities which functioned through their forms, the modern city obviously functions in spite of its lack of comprehensive form. The multicommunity is held together through the mobility of its members and through an intricate electronic communications network which is only loosely related to the physical structure of the city.

The direct links between subcommunities are thus supplemented by optional systems of communications which link individuals regardless of their status in subcommunities. But roads and electronic communications media have proved to be no substitute for direct personal contact. As Innes put it: "The printing press and the radio address the world instead of the individual."[7] Subcommunities linked to urban life exclusively through such

figure 4   (Above) *The traditional urban community was closed; its subcommunities were few and locally contained. (Below) In the modern urban multicommunity a network of subcommunities spans the globe with little, if any, respect for physical boundaries.*

media can easily become physically isolated and alienated from urban society. Slums contain typical trapped subcommunities; they are self-contained within clear physical boundaries beyond which meaningful contact with other members of the urban society is practically nonexistent in spite of telephone, radio, television, newspapers, and full freedom of movement. The isolation of many suburbs and even of apartment projects which offer their own communal facilities differs from that of the slums only in degree; the individual may choose from the range of traps he can afford.[8] The failure to integrate such subcommunities physically into the urban multicommunity is one indication that a satisfactory relationship between man and the modern city has not yet been found.

COMMUNITY AND TECHNOLOGY

Basic Communities and Basic Communications

Community and Communication. A community is a set of people in mutual communication. Communication, however, is only possible through a medium. And the medium through which its members choose to remain in touch determines to a large extent not only the nature of the community but also its maximum size.

The basic community depends entirely on face-to-face contact between its members which, to judge from experience and observation, limits their number to a maximum of about five hundred, the size of the village.[9] Within such a community all members know each other personally: by voice, by face, by name. It is obvious that even the small traditional city could not be built by, nor remain, one basic amorphous community. The city always had to depend on the interaction of subcommunities. To coordinate, direct, and control this interaction over generations, the urban community had to learn to rely on other media besides the spoken word. Ways had to be found to record and store communal data and ideas.

It is no coincidence that the founding of the first cities dates back to the time of the invention of writing. The written record, however, served initially only for the storage of communal data. As Mumford points out, "the earliest uses of writing were not to convey ideas, religious or otherwise, but to keep temple records of grain, cattle, pottery, goods, stored and disbursed."[10] For the bulk of mankind, and for several thousand years, writing remained exactly that and no more: a medium for recording and storing data. Not only were all except a small elite illiterate, but until the advent of the printing press, writing remained a medium of individual rather than mass communication. Through it, the educated could communicate free from the constraints of space and time.

For a long time the written word was therefore of little use for the propagation of communal ideas. The pre-Gutenberg media of mass communications were the signs and symbols which, through habit and tradition, had become universally understood: religious symbols, images, costumes and pageants, and, last but not least, fitting architectural forms. (Figure 5.) All were contained in the ever-dominant form of the city, which, as a result, became itself the dominant medium of mass communication.

In expressing the values of the community it contained, the traditional city was an organic whole. With the development of the printing press, however, the written word increasingly became the sole carrier of meaning. Expanding cities lost their formal unity which was no longer needed. In the literate urban society each member is able to assemble his own set of values from printed sources and express them fully within a loose and neutral urban framework. Buildings have become a medium through which individual or corporate owners can declare their personal convictions and preferences.

But as we enter the postliterate phase of human development, there is a growing awareness of universal membership in one single human community. The written word is once more seeming to become reduced to a depository of data and ideas for the few, while electronic media are offering direct links between individuals regardless of location, and through them between subcommunities everywhere. Concurrently, cities are slowly merging into what Doxiadis has called *ecumenopolis*, the "universal city" of the future. For the first time since the coming of age of the printing press, our sense of community and of urban habitat tend to merge once again.

Community and Space. In an urban environment designed to contain communities, urban space should obviously be arranged to aid communal communications. But rather than finding communal communications concepts readily translated into urban space concepts, the community may in fact be forced to adapt its communications process to the already implemented spatial conception of kings or bureaucratic elites, or to that of real estate developers, planners, or architects.

The natural complexity of a total urban communications network is further compounded by the fact that it has always been of necessity closely interlinked with, and in part coincident with, the transportation network. This is still so despite the fact that urban streets no longer serve, as they once did, simultaneously as channels for people, goods, messages, municipal services in the form of water supply at public fountains, and as waste and drainage collectors. Now the movement of people may diverge from that of goods; municipal services are disappearing underground; most communications functions have been assigned to print and electronic media; and public urban space has, in the process, come to serve the sole function of channeling the movement of people with maximum efficiency. The city, particularly in the technologically advanced regions of the world, has gradu-

figure 5   *Fitting architectural form was the dominant pre-Gutenberg medium of mass communications; it is preserved to this day in many European towns.*

ally become a basically utilitarian complex: not primarily a "machine for living in," to paraphrase Le Corbusier, but a machine to produce goods and services with, a megamachine in Mumford's sense of the word.

However, with the gradual automation of routine human functions, the usefulness of such megamachines is nearing its end, and the urban environment will have to be readapted to fulfill its original function of providing a communal habitat. Urban space will require redefinition in terms of its functions in order to meet the direct communication needs of the members of urban subcommunities. These needs are not served adequately by the electronic media, which permit communications of two kinds only: selective two-way communications between individuals, as for instance by telephone, and random one-way communication from a simple source to a mass audience, via television or radio. They furthermore transmit only incomplete amounts of sensory information. The low definition of such information must be compensated for by an excessive involvement of the receiver, who has to complete the information he receives from his own memory store of sense impressions.

The dependence on electronic media of communication will thus have to be balanced by a complementing urban environment offering ample opportunity for random face-to-face contact among individuals on the one hand, and for direct sensory exploration of the environment in all its manifestations on the other. Both requirements will make radically new demands on the spatial arrangement of cities.

Natural Limits of Communities. The maximum size of the traditional community is limited by the memory capacity of the human brain. The basic community, as discussed previously, is limited to a few hundred members, this being the maximum number people can, on the average, know intimately, keep a lifelong interest in, and instantly recall relevant personal data about. When a self-contained community grows beyond that size, it must split into separate communities, or it will gradually structure itself into subcommunities.

By its very definition the subcommunity does not demand the kind of lifelong personal involvement common in the village community. Subcommunities are based on individual choice and can be formed and dissolved at will. In contrast to the amorphous village community the structured urban multicommunity would seem not to have an organic limit. It can subdivide endlessly: on the basis of age and sex, on the basis of marriage and the extended family, on the basis of individual wealth and status, on the basis of trades and profession, on the basis of religious beliefs and minority interest, and so on. The multicommunity can grow indefinitely as long as its subcommunities remain effectively interlinked.

While the growth of the traditional city was limited by the amount of food that its hinterland could supply, the main problem of the modern megalopolis is how its inhabitants can remain in meaningful mutual communication. More specifically, the urban growth potential depends on amenities which at least permit, and if possible encourage, the continual formation of new subcommunities and which facilitate their continued existence. Without a continuum of interlinked subcommunities, the city tends to break up into the basic village-type communities of an earlier stage of development. Even when linked to the urban scene via telephone, television, and radio, such communities are in more than one way truly "suburban," meaning less than urban, and represent an obvious social retrogression.

Subcommunities can only grow out of the direct contacts between individuals, contacts that must be face-to-face to be meaningful in the urban context. But these in turn depend on the availability of social space. The future growth potential of cities therefore appears to hinge on the successful introduction of systems of public spaces which will interlace and complement the urban communications network.

It is doubtful if there is an alternative. To permit an urban breakup into pseudovillage communities and depend on their global interlinkage through electronic media would be equivalent to the dismantling of the urban environment. It is this very environment, however, which makes advanced technology possible by permitting and encouraging the close collaboration and interaction of vast numbers of individuals. No combination of village communities could either create or maintain a global communications network. A global technology must be based on a global urban community.

The Extended Community

Transportation: Extended Physical Space. Over the span of a few generations the effective boundaries of the urban community have been pushed from the traditional city limits to outer space, first through the creation of an integrated global transportation network and then by linking the world's urban population in an instant communications network. While the second phase of this process is being implemented, the first has been completed: urban space everywhere is interconnected and therefore without physical boundaries.

This global space continuum has been created through man's latest set of physical extensions to his body: the transportation apparatus, his machines to conquer space with. The means of transportation are by themselves hardly modern in concept: road networks were in use in Roman times, the railway was invented over four hundred years ago, and the idea of flying machines dates back to the Renaissance. What is new is the perfection and widespread use of these tools and their functional interlinkage in a comprehensive global transportation system.

The dominant characteristic of this system is the form of human transportation it provides—that of movement in capsules. (Figure 6.) The trend from the open to the capsule form has been unmistakable for all means of transport: for cars, trains, and planes as well as for passenger elevators and even ships. A partial explanation can be found in the steadily increasing speed of modern movement. However, the trend is not entirely based on utilitarian requirements, as demonstrated by the parallel trends in play equipment design where both open and capsule forms have been further developed: in sports cars and motorcycles, cabin cruisers and sailboats, not to speak of such open-air speed sports as skiing and skydiving.

The predominance of capsuled movement has meant that the experience of physical space has become almost entirely visual.[11] The window through which space and the movement through it are experienced filters out all but visual sense impressions. Space is no longer perceived directly, and even the scale of space is experienced only in relation to the scale of the capsule. This filtering process similarly distorts the relations between encapsuled individuals: interpersonal relations are reduced to their visual components; individuals become images, unreal and unimportant.

Significantly, the function in the modern city of its dominant means of capsuled movement, the car, goes far beyond that of providing individual transportation. It offers the driver an opportunity to temporarily opt out of the urban community and combine his escape with the exhilaration of space conquest. (Figure 7.) The car is thus both the average urban man's escape hatch from unwanted personal involvement and a popular version of a space capsule in orbit. From it the individual can sense his urban environment by moving through it, forming a composite image of megalopolis as a mosaic of sequences of views, and on that basis orient himself in urban space. What the urban transportation system at its present stage of development fails to provide is true continuity of movement, for the change from one medium of transportation to another is unnecessarily awkward. As urban space expands, vastly superior techniques of shifting from one kind of movement to another must evolve with the resulting continuity of movement on land, on water, and in the air.

Electronic Media: Global Space Awareness. With fast movement reducing the perception of space to its visual component there is an obvious limit to the scope of three-dimensional space awareness. Only by extending man's nervous system beyond its natural limitations is it possible to involve once again the full sensorium in the perception of space. The new extensions of the nervous system thus complement the older ones of the body: electronic media grafted onto the transportation apparatus make possible the perception and control of global space. Controlled space, however, is urban space, and the global scale becomes urban scale. And the individual becomes a member of a single global urban community as all space in a sense turns into social space, and the earth, once thought to be the universe, is dis-

figure 6 *Capsuled movement characterizes the modern transportation system.*

covered to be an inhabited but helplessly orbiting spacecraft. We are, in other words, entering an entirely new era of human settlement in which past criteria and patterns will rapidly lose meaning and validity, an era in which distances will have become irrelevant and natural boundaries dissolved.

The perfection of mass transportation techniques brought on the final demise of the traditional urban community. But the next step of technological progress—the perfection of techniques of electronic communications—is paradoxically reestablishing the closed urban community, only this time on a global scale. Unfortunately, the emergence of this new closed urban community does not reestablish the traditional city forms as models for future urban development. The traditional urban communications system depended on the transportation network to serve the added function of channeling messages. Plazas, squares, and streets were designed specifically for this purpose. (Figure 8.) News traveled from public spaces and buildings

figure 7 *The highway is an extension of the urban habitat into the natural environment.*

figure 8 In the traditional city, streets and public squares were specifically conceived to serve the channeling of messages. (Canaletto, View in Venice. National Gallery of Art, Washington, D.C., Widener Collection.)

along city streets to the gates of dwellings and onward from room to room. As news spread, public opinion was formed; the two were inseparable.

Electronic media, by contrast, reach every individual directly and simultaneously outside the bounds of three-dimensional space. Spatial arrangements have no longer any direct influence on the functional distribution of information. At best they may facilitate the cohesion and interaction of subcommunities within which public opinion can then take shape, at worst block such interaction with resulting public apathy. Hence the function of urban space is entirely different in the electric age.

The Extended Environment

Plug-in Communities. The new relationships between communications and urban space are naturally reflected in emerging new communal patterns. To the traditional set of links which the individual has always maintained in his subcommunities is abruptly added a new set of indirect links to a vastly expanded urban environment. Man's relations to his environment take on a dual nature: the simple life of three dimensions and events perceived in sequence becomes at the turn of a switch the extended one of simultaneity in space and time. Every individual suddenly has the option of switching from one set of links to another. He can withdraw from personal contact and plug himself into the global community, or he can turn his senses to the direct perception of his immediate environment. He cannot, however, maintain both types of linkages simultaneously. His awareness is split into two distinct levels: that of immediate and that of total environment.

As the individual plugs himself into the electronic communications network, he withdraws from his immediate urban environment. Like the fortified gates of the traditional city and like railway and air terminals, each room equipped with a television set becomes a gateway to and from a city whose part-time inhabitants become, much of the time, absentee occupants of urban space. When this absence starts to add up to a considerable part of the urban population's waking hours, the density of activity starts to drop.

In a way, this trend started before the age of electronic communications with the spread of literacy and the introduction of artificial illumination in public spaces and was strengthened by around-the-clock operations in industry. When cities lay in darkness after dusk, all urban activity had to take place during daylight, which in the cities of northern Europe might, during winter, amount to only a few hours a day. The activity density during these "waking hours" was therefore high. If, by contrast, people can now spread the same activities over a twenty-four-hour day and interrupt them at will in favor of such solitary activities as reading and watching television, then the use of public space is bound to be less intense. With urban activity extended beyond the daily cycle of individual lives, different parts of the urban habitat attract crowds at different times depending on their special appeal. (Figure 9.) Unused at other times, however, their average activity density is low. And the use of new communications and data processing equipment will almost certainly hasten this development further by encouraging the staggering of yet shorter working hours over longer daily periods.

If existing techniques of time scheduling, illumination control, and sound insulation were seriously applied to this problem, it should ultimately become possible to multiply existing gross population densities without affecting the present density of urban activities. Even now, vastly greater numbers of people are needed to enliven an urban core than was the case in the Middle Ages, when newly founded cities with no more than a thousand inhabitants could survive as independent entities. And this trend is likely to continue. The probability of mutual interaction among individuals is decreasing as their opportunities for withdrawal increase, and as the need for the functional interaction of different population groups lessens with the automation of work and communications processes. The maintenance of dense human activity in urban cores will come to depend on the continuing increase of the population these cores are serving.

figure 9 *Urban activity has long ceased to be bound to the natural rhythm of day and night.*

Man Lost in Space.   The plug-in features of modern life have changed both the quantity and the quality of environmental involvement. As it is, the bulk of the urban artifact, designed to satisfy the social needs of earlier periods, reinforces the dividing aspects of modern transportation and communications techniques. The urban environment offers little or no compensation for the great amount of time it forces individuals to spend in encapsuled movement and in plugged-in involvement in the impersonal world of electronic media.

Reflecting the all-pervading influence of the fading print culture, the dominant ordering principle of today's physical urban environment is that of lining up more or less identical elements vertically and horizontally—along elevator shafts, streets, and corridors—in a manner recalling the assembly line. In the truly modern city all human activities are made subservient to this linear pattern, frustrating any attempt at nonconformity. In the process life is moved off the street into the adjoining buildings and out of the corridors behind the closed doors that line them.

In an extension of this process, cities have, like centrifuges, created their centers by driving all life out to the periphery and rearranging it in stratified form. As modern megamachines they have become agents of a print culture whose ultimate aim is the isolation of every individual. Not surprisingly, the members of the resulting society tend to be, in Riesman's terms, "inner-directed." Although the world is entering its postliterate phase, our physical urban environment is still expressing and fostering the inner-directed values of the preceding print era.

It takes generations to create an urban environment, but the bulk of that environment can become obsolete in the span of a generation. The revolutionary nature of the present transition is suggested by McLuhan when he states: "The Elizabethans appear to our gaze as very medieval. Medieval man thought of himself as classical, just as we consider ourselves to be modern men. To our successors, however, we shall appear as utterly Renaissance in character, and quite unconscious of the major new factors which we have set in motion during the past one hundred and fifty years."[12]

Man of the electric age, in dire need of personal involvement, finds himself in a basically hostile urban environment specifically arranged to deny such involvement and to stress instead the values of efficiency and privacy. The modern city was designed to isolate. While the hermit of an older age had to flee from the city to escape involvement, the contemporary hermit finds his habitat in the urban center, so much so that much of the urban environment in its present form tends to force individuals into the role of hermits against their will. (Figure 10.) The resulting alienation affects not only individuals, but, since individuals form the connecting links between subcommunities, also the community as a whole. Without meaningful access to electronic media and barred from direct communication with others by

figure 10 *The modern recluse does not have to flee from the city; rather, the urban habitat can turn an individual into a recluse against his will. (Edward Hopper,* Nighthawks. *Art Institute of Chicago.)*

boundaries and walls, individuals and groups may range in urban space, but if they cannot relate to the urban community, they are lost in it.

URBAN CYBERNETICS

Environmental Feedback

Channels of Urban Communications.   The city is more than the count of its population, just as the human brain is infinitely more complex than the sum of its neurons would suggest. In both quantity and quality, the interactions between units are the significant factors, much more so than the number of units themselves. In these interactions each individual receives signals which he then transforms into symbols and interprets as messages. If found meaningful, they in turn affect his own transmission of signals.

To be received, such signals must be in a form adapted to the human sensory receptor system. In this way, a basic five-channel, person-to-person communications system is defined. The effective range of this system is, however, very short and suited only to the face-to-face communications adequate in the basic village community and within urban subcommunities. To serve the extended urban environment the basic communications system must be similarly extended, either directly by amplifying the strength of signals at points of emission and/or reception, or indirectly by moving senders and receivers within range of direct sensory communications.

Transportation systems thus become part of the urban communications system. However, when they enable the inhabitants of cities to meet with each other, they fulfill a function that is ancillary to the ones they were designed to serve. Their main functions are to move people from their place of residence to their place of work and to move goods from places of production to places of consumption. The highways and subways conceived to serve man's gregarious nature are rare indeed, and the type of urban traffic that is generated results very often directly from the lack of adequate means to extend the range of human signals electronically.

The amplification of signals involves their translation from one medium into another. This is usually a difficult process. Every medium favors signals in a specific form, a fact Harold A. Innes aptly expressed in the title of his book *The Bias of Communications*[13] and which McLuhan further dramatized in his famous dictum "the medium is the message." This applies to primitive amplification techniques using jungle drums, smoke, and fire signals, as well as to the more sophisticated urban communications media of art and architecture, writing, and electronics.

The dominant mass communications media of the traditional city were architecture and art; urban form was itself urban communication. To be adapted to these media, signals had to be transformed into symbols prior to their transmission and were interpreted by the individual receiver in accordance with a communal code. Every citizen could "read" his city. This direct relation broke down as writing ceased to serve merely personal communications and, with the perfection of the printing press, superseded architecture as the dominant urban mass medium.

In contrast to art and architecture, however, which appeal directly to the senses, the written message must be carried to the receiver and thus generates movement. Road and rail networks become extensions of the printing press in channeling its messages. The print age accordingly finds its physical expression in the systems of horizontal and vertical concrete and steel "channels" which have come to dominate the physical urban environment.

As printed advertisements and catalogs took over much of the function of the traditional marketplace, and as the conference room superseded the traditional civic square designed to permit public participation in the decision-making process (Figure 11), so are electronic media of communications now preempting the functions served by the channels of urban movement. Once again both individual and mass communication can and do take place outside the linear systems imposed by the print medium. Urban channels of communications have become invisible; another dimension has been added to the urban space-time continuum.

Jumbled Channels and Clashing Media. The need for urban communication is entailed in the high degree to which cities force the specialization

figure 11 *The traditional square permitted public participation in the collective decision-making process—a function it still serves in some Swiss towns where the voters gather to decide public issues in formal meetings in the town square.*

of individual functions. While the structure of village communities is one in which members live in parallel interaction, members of the urban community are interlinked in both parallel and series. The complexity of the resulting community structure grows at an exponential rate when compared with the increase in population.

The form of the traditional city clearly reflected its community structure. This overall image was lost only when production processes themselves began to be divided into subfunctions of steadily shrinking significance, be it on the assembly line, in administration, in research, or in distribution. As each of these subfunctions demanded increasing personal effort, leaving less time and energy for random communication and personal inquiry, the urban fabric began to disintegrate. Nor has this process been reversed with the gradual reduction of working hours, since the perfection of the production apparatus which permits the reduction of the individual work load has created in turn new problems of distribution, the only solution to which appears to be advertising, itself a communications activity. The increasing complexity of urban life, finally, has necessitated the creation of countless regulatory agencies whose primary function is the issuing of further "messages."

But the capacity of the urban communications system is ultimately limited by the total sensory intake capacity of the urban population. Beyond this saturation point the communications process starts breaking down. Incoming signs, symbols, and messages are either temporarily or permanently ignored. The difficulty of discriminating between important and unimportant messages leads to fatigue and stress in individuals and the malfunctioning of urban institutions. The relationship between the inadequate perception of incoming signals and messages and the loss of internal balance in the whole system is analogous to certain disturbances of the human nervous system known as ataxia.[14] Communications overload in the urban system can thus lead to a state of communal ataxia in which organic balance is lost and the community comes to depend on external controls such as police and military forces to maintain internal order.

The proportion of the urban population to which more information is directed than is able to be received, let alone processed, is increasing steadily. Through the still little understood mass media, the urban environment is flooded indiscriminately with signals, symbols, and messages in the hope that some of the information they contain will reach its destination. Feedback is minimal and indirect since these media are by definition directed away from the source, access to which is highly restricted. Lack of direct feedback is indeed the most serious basic shortcoming of the mass communications media, at least since Gutenberg.

Checks and Balances. The term "cybernetics" has been defined by its inventor, the physicist Norbert Wiener, as the science of control and communication in the animal and in the machine. Wiener himself expanded the frame of reference of this new science to include the disciplines of sociology and anthropology, but at the same time warned that while the main quantities affecting society are of a statistical nature, the run of statistics on which they are based is too short to make the application of mathematical technique anything but a procedure of doubtful value.[15] Nevertheless the concept of cybernetics can be helpful in understanding relationships that exist between communication and control in the urban social system, or at least, on a more modest scale, in its subsystems.

One of the basic functions of any urban community is to provide an environment for individual fulfillment in accordance with dominant communal values. These may vary widely, as is, for example, suggested by the tradition-directed, inner-directed, and other-directed personality types described by Riesman.[16] Any one of such types may predominate in different cultures which coexist in the form of subcommunities within one urban kaleidoscope. But the very term "community" implies a measure of stability. For the total urban system to remain basically stable, subcommunities of widely differing orientation must constantly react and adapt to changes occurring elsewhere in the system. To ensure that such reaction results in the reestablishment of balance rather than in increasingly wild gyration requires accurate and instant feedback within the urban system, supplemented by built-in stabilizers.

All this presupposes that the goal of the urban community is homeostasis, and that the games-for-individual-gain aspects of communal life can be successfully contained within the total system. Given these conditions, social homeostasis depends primarily on an effective communications system. In the traditional city, universal and constant face-to-face contact provided a system of maximum effectiveness, and public opinion, based on traditions, many of which had found expression in the form of urban spaces and buildings, tended naturally toward homeostasis. But then the concept of privacy within the urban habitat was unknown. Behavior and ideas deviating from the norm were soon enough public knowledge and could be dealt with.

While the only way to opt out of the traditional urban community was to leave its territory, the modern equivalent is individual withdrawal into a private world. Nature, which limited the size of the traditional city, no longer functions as a stabilizer for the urban community and, hence, for its values. Modern urban space is fragmented into private domains isolated from communal influences. In the absence of natural stabilizers, the state of homeostasis is protected by laws, codes, and conventions. In this way institutional stabilizers have replaced live public opinion, tradition, and myth as automatic communal controls.

Contrary to those of the traditional community, these artificial built-in stabilizers do not have the ability to adapt automatically to changes in the community by responding to information feedback. This is a particularly critical shortcoming in an urban environment changing as rapidly and drastically as the present one. Its correction must be sought not only through the elaboration of known electronic communications techniques, but also through the use of urban design techniques as tools of communal control.

Control through Design.   In an already quoted passage of his book, *Understanding Media,* Marshall McLuhan observes that civilized man tends to restrict and enclose space and to separate functions. In fragmenting space the print culture has consciously or unconsciously imposed controls on urban life. The functional subdivision of urban space, moreover, has resulted in a multiplicity of visually defined subspaces in the form of compartments and channels separated by buffer zones, sometimes "decorated" but more usually universally ignored. Thus urban space is used. And space not used is not perceived—is nonspace to McLuhan's civilized man.

Slums remain one place where the environment takes in total urban space, if only because the majority of people crowded into them have remained on a preliterate cultural level. Another is the city at night, when perspective vision becomes impossible, when urban containers and channels of movement alike lose their substance and disintegrate into lighted elements and sequences of points, patterns, and lines. (Figure 12.) Such fleeting glimpses suggest the possibility of making the direct sensory experience of urban space continuous with the kind of space perception possible through electronic media.

Rearranging the urban artifact to create one continuous living space involves nothing less than the restructuring of urban life. The controls exercised by the built, and therefore previously designed, environment must be gradually changed to bring about its enrichment. Whether the urban environment is considered machine or organism, its structure, in Norbert Wiener's words, "is an index of the performance that may be expected from it."[17] Urban design thus assumes a vastly wider meaning than that of adding beauty and harmony to an otherwise predetermined environment.

The design of any part of the urban artifact represents an intervention in the environment's control function. The consequences of such interventions are largely unpredictable, and their evaluation is only possible by studying the feedback information in all fields affecting and affected by design. The correction for undesired consequences can then be achieved by modifying subsequent design decisions. This process differs little from that which unconsciously directed the growth of cities over centuries. The need to develop it into a method stems from the fact that modern technology has developed the means for undertaking projects on a scale and at a speed which have clearly outstripped the ability of the urban community to direct them effectively for its own good. Unfortunately, the conventional approach to urban planning and design based on fragmented knowledge and departmental action does not yield such a method. And before an alternative approach can be suggested, the first step must be a detailed appraisal of the forces that influence the urban environment.

figure 12   *In the city as seen at night, perspective vision becomes impossible, and the sensory experience of urban space becomes akin to the perception of space through television.*

CHAPTER TWO

INDIVIDUAL AND

COLLECTIVE NEEDS

BASIC SHELTER NEEDS

The Concept of Minimum Shelter

Individual Survival. Man is conditioned by his environment. In confronting environmental forces, he may on occasion have the option of withdrawing. If forced to react, however, be it in adapting to changes outside his control or in attempting to counteract them, the individual automatically intervenes in his environment and subjects it in turn to change. Man and his environment thus participate in molding each other. The need to engage in this process creates what Selye has called the *stress of life,* and man's chances of survival under varying conditions are limited by the extent to which he can respond to such stress. The individual's adaptability to external influences may indeed reflect the degree of his aliveness.[1]

The adaptive response through which any stress is balanced results from the operation of a complex internal system which controls the organic functioning of the human body and the purpose of which is homeostasis, the state of organic stability. The maintenance of homeostasis requires unconscious effort through the exertion of "adaptation energy."[2] To ease it and to simultaneously improve the body's adaptive ability, human intelligence has tended to conceive artificial environments to envelop the body, thus in a sense extending the body envelope. Clothes are such extensions of the body as are the shells of buildings. Their creation represents man's conscious adaptive response to his outer environment.

The maintenance of the resulting expanded system, however, involves external controls in addition to the automatically functioning internal ones. Conscious effort must now be applied where natural adaptation energy might once have sufficed. The accumulation of such external and conscious controls defines civilization and leads to the wear and tear associated with civilized life. To the basic shelter's primary function of protecting man from elements of nature hostile to human life, a secondary one is gradually added: that of easing the strain imposed on individuals as a result of the side effects of, and the demands made by, increasingly complex environmental control mechanisms. In addition to sheltering human life from extremes of climate, floods, and fire and providing for necessary supplies and the disposal of wastes, urban building must now be designed to assure privacy in the face of ever-increasing communications needs, to defend against activity over-crowding in the face of vastly greater population pressures, and, finally, to help protect man from the degenerative consequences of technology and its environment-polluting side effects while depending on the same technology as the only conceivable weapon.

Technology so far has been applied almost universally to actively counteract environmental forces rather than as a method to help adapt to them. The result has been massive and continuing intervention in the natural environment with little or no regard for consequences, in the naïve hope that progressively stepped-up action could somehow make up for disturbances created earlier. The state of the urban environment in North America —the front line of progress—suggests the necessity to redirect technological development into adaptive molds. In the meantime, however, minimum shelter needs clearly have outgrown the ability of technology to satisfy them.

Survival of the Family. If the individual is the functional unit of the urban community, then the family can be regarded as its structural counterpart. The community is built of family units, just as the residential sector of cities is made up of housing units tailored to the needs of individual families. Family life of one kind or another is basic to human existence. This, however, should not obscure the equally important fact that the dominant concept of family can change and has indeed varied greatly in the course of history. Thus the medieval conception of the family as conjugal cell was replaced, as the state increasingly failed to ensure individual security in the tenth century, by the *line* in which ties of blood gradually replaced the medieval network of individual dependencies.[3] Out of this trend toward domesticity emerged the modern family, an isolated group of parents and children cut off from the world and in a sense opposed to society: the nuclear family of Riesman's inner-directed stage of social organization. And as we enter the postliterate other-directed era of McLuhan's "electric age," new concepts of the family will inevitably emerge.

Each of these stages is characterized by a specific pattern of personal relationships. The child in the medieval family was considered an unfinished adult, and marriage a basically contractual relationship supplemented by a great variety of communal ties. In the succeeding institution of the extended family, related adults of varying ages, their children, and dependents would live together under one roof. The child-centered urban family of a later epoch again generated entirely different social patterns.

Conceived to accommodate a social unit of a specific kind, the dwelling is thus far more than an extension of the human body's heat-control mechanisms. The spaces it defines modulate the personal relations of its inhabitants in definite if subtle ways, both within the dwelling and outward toward the community as a whole. The walled entrance court between dwelling and street implies a different family-community relationship than an inviting front door, and the interior court or backyard, which serves as the center of the family's outdoor activities, signifies a different type of linkage between family and community from that evolving when front porches serve the same purpose. (Figure 13.) The internal arrangements of dwellings similarly affect family life. The house designed to fulfill a public function, be it as status symbol or for extensive entertainment, imposes patterns on family life different from those encouraged in a dwelling tailored to the immediate needs of a child-centered family.

While the extended family had its own built-in stability, the modern family, much like its medieval counterpart, has a limited predetermined life cycle. But in contrast to earlier times, when people accommodated themselves in general-purpose rooms, the modern family moves from place to place as its space needs change. Each such place is selected to fit the functional needs of the particular stage in which the family finds itself, to be abandoned again as needs change.

Without an adequate amount of dwelling space the concept of the family cannot take shape or develop. This space must be arranged so that it supports the inhabitants' personal concept of family life. In a culturally homogeneous environment one family structure predominates; a single type of shelter and its architectural elaborations may in this case meet all requirements. But a megalopolis is obviously not culturally homogeneous; rather, it forces people from different levels of different cultures into close proximity. This fact should be reflected in the great variety of dwelling types that are available.

Survival of the Community. As the spatial arrangement of a dwelling modulates the personal relations of its inhabitants, so does the spatial arrangement of the urban habitat modulate the ways in which subcommunities are formed and interact. And since the survival of the urban community

figure 13 *The character of the entrances that lead to urban dwellings reflects the nature of the family-community relationship.*

depends on the viability of its subcommunities, the pattern of public space becomes a determinant of the community's future.

Public space is formed where the mental spaces of individuals consciously overlap; it is the place of mutual involvement beyond the immediate family circle. In this sense the traditional city was all public space (Figure 14); the very concept of privacy was unknown in its era: ". . . until the end of the seventeenth century, nobody was ever left alone. The density of social life made isolation virtually impossible, and people who managed to shut themselves up in a room for some time were regarded as exceptional characters."[4] The big houses were the centers of social life. Always crowded, their rooms opened onto one another without serving any specific function: "In the same rooms where they ate, people slept, danced, worked and received visitors."[5] Curtained beds could be found all over the house, often several to a room. Even so, one apparently rarely slept alone in any of them. The concept of privacy only emerged in the eighteenth century along with general literacy. From there it led to the increasing isolation of individuals, families, and subcommunities. Communication became a problem.

This trend toward isolation culminates in the modern city, where urban space is reduced to the two categories of private space and nonspace. With the social function of subcommunities accommodated in the basically private domain of club, church, and community center, bar, restaurant, and hotel lobby, it remains for schools and universities to allow, if not force, the establishment of meaningful random contacts within the total urban population. Even there the special interests of subcommunities afraid of intruders can lead to withdrawal from the "dangers" of such contacts through the media of private and denominational schools. Meanwhile, street and promenade, corner store and public house have long lost their function as places of urban interactions.

The trend toward the withdrawal of individuals and families from society and into urban subcommunities shows clearly in the mid-twentieth-century school-centered residential subdivisions which manage to isolate whole parcels of urban land from the public domain and turn them into private space. The possibility of capsuled movement from such residential to equally exclusive work communities completes the mutual isolation of urban parts. At this point the urban community has ceased to exist; the concept of community has been replaced by that of forced urban coexistence.

The phenomenon of urban nonspace consisting of space left over between building enclosures is the perceptible result of the isolation of people and their activities. The obsession with privacy and urban noninvolvement has found its natural expression in space-repellent buildings. Similarly, however, a spirit of urban involvement will result in a new environment in which private and public space needs find a healthy balance, and joint use of communal space will supersede the conflicting uses of overlapping private spaces. (Figure 15.)

figure 14 *Within the traditional city, private and public spaces merge in one communal space.*

figure 15 *The search for a contemporary balance between private and communal space needs will result in a new spirit of urban involvement.*

The Conditions for Cultural Evolution

Beyond the Hive. An urban environment of which no more is expected than that it ensure communal survival could conceivably be designed by using the animal hive as a model. In the resulting human hive every individual would be conditioned to fulfill specific communal tasks without question and to behave in strict accordance with preset patterns. Its survival would, however, depend not only on the success of the programming of each individual's behavior but also on his inability to communicate or absorb new learning. The realization of the city as hive, as collective social organism, would thus necessarily be predicated on the dehumanization of its inhabitants.

Man's superiority in nature rests on his awareness and foreknowledge of death. This knowledge makes it impossible for him to, in Susanne Langer's words, "live from moment to moment in an endless Now."[6] Being able to envisage his own life-span as the culmination of a long past and the beginning of an unforeseeable future, man cannot help but value his time higher than as an accumulation of sense impressions: "Since we cannot have our fill of existence by going on and on, we want to have as much life as possible in our short span. If our individuation must be brief, we want to make it complete; so we are inspired to think, act, dream our desires, create things, express our ideas, and in all sorts of ways make up by concentration what we cannot have by length of days. We seek the greatest possible individuation, or development of personality. In doing this, we have set up a new demand, not for mere continuity of existence, but for self-realization."[7]

The individual realizes himself through the medium of the culture he identifies with. His potential is thus limited by the level of his cultural environment; by raising it, the density of human life is increased. The process through which this is accomplished is that of cultural evolution, in which levels of communal awareness are raised through the actions of what Margaret Mead has called "evolutionary clusters."[8] But the urban hive by definition excludes the possibility of such clusters. The process of cultural evolution, dependent as it is on the combined action of groups of individuals each of whom is open to outside influences, is obviously at least indirectly dependent on certain environmental conditions. "The existence of these conditions, or the hope that they may exist, is the reason why high civilization flourishes in cities. . . . In a city, especially a city in which there is provision for many kinds of people to meet in clubs and cafes, in theatres or at the opera, the gifted are drawn together by no master plan, but they move toward one another as inevitably as moths toward light."[9] This clearly implies that the urban environment can be consciously arranged to facilitate and speed up the evolutionary process.

The viability of the urban environment is a direct function of the number, location, and quality of its meeting places. The term "quality" refers to their attractiveness and the degree to which they permit and encourage informal contact between members of the community who might be interested in meeting each other. (Figure 16.) Their number must be adequate to avoid conflict between different interest groups with little in common and their location such that they can be reached easily, conveniently, and safely from both places of residence and places of work. Superimposed on these conditions, finally, are those necessary to guarantee the health and survival of the total urban community: the involvement of all subcommunities, all parts, in the fate and destiny of the whole, both on the local and the global scale.

Technology and Society.   For the vast majority urban life is not a result of free choice between alternatives. "People seek in the big city not primarily a way of living, but a way of making a living . . . there can be no good living without making a living."[10] Working in the city, however, may mean becoming a part of the global production apparatus and submitting to the unrelenting command of mechanization.

Mechanization is anti-organic. The method which forms the basis of all mechanization has been described by Sigfried Giedion as, firstly, the transformation of all movement of the human body, in particular the hands, into endless rotation and, secondly, its application to the production of standardized and interchangeable products and parts.[11] Human involvement in the mechanized process inevitably forces man into the role of an interchangeable cog. Depending on the degree of involvement, his body may actually be forced into a machine-directed pattern of movement, be it on the assembly line or at the typewriter. Even if freed from direct physical participation, a man may spend his life in seemingly endless artificial cycles of clock-controlled specialized activity related solely to the production process. The advent of automation has, at least in its first phase, not as yet changed this fact, but only redistributed the functions of individual cogs.

Technology, the fountainhead of mechanization, thus tends to force society, and with it the urban community, into the mold of the hive. The individual's reaction may be passive withdrawal, but it may also be an escape into the irrational with the most obvious escape route leading to aggressive behavior: "Man's aggression is more than a response to frustration; it is an attempt to assert himself as an individual, to separate himself from the herd, to find his own identity."[12] The human hive thus produces the seeds of its own destruction.

THE NEED FOR OPTIMUM SHELTER

Housing Unit, House, and Home

The Optimum Dwelling.   An environment which satisfies man's basic shelter needs may ensure his survival as an individual and possibly even that

figure 16   *The public meeting places which cities provided in the past are almost nonexistent in the contemporary urban environment.*

of primitive communities. The emerging postcivilized urban world community, however, depends as never before on the continuing growth of human knowledge. For such growth to be maintained, increasing numbers of people will need to develop and devote their talents and abilities to their limits. Yet such performance cannot be expected from individuals housed in minimum dwellings that offer no more than bare shelter. With the increasing sophistication of urban life, the sheer survival of both the community and most of its members paradoxically requires the provision of optimum dwellings in an optimum environment. The optimum is becoming the minimum.

Unfortunately, the concept of man's dwelling is irretrievably interwoven with his subconscious memory and ancestral attitudes—with drives, motives, and desires the individual may not himself be aware of. In the *home*, the individual wraps a container around himself and his family, whereas his *house* is the symbol through which he presents himself to the community. *Privacy* and *community*—as opposing aspects of the human dwelling—thus find expression in the concepts home and house. And in the optimum dwelling both aspects of the individual housing problem find their simultaneous solutions.

But individuals age, and while their aspirations may for a time remain the same, their needs change. The child's initially quite limited, and only slowly expanding, capacity to interrelate new sense impressions seems to demand above all a stable and relatively isolated environment. This same stability and isolation will be experienced as stultifying by man at the height of his physical and intellectual powers, and only when he is faced with old age and reduced capability to cope with new facts and external stimulants will he eventually choose withdrawal to the safety of the already familiar. In the traditional dwelling this whole range of needs had to be accommodated within the same space container and had to find expression in the same form. The complexity of this problem is today compounded by the regional and even global mobility demanded from, and enjoyed by, increasing numbers of people during their productive years, as well as by the trend toward a looser and less stable family structure.

The form of the traditional, self-sufficient dwelling is obviously at odds with the modern household, which is dependent on communal services not only for light, heat, health services, and communications, but increasingly even for food preparation. Such services relieve the individual from drudgery and will increase in kind, scope, and number. In the process, however, they will alter the urban style of life further, and dwelling forms will have to be found both to accommodate and express this change and to establish a new balance between form and content, house and home.

Any one solution to this evolving problem will be, of necessity, merely a part of a whole range of solutions. Not only will an individual's life-style change many times during his life-span, and hence the dwelling satisfying his needs; its appropriate location and position in the urban megastructure will also change. One range of optimum dwelling types might thus consist of movable and expandable containers which can be plugged whole into the urban service network (Figure 17); another may consist of space readily adaptable to individual needs but part of a permanent structure. The optimum dwelling can almost be defined as the one most easily adapted to the individual's every changing need.

Optimum Relations between Dwellings.   The urbanite who is accustomed to thinking of his environment in terms of houses, apartments and hotels, streets and sidewalks, automobiles and trains, and offices and factories will find it almost impossible to apply any but conventional thinking to the interrelation of inhabited spaces in the city. To break out of such intellectual confinement, he must restate the problem in more abstract terms: urban design as a concern with the conditions governing the distribution of people in urban space. This distribution obviously varies with time and with the range of local activities. From it, the distribution of people within their dwelling spaces and the pattern of movement and communication to, from, and between these spaces can be isolated and optimum relations determined.

Human dwellings are of necessity open toward the community, even if the degree of openness varies widely depending on environment, cultural conditions, and individual choice. At one extreme life spills outside a dwelling's boundaries onto street, lawn, and balcony (Figure 18); at the other,

figure 17   *Mobile homes, so far thought of only as detached residences, could be designed equally well for installation in urban megastructures.*

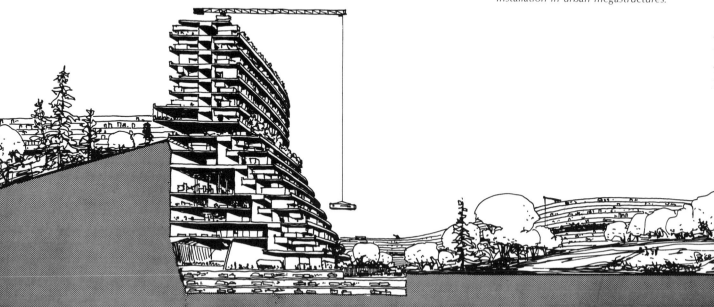

figure 18　*Life spilling outside the boundaries of private space.*

walled-in formal entrance courts add zones of disengagement: neutral spaces between public space and the private space of the dwelling that filter contact to its visual component, the view through the window. Such devices help to control the extent of random contacts forced on the individual and also the amount of physical communication which such contacts demand.

All communication involves the dissipation of energy. While there is a basic human need to communicate with others, there is also a limit to any one individual's capacity to communicate. In contrast to conditions in the traditional city, the communications load is by no means equally distributed within the modern urban community. The links beyond the local community are maintained by a limited number of individuals—both in space, through travel and electronic media, and in time, through, for example, graphic media such as the written word. The urban environment must allow such individuals periods of privacy at their option during which they may withdraw from the local communications process without danger of permanent isolation from it.

But the withdrawal of part of the urban population reduces the chances for direct communication for the rest. To offer wide opportunities for random contacts at any time, the urban environment must therefore accommodate people at high densities. This is particularly important since family

figure 19　*"Urban dwellings must be arranged spatially in a way which offers residents the options of varying degrees of privacy. . . ."*

members sharing a dwelling have quite different communications needs which may range from high and indiscriminate for grown children and medium for housewives to low for the professional people and executives whose capacity to communicate is preempted by their work. Communications needs naturally vary for people living permanently or temporarily alone and for old people without routine function in the community. However, from our knowledge of both life in primitive societies and urban life in the Middle Ages, the reasonable assumption is that no such thing as a basic human need for privacy exists.

Urban dwellings must be arranged spatially in a way which offers residents the options of varying degrees of privacy short of complete isolation, but which at the same time encourages random contacts and physical communications outside the confines of established subcommunities. (Figure 19.) Through such contacts the urban environment becomes one; without them it breaks up into ghettos. The integration of all parts, however, demands the effective use of design tools in shutting out any unwanted communications load brought on by propinquity: in the dwellings as well as in related joint facilities, and on all connecting channels and paths.

Space Needs

The Hierachy of Urban Space. All urban land and buildings are owned by someone, but since the senses do not recognize legal boundaries, all urban space is not occupied. Space is intangible; its boundaries are in the individual's mind. Its definition starts with the very small child's first space awareness: a vague complex of sense impressions enwrapping the body. Depending on how these sense impressions become ordered by the developing mind in later life, space is perceived differently. During this process, consciously or unconsciously, directly or indirectly, the mind's development is guided by the forces of community and environment, resulting in a strong cultural bias in the individual's perception of space.

The first stage of the worldwide process of urbanization has tended toward the separation of private from public space on the basis of ownership and land use. Such space is defined by the vertical upward projection of the land area with the resulting space modules containing different activities. Zoning regulations are extensions of and a last effort to maintain this geometric conception of space in the face of its obvious failure as an environmental ordering principle. This geometric subdivision is increasingly unrelated to man's direct experience of space, with the result that private and public spaces are either overlapping, with ensuing friction, or are mutually isolated by unclaimed space: nonspace as far as the senses are concerned.

Private and public space are mutually exclusive. The very use of the terms suggests individuals alienated from the society of which they are part. Yet the fact that thinking in terms of a global community has become possible indicates that, as in the Middle Ages, urban space may once more become communal space. Communal space is extended private space, while public space is akin to nonspace set aside to permit public movement and activities. Streets, highways, and parking lots thus define typical contemporary public spaces. At the pedestrian scale, plazas in front of office buildings, sidewalks, department stores, and movie theaters serve the same function. They are spaces of noninvolvement, contrasting unfavorably with the few urban features that have in some places been carried over from an earlier age: the open market, the informal park or square, the treed sidewalks and promenades, a few old-fashioned restaurants, and the live theater—spaces, in short, which demand the public's full sensory participation and which draw individuals out of their private space boundaries. (Figure 20.)

In the medieval city the individual was totally involved in the urban environment—to the point where privacy was neither sought nor known. At the other extreme, in the industrial city at the culmination of the print culture, involvement with the environment was correspondingly unknown. But as we enter the electric age and learn to use the new extensions of our awareness, individuals are learning once more to sense the urban environment, vastly expanded now and increasingly enveloping the globe. While the medieval, direct environmental awareness could exhaust itself in the communal space defined by city walls and shaped by houses, streets, squares, and spires, our expanded awareness now demands an urban environment conceived on a scale equally expanded, where buildings lose their box shape and emerge as elements of landscape: islands, mountains, cliffs, and promontories, molded and shaped to reflect the dynamism of man's new global community while drawing the individual out of the privacy of his spatial cocoon into the extended environment of the new community. (Figure 21.)

Private Space. If urbanization has resulted in the separation of public from private space, the further decomposition of what was once communal space into a multiplicity of individual space cells has been even more significant for the development of the urban environment. Except in some isolated pockets, usually in older parts of cities where life continues to spill over property lines, invading the streets and merging private spaces into its common communal extension, private space has been banished behind the walls of dwellings and made to fit into the confinement of secluded rooms.

Physically subdivided space is visual space and does not involve and satisfy the senses of hearing, touch, smell, and even taste to which a richer urban environment could and did indeed cater in the past. The medieval urban environment offered a vastly richer mix of sensory stimulation than any modern city. But more importantly, it offered the individual security. Once the community disintegrated under the impact of new cultural and

figure 20 *Remnants of past ways of life suggest how the senses can become more fully engaged in the urban environment.*

economic forces, individuals were left to fend for themselves. Withdrawal into private space meant finding a new kind of security—finding it, alas, at the cost of urban decay.

There can be little doubt, however, that as communal values were neglected, urban man in the privacy of his home enriched his inner life. And as communal security on a global scale becomes a distinct possibility, a return to traditional communal life now would, if it were possible, result in no less of a loss than its earlier abandonment. Sacrificing personal values to communal values is neither necessary nor desirable; the medium need not become the whole message. Private life can and should add another dimension to communal life. Hence, even as it loses its predominance in the urban environment, private space takes on new functions and meanings.

Private space need thus no longer be defined as the individual's room or house, even if the two may for a time coincide. The physical conception of private space is being superseded by its psychological conception: the purely visual space definition has ceased to be adequate and is being supplemented by definitions involving all the senses. Private space, no longer necessarily a static container even when stationary and enclosed, may employ transparent and translucent elements to relate the interior to the total urban environment, to nature, and to sky. It may be wired for sound and shaped and furnished for tactile involvement, and it may be plugged into the global communications network.

Beyond the special case of physically enclosed private space, however, a wide range of possibilities remains open in which private space needs may be satisfied outside the dwelling. Privacy is the condition of being away from others, and the erection of walls is but one way of achieving it. The solitary mountain climber, sailor, and hunter knows private space, the limits of which are beyond perception. Given the crowded conditions predominant in the sprawling modern city, it is no accident that skiing, boating, motorcycling, and skydiving are popular urban sports. In movement, particularly at high speeds and when combined with concentrated activities, the individual creates his own dynamic space, the boundaries of which are impervious to human relationship, even while physical space is shared by many.[13] Even concentrated mental activity can result in individual isolation; hence the popular image of the absentminded professor who has successfully created his private space amidst family and friends. Private space needs are obviously not served by providing each family with an opaque, soundproof cell. Space needs change with age and climate and from individual to individual; they may be satisfied through physical isolation or motion or activity. The optimum urban environment for the individual is that which guarantees maximum choice.

Art and the Need for Stimulation. The fact that space needs are basically psychological and elude physical measurement does not make them any less real. The same holds true for the human need for stimulation which has been variously described as a "desire for tension" and a "craving for mental dissatisfaction,"[14] as a "rage for chaos" as opposed to the rage for order,[15] and explained, as for instance by Cantrill: "As human beings, we seem to seek a quality of experience far different from that sought by any other type of organism we know. Man's capacity to experience value satisfaction propels him to learn and devise new ways of behaving that will enable him both to extend the range and heighten the quality of value satisfactions and to ensure the repeatability of those value satisfactions already experienced."[16]

Stimulation results from those changes in the environment which man perceives as signals. Such signals may be directed at the receiver by other members of the community; they may be picked up in the coded form of a language; they may be caused by natural phenomena such as a change in the weather or originate from the presence, absence, or movement of familiar artifacts. The cognitive process, however, is highly selective. When survival is or appears to the individual to be threatened, all irrelevant signals are filtered out. The subsistence farmer watches for signs affecting crop and livestock and has little if any time left for formal education and social intercourse. Similarly, within the urban community the majority often appear too occupied with problems of production and concern for continued acceptance within their subcommunities to find the leisure necessary for full personal development. In the functional community in which production as means to survival is itself an end, the need for stimulation is thus deliberately suppressed for those who have reached productive age.

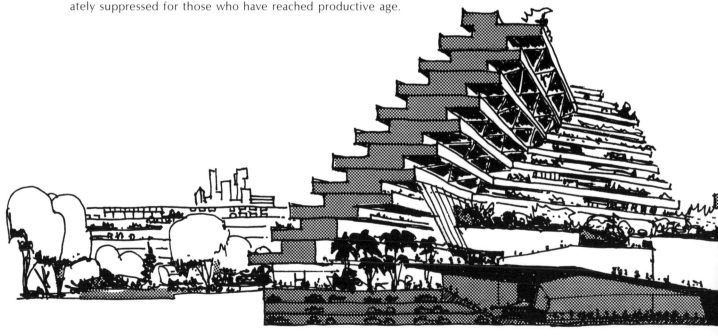

figure 21 *Modern man's expanded awareness demands rich building forms that are conceived as landscape elements and elaborated at every scale down to that of intimate spaces and minor components.*

The role of the human producer, however, is losing significance. Once machines provide the bulk of goods and services necessary for physical survival, the need for sensory and intellectual stimulation will widen and eventually become universal. This trend would demand that elements of change be built into the urban environment, giving it a dynamic quality and a new dimension. Elements of change may be new faces in a familiar environment or an opportunity to experience movement at greatly varying speeds. They may be bui'dings with movable parts or structures designed to change form with time. Above all, however, change may be experienced simply through exposure to the natural environment: wind and weather, the movement and sound of animals, the growth of plants, changing light and changing seasons. Such exposure finds its symbolic expression in an architecture of total involvement in which forms change with the quality and intensity of light—an architecture which invites movement through buildings and with it a penetration of their form as well as tactile involvement through the texture of their surfaces. In short, it finds expression in the antithesis to the air-conditioned glass box.

Under conditions of machine-produced abundance, the total urban environment, rather than mere parts of it, can be conceived once more as a work of art as it was in earlier times when slaves produced equivalent abundance for the citizens. As the need to produce is replaced by the need for stimulation, the city as megamachine must become the city as work of art. Once the escape into routine work is blocked, many more will have to face the reality of human existence. To use Morse Peckham's words: "Art is the exposure to the tensions and problems of a false world so that man may endure exposing himself to the tensions and problems of the real world."[17]

Status and Its Symbols. The needs for individual and communal containment and stimulation are basically passive in nature, but beyond their satisfaction the urban environment must offer scope for creative action. Communications, movement, and routine production are all functions fulfilled adequately and even admirably in the animal hive. Only the added discontinuity of human creativity distinguishes urban activity.

All creativity springs from individuals who, sometimes alone, but more often jointly with others, act as the agents for cultural evolution. For their contribution these individuals are rewarded by the community by being granted special status. The urban environment is the place where both evolving cultural forces and accruing rewards leave their mark. In this sense all art, and particularly buildings conceived as works of art, can be regarded as lasting reminders of past creativity. Individual status thus finds its permanent expression in symbols embedded in the townscape.

Such symbols have assumed a great variety of forms through history. Status has been expressed in dominant burial places, in dominant places of worship, in dominant places of residence, and in dominant places of work.

Through such monuments individuals extend their status beyond their own life-span into following dynasties, religious orders, and heirs. Individual status need not, however, be deposited in the physical environment of succeeding generations in the form of monuments. Each society has its own way of rewarding its members, and revolutions have been and are being fought over the criteria to be applied in the determination of status and the distribution of rewards.

The individual scope for monument building has indeed nearly always been narrowly limited except during times of economic, political, or social upheaval, such as during the industrial revolution. Other eras favored the action of individuals within the framework of the community, with the consequence that dominant buildings tended to serve collective functions, as in the medieval guildhalls. Neither denied the importance of individual excellence, which in one case was channeled in the direction of maximum efficiency in the exploitation of communal resources and in the other in the direction of the greatest refinement in the performance of specific tasks.

Status within the urban community is based on access to power. The resulting ability to influence the course of events may rest on wealth, political following, or knowledge. Correspondingly, the community rewards achievement with money, popular support, or by granting access to the sources of learning. Either base assures the all-important access to the media of communications, but beyond that the holders of such power can be expected to want to express it symbolically. With the community dependent on the services of such individuals, such demands can be regarded as nothing but legitimate needs.

The urban environment thus becomes a medium for status display. Details of clothing, grooming, and manners in the face-to-face contact of the pedestrian precinct and the shape, size, and condition of cars on the roads, in combination with the location, type, and size of dwellings and other possessions, add up to the composite individual status image. Where individual exertion in pursuit of tangible goals is highly valued by the community, the urban habitat must accommodate the symbols of individual success, even at the risk of creating utter visual chaos. Where, on the other hand, individual energy is automatically channeled into collective effort, the resulting habitat will inevitably tend toward complete anonymity and in the end come to resemble the hive.

CHAPTER THREE

THE SOCIAL

CONSTRAINTS

NEEDS AND CONSTRAINTS

Needs in Conflict

The preceding discussion of individual and collective shelter needs will be expanded and elaborated in later chapters. The immediate objective is to investigate the possible and probable ways in which urban needs interact. Due to the complex interdependence of the elements of the urban environment, these needs can be isolated and met separately only at the risk of tearing the urban fabric. Being interrelated, they establish the social constraints which limit the number of forms the urban environment may ultimately assume.

The Conflicting Needs of Individuals. Awareness of needs leads inevitably to the consideration of ways and means to satisfy them. Unsatisfied needs thus become latent drives. Yet the satisfaction of all needs at any one time will clearly never be possible; some are contradictory, while others are impossible to satisfy because of the presence of fixed constraints that are built into the environment. Hence there will always be drives that remain, for a time at least, consciously repressed. The results are conflict and tension.

The chances for conflict are the likelier the more varied, exacting, and urgent the demands that are made on the environment. At the subsistence level few needs are related directly to the urban environment; besides basic shelter the need is for food and clothing, and even private space is a luxury. Once basic needs are met, however, the individual's concern shifts to demands for specific quantities of, and qualities in, urban space, for features that offer intellectual and sensory stimulation, and for facilities that accommodate complex communications processes. But the rise in standards of living which buoys up urban expectations is accompanied by a simultaneous increase in the density of activities and movements, and the resulting quicker pace of urban life inevitably introduces new potential for conflict into the environment.

Most conflicts that result directly from urban conditions are related to one or another aspect of crowding. For a minority, these conflicts can obviously be avoided by dispersing a part of the urban population evenly over the countryside.[1] Such a solution, however, ignores the preferences of great numbers of people who enjoy the tensions associated with living in a population center and would not dream of trading it for pastoral peace.

Individuals whose dominant need is for quantity of space can be satisfied with relative ease outside the areas of urban concentration. Their demands can furthermore be scaled down considerably if dwellings are assorted according to their occupants' personal preferences. In the absence of fences, for example, an illusion of ample property obviously may be shared by many. The preferences of individuals, however, are not freely acquired, but are the result of different cultural and economic backgrounds. The separate accommodation of different space needs, while avoiding some conflict, leads therefore inevitably to the kind of social stratification fostered by both conventional suburb and conventional apartment tower.

A need conflict becomes inevitable where people search for direct personal involvement within a high-density habitat. When an urban population is homogeneous and stable, as is the case in many of the older European centers, the conflict is partly resolved because patterns of behavior coincide: if every tenant in an apartment building sleeps, eats, and watches the same television program at the same time and keeps quiet and to himself on all other occasions, there remains very little scope for open conflict. But even then built-up hostility and frustration have a way of surfacing in other spheres of urban life, as for instance in the attitude to social outsiders, be they foreigners, artists, or simply nonconformists.

In the open society of the metropolis, however, there is no such uniformity of collective values. Almost by definition, the metropolis is the seat of human extremes, however they are measured. It includes at one extreme the human casualties and the aberrants, at the other the elites.[2] Complete social homogenization is therefore clearly unthinkable. Quite the contrary, an urban region that wants to maintain a metropolitan core must provide just as many facilities for individual and group isolation as those encouraging

social integration. Otherwise, the ever-present possibility of open need conflict becomes a certainty.

Individual versus Society. Conflicts rarely arise at clearly defined space boundaries. They are likely to occur, however, whenever an individual's sense of his private space extends beyond the legal space boundaries which are defined in abstract rather than in sensory terms. A distant view from a private dwelling may thus come to be considered part of the private space claimed by its occupant. On the other hand, industrial or commercial users of urban space may pollute the environment far beyond its legally defined boundaries. In such cases individual needs clearly conflict with those of society as a whole.

Conflicts between individual and social needs used to be slow in developing and could, if all else failed, be resolved through the emigration of dissenting individuals. However, as a consequence of technological developments which have forced frequent and drastic changes on the urban environment, new needs now arise faster than old ones are satisfied. Simultaneously, global urbanization is tending toward an increasing uniformity of social values so that nonconforming individuals face the problem of need conflict with society wherever they may turn. The emerging global urban habitat, therefore, can no longer exclude socially disruptive elements, be they unpopular philosophers, iconoclastic artists, or potential criminals. (Figure 22.) The existence of considerable numbers of people who at some

figure 22 · *Nonconforming individuals tend to be pushed to the fringes of planned urban development. But as the global environment itself becomes urban in character, the fringe must be absorbed in the urban habitat. This fact was first recognized in the design of towns located in forbidding natural surroundings where the fringe is uninhabitable and which, as a result, must include zones that permit uncontrolled development within the planned environment.*

time during their lives may choose to withdraw from society or fight its dominant values cannot be ignored any longer, even if recognition of the fact only means the deliberate continuation of undeclared policies which accept social decay and ferment in the parts of cities which are decaying physically.

The individual and society have traditionally been linked in the family. There the individual and society in its most basic form are one. The family thus serves the individual as social extension and interlinks him with the community as a whole. Where the social fabric is reinforced by extended and enduring family ties, need conflicts between individual and society are greatly reduced.[3] In this case environmental shortcomings are compensated for by the survival of an institution that has maintained its traditional form. But once this basis weakens as a result of loosening family bonds, the conflicting needs of individuals and society find new focus, and the urban community must once more come to depend on a suitable urban environment to survive. Its eventual form will reflect the strategy applied in the balancing of individual versus collective needs—whether it is defensive in character[4] or aggressive and aiming at solutions appropriate to newly emerging ways of living. (Figure 23.)

Conflicting Social Needs. The defusing function of the extended family may, under certain conditions, be taken over by urban subcommunities. While they last, the wear and tear of life is shared by its members; urban needs that cannot be met for each individual separately are satisfied at the social level. It follows that individual and social needs are not only closely related but also in many cases interchangeable.

But social needs may also be shifted onto individuals. The typical industrial city is a clear example of this condition, with the satisfaction of cultural, recreational, educational, and even health care needs delegated without mercy to private initiative. The medieval city, by contrast, seemed to favor the satisfaction of individual needs at the corporate level; hence, for instance, the anonymity of the art of that period. More recent developments suggest a continuing search for a balance between the two basic approaches. Identification with institutions, business corporations, unions, residential subcommunities, and minority groups appears on the increase, while the option for individual self-realization remains open. The resulting social needs manifest themselves mainly in the realm of philosophy and politics.[5] Their conflict can, however, affect the urban environment directly, in particular its land use and communications patterns.

Communications overload does to the social processes within the urban community what activity crowding can do to the mental health of an individual.[6] The viability and even the survival of subcommunities therefore depend on the ease of communications possible within the urban environment. And since individuals are very limited in their ability to receive signals

figure 23 *If the existing urban cores are to remain in use, they must be drastically altered to shed their basic hostility to life.*

and messages and to store them for subsequent use, the problem of communications overload is easily one of the most critical of urban problems.

Technological developments have tended to reduce the suitability of the urban environment for direct human contact. This happened, for instance, through the introduction of automotive traffic into every part of the city and the ruthless sacrifice of any landscape elements or structures that interfered with it. It happens through the unchecked raising of noise levels everywhere, and it happens through the littering of the townscape with commercial signs. (Figure 24.) While reducing the possibilities to communicate through traditional media, the new media have been largely left to be exploited by special interests.[7]

While prime urban land, traditionally reserved for the whole community, is consistently preempted for private and corporate use, public spaces have simultaneously been replaced with private ones, the use of which is for hire: restaurants, clubs, meeting rooms, etc. The overall result is a distinct narrowing of opportunities for nonfunctional communication and a consequent conflict over the use of the remaining facilities. Where group differences were at one time expressed in the diversity of dress and living habits, today's prime manifestations of urban diversity take the form of public demonstrations and strikes.

When conflicts between individual needs remain unresolved, a reserve of adaptive energy is available to absorb the resulting stress. Social needs, however, are those of subcommunities—organizations rather than organisms. Instead of adjusting to stress, they tend to disintegrate when subjected to it. An urban environment not designed to accommodate differing social needs forces the fragmentation of society into the defensive closed subcommunities formed by the central business district, ghetto, suburban subdivision, retirement colony, etc.

figure 24 *The transition from traditional municipal services and media of communications to those of the electric age has left its unmistakable mark on the urban habitat.*

Built-in Constraints

Time and the Value Bias. Human values change with time—with the rhythm of day and night, the monthly cycles, the yearly seasons, the ages of man, the life-span of urban artifacts. But they also change as a result of cultural and technological developments which are in turn supported by the value bias that dominates the community at a particular time. Some such needs are basic, for example those for shelter. Others, transitory in nature, may for a time appear equally pressing. Still others are clearly passing needs whose satisfaction is optional.

But needs not catered to may subject some individuals to increased stress. And past the threshold beyond which homeostatic processes cease to function, added stress leads to injury. Unfortunately this threshold is neither fixed nor is its level known. Only the prevalence of degenerative diseases and certain mental disorders vaguely suggests that the urban environment subjects some individuals to greater stress than their systems can absorb.[8]

The very fact that most of the needs related to urban shelter and amenities appear deferrable—if they are recognized at all—makes the time factor one of the major constraints to the alleviation of such needs. The result can be a self-feeding process of need accumulation in which new needs develop faster than old ones disappear, often as the direct outgrowth of neglect. Or it may alternatively take the form of need inflation in which successive needs are artificially created through the use of mass media.

The value of any urban artifact must be judged in terms of two complementary sets of functions: one is defined by the specific needs it was intended to serve, the other by the needs that were disregarded in its conception and the satisfaction of which may as a result be obstructed. At different times the same structure may be an urban asset or an urban liability depending on the conditions governing at the moment. These conditions may, moreover, change several times in the course of a single day or week, with the yearly seasons, or from human generation to generation. The constancy and change of human development are reflected in these conditions and related to the life-span of urban artifacts.

A community's priorities may be based on needs that prove to be transitory. But with time, the resulting value bias is frozen into interlocked administrative systems and guides the subsequent molding and structuring of the urban environment. The transportation system, the systems of arrangement of dwellings and work places in space, the fiscal system reflecting the tax policies of different levels of government, park systems, systems of municipal water and power supply and refuse collection, systems of education, etc., do not develop directly out of people's needs. They are outgrowths of systems of urban administration assembled initially to serve social needs. Such systems are the necessary links between needs and their satisfaction. They are, however, by nature rigid and not adaptable to unexpected change. For this reason, changing communal values are in the end locked into obsolete systems that are unresponsive to new needs.

Clashes between values are inevitable when different communities share the same space, be it visual space or the aural space created through the media of telecommunications. When communal space is visually defined, conflicts can be confined to its boundaries. With technological progress, these have gradually expanded from the fortified city's wall to the nation's defended border. However, the advent of electronic media of communications is now destroying the very concept of boundaries, and the scene of conflict is moving within the urban multicommunity. There, people of widely different aims and backgrounds, rich and poor, educated and illiterate, fulfill a growing multiplicity of functions in a multiplicity of spheres of activity. Potential areas of conflict become infinite in number.

Communal values at their highest are those of religious belief; at their lowest, in the form of blind prejudice, they turn from value to liability. Their whole spectrum, however, influences the urban environment, and so do the conflicts between communal values. In competing forms of adjacent buildings, in the dissection of residential areas by highways, in the fortresslike aspect of some urban schools, conflicting values within the multicommunity find their reflection. By their nature such conflicts become more clearly visible in the environment than does the unquestioned, and thus dominant, communal value bias. The dogma of the sanctity of private ownership of urban land, the belief in the inherent superiority or inferiority of different subcommunities, and the unquestioning commitment to ruling tastes inevitably find their sedimentation in the environment even if the process is imperceptible to those involved in it.

Establishments as Constraints. The vast majority of people are never more than vaguely aware of their individual needs and do not know how to satisfy them. They pattern their lives on sets of priorities handed down by elites made up of the individuals they have accepted as their betters and with whose attitudes and actions they identify themselves. The members of elites in turn tend to consolidate their positions of control by exercising them through institutions—either existing or established for the purpose in the form of government agencies, corporations, educational and cultural institutions, foundations, political and professional organizations, etc. Individuals occupying corresponding control positions in different institutional hierarchies form the various levels of the establishment.

The rules which govern the evolution of the urban environment are made within this establishment. Priorities of needs are decided on, new needs created, the satisfaction of existing ones encouraged or denied, and individual energy channeled; in short, the establishment determines communal values. Within any establishment, however, the relative positions of the different institutions vary constantly. The church hierarchy, for instance, once at the pinnacle of power, has sunk to the lower rungs of the establishment while government bureaucracies and business corporations have taken the leading roles in shaping the urban habitat.

There is no doubt that coming shifts in the urban power structure will affect the urban image correspondingly. The city dominated by office buildings will prove just as much a passing phase as was the city dominated in turn by castle, cathedral, and palace in earlier times. Yet new urban forms will result not from revolutionary social changes, but primarily from the regrouping of forces within the establishment made necessary by the absorption of newly emerging centers of power.

Establishments are in essence conservative. The more deeply entrenched they are, the less scope there is for new development and unprecedented action. Only during the recurrent periods in history when establishments fail to cope with new forces emerging within the community or are successfully challenged from without is radical change possible. This has been particularly true of the present period of rapid technological development, ushered in by the industrial revolution whose flood of inventions continues to bypass old and new constraints. The continuing inability of establishments to effectively constrain new developments may paradoxically be the very result of universal longevity. Since traditional institutions tend to provide for personal power to accrue with age, establishments often end up being controlled by individuals who are separated from the sources of newly generated knowledge by an unbridgeable generation gap.

Modern establishments are anything but monolithic and are often split and torn by internal conflict. They are, moreover, practically nonexistent at the international level. Only on the local and national scenes can establishments thus exercise considerable constraints on urban development, and only over limited periods of time. Under such conditions conventional wisdom combined with ruling taste, when sufficiently entrenched, often force building into thoughtlessly applied molds, such as those of endlessly repeated bungalows, apartment blocks, and office boxes. The state at which no further thought impedes established processes is only possible, however, when all members of the establishment concerned have reached permanent agreement or been brought into line. Potentially disturbing outside influences can then be quickly neutralized through concerted action. But this is a situation that clearly cannot last in a pluralistic society.

Artifacts as Constraints. The existing urban environment, thanks to continual adaptation, adequately meets most of the demands made upon it most of the time. Demand, however, is not necessarily a true reflection of need. It may be far in excess of need, or it may express transitory needs, or even whims, and ignore basic needs whose satisfaction may later prove to be of crucial importance for the survival of the community.

Creating an urban environment means superimposing human values on nature. Each artifact added to it represents a further intervention in the natural order of things. At the same time, it adds clarity to the definition of the human values expressed, which becomes complete when the forces of nature are effectively subdued and the environment is fully defined in human terms. Only at this point does the environment become truly urban. The completed city, however, is fitted tightly to a particular set of collective values. As these change, its inhabitants must adapt their own values to those incorporated in the existing structure or leave—or adapt the environment to their new needs by replacing parts of it at the expense of possibly greater effort than would be required by building afresh.

Once completed, both the city conceived as communal container and the dwelling conceived as container for individuals are inflexible. If they are built originally to serve constituent needs, they offer relatively little

figure 25 *Urban form conceived to meet constituent human needs offers little resistance to its adaptation to later changes in living habits.*

resistance to being adapted to later demands. Constituent needs are basic and not subject to change; only the means to their satisfaction change. Parts of medieval cities and early North American towns are thus often quite livable even today. (Figure 25.) When, on the other hand, the urban habitat has been assembled primarily to fulfill demands unrelated to basic needs, the resulting environment may reveal hostility to life as soon as new demands supersede the old.

In the past, living conditions and needs changed slowly and imperceptibly. Cities, furthermore, were periodically destroyed by fire, through accident, by the action of enemies in war, or by natural disasters such as floods and earthquakes. In the rebuilding process the urban environment could be refitted to slightly changed conditions and adapted to new demands as seemed necessary. (Figure 26.) Today, by contrast, the destruction of cities in war invites the risk of global nuclear holocaust, while potential damage from floods, earthquakes, and accidental fire have been reduced to the point where they no longer seriously endanger life in the modern city. In the process, the urban artifact has become almost impervious to change except through planned action. The traditional random process of adapting the urban environment to needs through accident has given way to planned renewal of the city as the only alternative to its progressive decay.

Planning is dependent on a clear understanding of basic trends and of the forces constraining them. Yet all thought of planning is shaped in turn by the structure and form of the existing environment. The urban system of artifacts, therefore, not only restricts renewal action but also constrains all thought about intervention in the urban environment. Unless approached

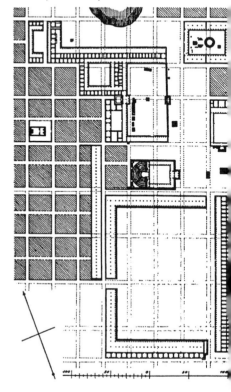

figure 26 *Completely destroyed in the course of a war in 494 B.C., the old city of Miletus was rebuilt on the basis of a radically different plan.*

through the media of anti-environment, that is, of art, the existing urban habitat can become a trap for both action and thought.

THE FORMS OF SOCIAL CONSTRAINTS
Traditions and Habits

The Pall of Traditions. As artifacts accumulate in urban space they gradually displace all elements of nature, ultimately leaving an urban environment that is completely artificial: man's habitat itself becomes an artifact, and nature's function as the city's anti-environment is ended. Where the last semblance of integration of the natural with the urban environment is lost, the latter can only continue to sustain human life at anywhere near optimum levels to the extent that it is art.

The traditional city had few alternatives of development. Its needs for fortifications and close communal integration ruled out the option of introducing nature as a major element into the urban environment except in rare instances and at great cost. The city was conceived as a work of art and this conception has dominated its form to this day. The value of art, however, is tied to the values dominating the thought and action of a community. As long as communities remain closed and values unchanged, environmental art in the form of cities is possible. But as urban communities break up into loose subcommunities, traditional values lose their currency and what was once art may remain as empty form.

But these empty forms remain in use if only for economic reasons and end up serving new urban activities. Motorized traffic, as a result, attempts to follow the paths originally laid out for pedestrian circulation and communication, and the spaces that were scaled to the speed of natural movement are now traversed many times faster. The existing environment, moreover, by its very presence tends to force human thinking into established channels, and the urban designer's options are likely to be compromised by the mere presence of traditional artifacts.

As long as communal survival depended on the continuity of established values, traditions served a vital purpose. The dissolution of the closed community, however, has blinded the force of tradition. The word "traditional" has taken on an ominous synonymity with "reactionary," even while the numerical majority of the world's population is emerging only slowly from the security of tradition-directed values.[9] But survival depends increasingly on a clear understanding of all environmental forces and their interrelation rather than on tribal memories. Instead of being preserved, all parts of the urban habitat need to be constantly and basically rethought and re-created.

An artificial environment has identity to the extent that it is art. Works of architecture preserved from the past extend such identity in time; this

figure 27 *Urban form could conceivably be created for the express purpose of providing escape from the monotony of everyday life. Expo 67 is a prototype of urban form conceived as anti-environment.*

is the ultimate reason for their continued existence. However, once the inventory of functionally obsolete artifacts starts to constrain urban life, tradition gains a stranglehold on further human achievement, and individuals in gradually increasing numbers may concentrate their creative energies on finding an escape from a dying environment. They may withdraw from it by immersing themselves in work, through involvement in expressive art, by yielding to the promise of alcohol or drug-induced hallucination, or simply by physically and socially isolating themselves and their subcommunities from the larger environment. The strategies of noninvolvement are innumerable. (Figure 27.)

The Price of Togetherness. Cities were once limited in size by the food that could be grown in their immediate region. But as the world's regions became linked in an international transportation network and as the global population became independent of local food supplies, urban densities have been freed from their traditional constraints. New limitations have appeared in their place, but so far they have been only vaguely perceived.

The density of urban activity varies with daily, weekly, and seasonal cycles. It depends on the age, status, occupation, and place of residence of the individuals responsible for different activities and on their grouping in subcommunities. Through control of the spatial relations between places of residence, of work, of leisure time activities, and of channeled movement, activity densities can therefore be changed in degree or in time or shifted from one location to another.

The individual adapts himself to such changes in the environment by adjusting his living habits. If the physical distance between neighbors increases, social intercourse becomes easier and less formal, just as the reverse—shrinking distance—increases activity crowding and forces human relations into more formal patterns. (Figure 28.) This latter process, however, presupposes the ability and willingness of individuals to learn and their membership in stable subcommunities within which the values of individual achievement can be communicated and transmitted to following generations. Without the support of such communal ties the demand for formal restraint may well exceed individual ability to comply. Unfortunately, rapid increases in urban density may destroy the very communal ties which might otherwise enable individuals to adjust to added crowding. This tendency is all the more disastrous since the buildup of population pressures hits the poorest parts of cities hardest; the inhabitants there have the least option to move elsewhere.

Only when communal ties are not place-related, as in the middle and upper strata of the urban population, does increased crowding of urban activities, whether at home or at work, appear not to have any demonstrable negative effect. It may, however, partly explain the emergence of Riesman's "other-directed" personality: open, lacking inhibitions, interested in others, and thus able to move freely in the crowded urban habitat, thanks to the controlled "informality" of his manners.

Problems of Mixed Urban Populations.   In the urban environment individuals interact directly as well as indirectly—through membership in the same all-inclusive society and through the joint ownership of public assets. Under the circumstances different individual attitudes may become, with time, increasingly attuned to each other. In this fashion the urban environment acts as a melting pot. As cities lose their separate identities and connect up in one globe-encircling habitat, a distinctive type of urbanite emerges who dresses, behaves, and thinks one way regardless of his place of birth and residence: the prototype of the human products that emerge in growing numbers from the new global melting process.

It is possible that individual and communal differences will progressively be dissolved through such personal urban interaction. But, while the mold may be ready, a great proportion of the urban population seems to resist being cast in it. Also, the melting process, even when in action, may be effective only to a degree, thus adding yet another variable to the range

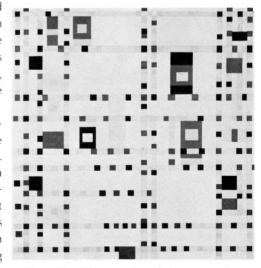

figure 28   *The more formal the patterns into which human relations are forced as a result of activity crowding, the greater the challenge to the human spirit. Mondrian's painting* Broadway Boogie-Woogie *(1942–1943) provides a classic example of the way in which self-imposed geometric constraints can be transcended through art. (Collection of The Museum of Modern Art.)*

of possible urban attitudes. Compared with the homogeneity achieved in the traditional city, the performance of the contemporary urban habitat as a melting pot for divergent individual attitudes has been rather poor.

Unfortunately, contemporary society does not have the collective sense of purpose which permeated earlier eras. Even the materialistic values that have long dominated thought and action throughout most of the world are in the process of losing currency. Only in the growing realization that there may be value to life itself besides in the production of goods is there hope that new purpose can be instilled in urban activity. But if this realization is growing, it is by no means universal. Rather than being concerned with the creation of new values for a global community, the overwhelming majority of the world's urban population, no doubt, cares primarily and instinctively for the preservation of the status quo. For some this may mean loyalty to the values locally current in their youth, for others the futile attempt to bring present-day reality to terms with ancient traditions.

The creation of new values and, even more, their dissemination, depends on a multiple two-way communications network that tightly interlaces the urban environment. In the modern city this network is neglected. The functional, that is, "paying," aspects of communications are served well, but others, particularly the subsystems based on random-direct communication from person to person, remain largely ignored. The isolation of individuals and groups from unwanted face-to-face contacts is thus encouraged, with the result that different clusters of interlinked subcommunities have no mutual ties except the indirect ones provided by the mass media. Mass media, however, permit no dialogue, and the disjoined urban environment increasingly fails in its vital function as an all-involving communications system.

Conventional Wisdom Codified

Constraints as Stabilizers.   Constraints are a component part of all civilization. And one of the media through which civilizations constrain life is the form of the urban habitat. As it fixes communal values, directs thinking, and channels action, it stabilizes social forces through the imposition of order. Order, however, can be conceived at vastly differing levels of complexity. The spirit of frenzied pursuit of monetary gains, for instance, imposes a distinct visual order on the resulting urban growth. (Figure 29.) Similarly, the unchallenged exercise of political power or the dominance of the military mind or highway engineer expresses itself clearly in urban order, which may be explicit or implicit depending on the degree to which the spirit it expresses is imposed on or absorbed by the builders of cities. Thus the lower Manhattan skyscraper complex is the near perfect fossilization of the unchecked spirit of private enterprise, while Penn's plan for central

Philadelphia represents equally clearly an imposition of external order on urban growth. (Figure 30.)

Order can be internalized at different levels of the urban hierarchy. If a power elite is sufficiently determined, it may force its concept of order on the environment. If, on the other hand, a dominant concept of order permeates the urban community as a whole, it will in turn find its formal expression, be it in skyscrapers or in a traditional city. (Figure 31.) The difference to the community is that between being regimented and submitting to an order that is self-imposed. Self-imposed order, by its very definition, changes with the composition of the self—the community. As its values undergo gradual modification the concept of order is constantly readapted. In this process the urban environment retains its fitness to support life. Self-imposed order, in the urban context, is organic order.

As soon as order is imposed on the community rather than by the community, it becomes rigid and insensitive to changes in communal values; instead of ordering urban activities, the environment confines them. Perfect order, as judged from any one individual's point of view, inevitably comes to mean the successful confinement of all urban activity. Ultimately, a community can achieve a state of complete stability only at the cost of its life.

For organic order to be visible in the urban environment, a community must be defined by clear physical boundaries. In the age of the global urban multicommunity this condition is rare indeed. The tip of Manhattan Island projects a definite image because its dominant buildings accommodate a homogeneous body—the business community—whose leading members were, moreover, in a position to exercise direct control over the essential details of the form of their habitat. Normally, however, neither clear community boundaries nor opportunity to exercise environmental control exists. Subcommunities are based only to a negligible extent on the propinquity of its members' dwellings or places of work, and few people are in a position to determine even the features of their intimate surroundings. Thus order can no longer be directly self-imposed. The indirect process, however, involves both the reaching of a consensus by many subcommunities and the consent of potential veto groups. The maintenance of organic order in the urban environment depends, therefore, on changing sets of codified constraints arrived at and continually adapted in an all-involving process of decision making.

The Forms of Codification. As Keynes noted, we are ruled by ideas and very little else. Ideas, however, can assume dominance only after they have been widely disseminated and absorbed in what Galbraith has termed the "conventional wisdom." It is on the basis of the conventional wisdom of the moment that laws are enacted or revoked and policy statements issued. Thus codified, the conventional wisdom current in the establishment exercises the direct constraints on urban development.

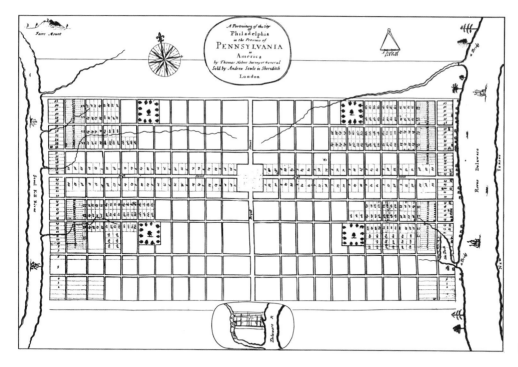

figure 30 *Order imposed by decree.*

figure 31 *Order self-imposed by the community.*

In this manner codes of one kind or another regulate every aspect of the modern city either directly or indirectly, whether it be the path of its development, its network of services, the shape of buildings, most details of their construction, the possible spatial relationships between buildings, the distribution of people within them, the location of paths and acceptable speeds of movement on them, and so on. Codes need not emanate from governments; the conventional wisdom dominant within the management of an international corporation, for example, will find its expression in codified form and affect the quality of its contribution to the urban environment. Similarly, at a different level, the conventional wisdom governing the policy of professional bodies—town planners, engineers, land surveyors, architects— finds its sedimentation in such things as the forms of contracts its members may enter and the curricula upon which candidates' studies must be based. Even books and technical information, once printed and distributed, may be considered a form of codification which can directly influence the urban habitat.

The maze of relevant codes is truly impenetrable, particularly since a great part of it is submerged in imagery and specialists' jargon and thus invisible from any single point of view. Only when ideas are embedded in myths do they become equally invincible. All the possible meanings of land-use legislation may be as little apparent to an architect as its latent aesthetic and social meanings may be to a lawyer. The danger of any wisdom in codified form is its relative invisibility and resulting latency as a constraining force. The more explicit the codified form of an idea, the clearer can be the reevaluation of its relevance to the urban environment at any time.

Since the end of the Middle Ages the printed word has dominated all forms of encodement, taking over the function imagery fulfilled before. The increase in electronic communications means that new forms of coding are for the first time successfully challenging the predominance of the printed word and are ready to preempt the meaning of printed words to a similar extent that they at one time had drained images of their meaning. This process will require a complete reencodement of all past information and offers a unique opportunity for its total reevaluation. A new order will come to mold the urban environment, and among the determinants of its qualities will be, on the one hand, the amount of thought and wisdom applied to the new approach to coding information and, on the other hand, the built-in bias of the media used.

Guides and Straitjackets. Once an artifact is in place, it acts as a constraint on further development. In the sense that any such object inevitably takes on symbolic meaning for some members of the urban community, its form can become a medium in which elements of conventional wisdom are encoded. But conventional wisdom conventionally codified becomes in turn a constraint on subsequent changes of the communal value bias once it is translated into the medium of urban artifacts. Urban development is thus constrained both by current conventional wisdom and by the accumulation of reinterpreted past conventional wisdom.

Constraints can act as guides, but beyond a certain stage they become obstacles to further development. When different codes combine to block the growth of the urban habitat or internal adaptation to changed conditions, they clearly become adverse to urban life. When, as in numerous ancient and not so ancient European cities, no modern architecture is tolerated regardless of its quality,[10] man's creative spirit must find an outlet in spheres other than those of urban design, or in other parts of the globe. But similar sets of constraints are present in all established fields of endeavor; one need only think of the bureaucracies of government and big business. And as the urban environment enfolds the globe, escape in space is blocked. The need to constantly reevaluate all constraints becomes vital.

All codes become obsolete in time. The more general their terms, the longer their potential life. This accounts for the extreme longevity of codes clothed in mythical terms. Inversely, explicit codes tend to be the first to appear obsolete: building plans, technical information, regulations, etc. They are also the ones that offer ready access to their sources and are thus easy to uproot.

The method of storage used for codified information changes with the medium: from human memory to manuscript to printing press to machine memory. And as the method of storage changes so does the problem of information retrieval. The present environment is clearly the result of an uncontrolled accumulation of independently devised codes, too many of which are basically authoritarian: they state in detail what is or is not allowed, desirable, or practical, but rarely do they program alternatives and goals explicitly. Their accumulation is not only uncontrolled and fraught with redundancies but beyond analysis. The cataloging of written information has proved impractical beyond a certain volume and when time is of the essence, and both of these conditions apply in the case of encodified material concerning the urban environment. The hope for the effective manipulation of social constraints within this environment rests with the emerging electronic technology and, even more, with the new approaches to problem solving which it has made necessary.

The degree to which conflicts between social needs can or should be resolved is in considerable doubt. Natural conflict could conceivably be planned out of the urban environment, only to be reintroduced in artificial form to combat the paralyzing boredom that would result from a total lack of mental or physical stimulation. Before this stage is reached, however, it will be necessary to reduce the physical and economic constraints that still limit urban development everywhere, and to which the discussion now turns.

CHAPTER FOUR

THE PHYSICAL AND

ECONOMIC CONSTRAINTS

LAND AND ITS USES

Urban Land Resources

The Uses of Land. The urban habitat is the battleground where different uses compete for limited land resources. When clashes ensue, the deciding factor is the community's value bias or, more accurately, the value bias of the subcommunities dominant at the time. Land once consumed, however, is used up, expended, and possibly wasted for generations to come. As with industrial products, some of this consumption may actually contribute to life's enrichment. But the bulk of it satisfies, at best, only transitory needs.

When regarded as real estate, land and buildings are mere economic assets from which all monetary value is to be extracted as effectively as possible. But as the promise of abundance through automation brings the value of economic activity into question, cities may now revert to their original roles as centers of human life rather than as centers of production. In that case, existing cities will have to be adapted to serve new life-supporting functions, or urban cores will move to new locations.

Both choices are constrained by sets of forces the strength of which varies from place to place. The creation of new centers is hindered by the fixed image that any city has in the minds of its inhabitants, and even more so

63

by the fact that all established paths of urban movement—highways, railways, subways—are oriented toward the existing cores. The adaptation of old centers to new concepts of urban living, on the other hand, is seriously impeded by the life-choking activities which pollute their every aspect—the physical environment as much as their image and intellectual climate. (Figure 32.) But the constraints affecting both alternatives are relieved by the same remedy. A well-conceived transportation system diffuses the forces which threaten to strangle the city, both by relieving congestion and encouraging the removal of productive industries, and by creating new nodes which can absorb the excess growth potential of established urban cores.

Continued urban growth implies stepped-up competition for previously undeveloped land and human intervention, not only in the existing urban habitat but also in the larger natural environment. Any such intervention in turn releases chains of unpredictable reactions and counterreactions. Thus, even at the present scale, cities modify their own climates through the formation of dust domes over built-up areas;[1] and spreading urbanization may eventually cause climatic changes affecting whole continents and their plant and animal life and draw agricultural production ever closer into the widening urban orbit.

In a sense the process of urbanization has always involved the despoiling of land. As long as cities were directly dependent for their survival on the agriculture of their immediate region, however, there was an obvious incentive to waste as little of the available natural resources as possible. The land required for urban purposes, moreover, represented only a minute part of the total. Since then, technological development has created the unfortunate illusion that food is grown "elsewhere" in unlimited quantities. Yet, as population growth and the corresponding urban sprawl force thinking into terms of regional and even continental cities, the conventional scorched-earth approach to urbanization leads inevitably to the stage where "elsewhere" will become part of the city itself. The only approach to urban planning that is sound in the long run is thus based on concepts that integrate urban land-use patterns into the ecology of nature.

Population Densities. In a distorted fashion, population densities reflect the intensity of the human use of urban land. The distortions are caused by the daily, weekly, and seasonal variations in the use of different parts of the urban habitat. In the central business district of any typical North American city, for example, the population density thus may vary from zero at night and on weekends to tens of thousands of people per acre at other times, a contrast amplified by the effects of synchronized working hours. In residential suburbs the fluctuations are less pronounced. But only in the obsolete parts of cities are densities nearly constant: in slums because of the great number of idle or locally employed men, and in other enclaves similarly bypassed by technological progress.[2]

What limits local population densities are the type, size, and density of buildings; what limits their fluctuation is the capacity of the transportation system that serves them. Density figures generally used for purposes of comparison are based either on the resident population within political boundaries or on the resident population within the limits of specific projects. Neither means much. If based on areas which include land that serves industry, transportation, and commerce, density figures give no information on the amount of land used exclusively by local residents. Project densities, on the other hand, count numbers of dwellings or numbers of bedrooms per acre and say little if anything about the residents' activities outside the project area and the resulting effect on the density of activity elsewhere. The Midtown Manhattan Study, for example, quotes a gross population density of 90,000 per square mile for the whole of Manhattan in contrast to an average net density of 380,000 people per square mile of residential land.[3] The constraining effect of such densities on an individual's activities clearly depends on his ability to move freely within the zones of differing population density and to escape the most crowded parts at least temporarily.

To yield any meaning, residential densities must be linked to local activity densities, and these in turn must be considered in relation to time, since the patterns of urban activity may change with the hour, the day, and the season. But activities are also affected by the presence of urban artifacts which can be measured in terms of building density; for instance, as building volume per unobstructed ground area. By assigning different weights to different types of buildings, the amount, kind, and timing of activity generated at their gates can be evaluated. And from the correlation of the resulting data, a true picture emerges of the life and activity characteristic of different parts of the urban habitat at different times.

Particularly when the various urban functions are mutually isolated in different zones, the very functioning of the city depends on its facilities for mechanized mass transportation, be they highways, railways, or airways. In this case, a centralized transportation system replaces the centralization of resident populations, and land is devoured both by inflated residential demands and by the corresponding land needs of transportation and distribution systems. In a curiously perverse manner, planning practices embodied in zoning legislation can actually enforce the waste of dwindling land resources. If, alternatively, residential land needs were directly integrated with those of industry, commerce, and transportation, the use of urban land could obviously be intensified. (Figure 33.) And since such an integration would reduce urban dependence on the transportation system, its land needs might, as a result, be less.

Potential damage to individual well-being arises not from high population densities, but from the resultant overlap of concentrated urban activities, i.e., from activity crowding. When activity is decentralized, such crowding is relieved, but the potential richness of urban life suffers proportionately. Only by interrelating concentrated activities in ways which avoid their mutual interference can activity crowding be avoided without loss of urbanity in the environment. And with the help of electronic data processing equipment, the integration of rest and activity in urban space and time may be achieved for the first time.

Urban Land Values. When stepped-up demand leads to competition for the use of resources which are in limited supply, their cost rises. Climbing land values may be considered as a capital gain or as an index of rising land needs; in either case, they reflect the fact of intensified competition for urban land and foreshadow its subsequent intensified use. The degree of potential use intensity depends, therefore, on factors which invite needs to focus on particular parcels of urban land. A few of those are natural factors, such as the features of the landscape and local peculiarities of topography and climate. The most important ones, however, are made and controlled

figure 33 *The land needs of administrative organizations and of commerce can be integrated harmoniously with residential and recreational needs, and urban space utilized more intensively as a result.*

by man. Increasingly, this is true even for the dominant elements of land-scape: artificial lakes, buildings in the same scale as hills and cliffs, etc. The potential value of any parcel of urban land thus results almost exclusively from human intervention in the natural environment.

The kinds of intervention directly relevant to the value of urban land are those which affect its use for urban activities and their maximum density. Values are thus clearly related to services provided and their cost, particularly road and rail access, communications links, water supply, and waste disposal. They are modified, however, by interventions that operate on different planes, such as zoning and other legal restrictions on land use, and by the type and intensity of use made of neighboring land. Values, finally, may be influenced by the ingenuity applied in making maximum use of land within the framework of existing constraints. (Figure 34.)

All but the last-mentioned factor are directly or indirectly under public control. If the value changes that result from public intervention are passed on to individuals, newly created wealth is clearly transferred from the public to the private domain. The dismal financial situation in which most growing North American cities find themselves may, to a large extent, result directly from this transfer of locally created wealth, which is subsequently taxed at senior levels of government only. This situation is made worse by the fact that public investment in the servicing of land raises values, while private investment in buildings often reduces the value of the surrounding land. Too often publicly serviced land is used up privately, in every sense of the word, by the buildings erected on it, be they of the environment-polluting

figure 34   *A previously useless airspace over railway tracks in the center of Montreal became the location of a major convention and trade center. (a) Hotel Bonaventure, (b) International Center of Commerce, (c) five-story market, (d) mezzanine, (e) Hall Concordia, (f) Galeries Bonaventure.*

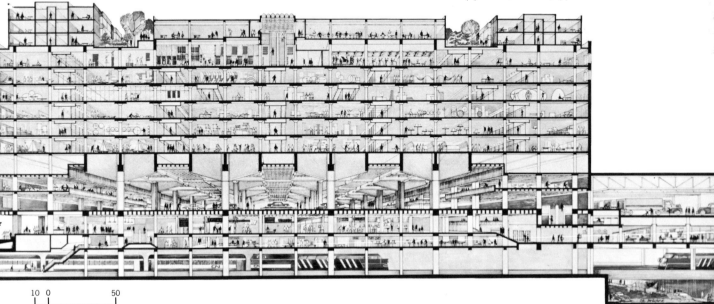

10 0   50

commercial or industrial kind or the less malignant expressions of extractive land use—office and apartment blocks—which nevertheless manage to deaden their surroundings under covers of asphalt and concrete. Urban buildings which truly enhance their environment are rare indeed. (Figure 35.)

Different urban activities are assigned different values by different communities. Whichever function weighs most heavily on the scale of communal values tends to drive uses of lower priority out of choice locations.[4] Once uses are established in buildings, however, they are difficult to dislodge. Unfortunately for North American cities, their formative period coincided with the era of the industrial revolution, with the result that their urban cores developed unchallenged into the ubiquitous central business district. That this bias was never an exclusively North American monopoly is illustrated by Le Corbusier's proposal of 1925 for the razing of Paris and the replacement of that city's center with eighteen 60-story office buildings, meant to dominate France symbolically.[5] The dominant value scale is still very much pervaded by this same spirit, which permits the deduction of office but not apartment rent payments from taxable income, to mention but one example. In the long run, land values do not influence urban land use; quite to the contrary, they reflect the dominant value bias of the community. (Figure 36.)

figure 35   *"Urban buildings which truly enhance their environment are rare indeed."*

figure 36 *Even an international financial center need not be dominated by skyscrapers.*

Trends in the Uses of Land

Trends and Their Extrapolation.   The larger his family, the better a peasant's chances for economic survival and the greater the urbanite's protection from communal isolation. Thus, compounded by the effects of the rapid progress of medical science, the desire for social security in the widest sense has made its contribution to the current global population explosion.

If there is one indisputable trend, it is toward an increased global population density which is crystallizing in the world's urban areas. The projection of current trends of population growth suggests that it may become increasingly hard and eventually impossible to maintain current standards of living anywhere, quite apart from the obvious necessity of raising them in the economically underdeveloped areas of the world. However, "trends are the composite results of human actions, born from human desires,"[6] and as such, expressions of the human will. The very urbanization of the planet may thus lead to an eventual stabilization of this growth, particularly if the communal structure in the emerging conurbations can be fashioned to guarantee individual security regardless of family attachments.[7]

Meanwhile, the clearly foreseeable increase of the world's population, housed at the average Manhattan density of 90,000 persons per square mile, would only require some 110,000 square miles out of a total of 55 million square miles, or some 0.2 percent of the globe's land surface. Even applying the more common figure of 10,000 persons per square mile, equal to the density prevailing in cities like Metropolitan Toronto or the Greater Hamburg area, less than 2 percent of the available land would need to be assigned to urban uses. But the areas these residential densities are based on are unrelated to the activity areas claimed by the inhabitants of urban centers. They take no account of the regular exodus of city dwellers to the beaches, resort areas, and parks beyond their immediate habitat. They ignore the urban cores' physical extensions—the land, air, and sea routes that transform the world into an urban domain. But urban uses of land are not necessarily incompatible with the needs of agriculture, hunting, and the fishing industry, even if their integration may require careful planning.

The continuation of current planning practices may well lead to an excess of land needs over land resources. (Figure 37.) But any extrapolation of single trends, particularly when considered on the global scale, are made up of uncounted secondary and minor trends, many of them contradictory and all constantly changing in force and deflecting one another in the process. Analyzing them requires not only a complete understanding of their multiple interaction but the simultaneous comprehension of the nature of each relevant subtrend. This complexity renders the interpretation of all but the most basic urban trends open to a vast range of questions.

Present difficulties, therefore, cannot be simply projected into the future, nor can approaches that are successful at the present scale of urban development be expected to prove equally successful at a vastly larger scale. The average density at which Manhattan is populated might well become unbearable without the relief offered by open space in close proximity—and when applied to urban concentrations housing populations approaching the 100 million mark. At that order of human settlement, urban land use may once more have to become integrated with the agricultural use of land, as is happening now to a limited extent and, independent of public planning, in the agricultural estates maintained privately around major cities.[8] And since it is unlikely that land once urbanized will ever revert to agricultural use, the preservation of remaining agricultural areas near the potential international focal points of urbanization may well be of crucial importance for the well-being of future generations.

Variations and Alternatives.   Futile as it is to attempt any but the most general predictions concerning the future course of urban development, the analysis of trends permits an evaluation of their potential consequences. Of the great variety of possible futures, the one that appears the most desirable at any one time can then be achieved by deliberately guiding trends and by influencing the rate of their progress. The art of long-range planning becomes the art of manipulating trends.

Few trends are urban per se. Phenomena such as the population explo-

figure 37 *The continuation of present planning practices will inevitably lead to shortages of urban land or to restrictions in the use of private automobiles.*

sion, the bias of dominant communications media, communal value scales, and so on, although linked to urban development, may remain largely independent of it. They are accommodated in the planning process and given expression in urban form; and by forcing thought into specific channels, they become the primary trends that mold the urban environment. With the waning of centralized control, however, their primacy no longer excludes the action of secondary trends. Multilayered land uses have been possible in spite of established zoning practices, and aesthetic considerations have at times been strong enough to block or redirect the construction of urban expressways.

Secondary trends are often hidden by the more obvious aspects of the conventional development processes. The trend toward global mobility, for example, as yet hardly reflected in urban form, helps millions of travelers gain a firsthand experience of the amenities available in other parts of the world, and, by inviting comparison, it will ultimately result in changes in their home environment. Similarly, the international character of capital investment in urban land and buildings can help contribute to the mutual enrichment of remote urban centers. (Figure 38.) In addition, however, increased mobility will ease the occasional escape from urban crowding and, assuming there are places to escape to, render life bearable in increasingly crowded urban core areas.

Other latent trends can be detected in the growing diversity of living habits and corresponding housing types, in the new communications techniques which permit a growing number of specialists to work from their

figure 38 *The international character of capital investments and of tourism helps contribute to the mutual enrichment of urban centers everywhere.*

place of residence rather than in an office, and in the automation of previously human labor. Countless others could be mentioned. They all contribute with varying force to the constant shifting of constraints which affect the use of urban land.

The tendency to use urban space in more sophisticated ways than the conventional zoning practices envisage may contribute to the acceptance of higher building densities. As a means to separate incompatible activities, zoning, after all, need not be conceived in two dimensions only. When extended into the vertical dimension and the dimension of time, however, space- and time-use zoning replace the conventional concept of land-use zoning. The vastly greater complexity of its application is matched by the data processing ability of electronic equipment, and the added cost of building multiple-use structures is balanced by savings in land and development costs.

MATERIALS, ENERGY, AND TECHNIQUES

Stages of Production

Basic Urban Shelter. The very concept of an urban environment presupposes a relatively high level of sophistication in social organization and, in particular, the prior emergence of specialized skills. For this reason urban shelter has been at all times technically superior to comparative rural housing in the same region. The very specialization of local skill, however, combined with the dependence on building materials available in the immediate area, imposed fixed constraints on initial urban development. For this reason traditional cities arrived early at standardized forms of dwellings in which heights and clear spans were dependent on the kinds of stone, clay, and wood available locally and on the level of ingenuity and skill acquired in their application. Except for a certain elaboration of details, standards once established might not be questioned again for centuries. (Figure 39.) Standards of sanitation and other environmental services also tended to remain static. Changes occurred only as a direct result of major disasters, such as destruction by war or fire, or following social and political upheavals.

Traditional urban shelter remained unchanged because the limitations inherent in existing methods and materials remained invisible. Even if they were perceived occasionally, as they must have been, the restrictions remained acceptable because experimentation in new approaches was neither economically feasible nor socially desirable. Basic traditional housing evolved gradually from rural practice—adapted to the demands of early urban life. The evolution was successful because the difference between rural and urban ways was still relatively minor. As this gap has widened, however, the successful transition from the one way of life to the other has

figure 39 *The suitability of traditional building methods might not be questioned for centuries.*

become increasingly difficult to make. At the same time, rural life has, for increasing numbers of people the world over, come to mean destitution in comparison with the seemingly unlimited opportunities offered to the inhabitants of cities.

The accelerating flight from rural areas has led, paradoxically, to a new era of urban life in which basic shelter is in no way comparable to what it once was in the traditional city. In the contemporary encounter between the rural immigrant and urban civilization, people without skills or capital are confronted by a social system in which individuals are valued as secondary to the assets at their command. In rapidly expanding economies, unplanned urban renewal, which involves people moving steadily from old dwellings to new, allows a residue of obsolete dwellings to serve as emergency housing for the incoming migrants. Elsewhere, however, or when the movement to the cities exceeds the cities' capacity to absorb the resulting population growth, the migrants are left to provide for themselves. Without access to conventional building materials and without any training in the skills necessary to use them, their last resort is to squat on unoccupied land and assemble their dwellings in makeshift fashion from urban waste materials.[9] The chance availability of land and basic building materials becomes a major determinant of urban growth. (Figure 40.)

The Craft Stage of Building Production. The continuity of life in the traditional city led inevitably to the specialization of building trades and their gradual refinement into crafts. As guilds established rising standards of skills, the constraints inherent in the limited number of available building materials were slowly reduced. Experience in their use and the imaginative application of skills permitted an increasing range of building solutions. Raised aspirations could find their appropriate expression in great communal enterprises, as in the construction of temples, cathedrals, palaces, and city halls. And increased travel gradually enriched this development further by introducing both foreign materials and foreign methods to the local scene.

The crafts involved in the construction field have been so successful at adapting to changing conditions that they have been able to control building processes in most parts of the world to this day. Rather than become obsolete or absorbed in industrial processes as were the crafts engaged in the production of consumer goods, the building trades have tended to adapt industrial materials and tools to their purpose.

At the peak of craft development the constraints inherent in materials and building methods become minimal, and any form becomes possible. This ultimate stage can only be reached, however, from a broad and mature industrial base where average productivity of labor is very high and increasing and working hours are short and decreasing. But by the nature of his work the craftsman's hourly output grows at a much slower rate, if at all. And since he naturally expects his working hours to remain in line with those applying in other sectors of the economy, building costs rise out of all

figure 40 *Urban squatter dwellings in Hong Kong. "The chance availability of land and basic building materials becomes a major determinant of urban growth."*

proportion to general price increases. In a developing economy, craft-based building inevitably prices itself out of the market; it represents at best a passing phase.

This process runs its course gradually, during which the part played in building by the crafts dwindles steadily as cheaper, industrially produced components take the place of handcrafted ones, and as standards of workmanship drop in the effort to save labor costs. Craftsmanship of inadequate quality, moreover, serves to emphasize the effectiveness of industrial quality control, a contrast which further accelerates the trend toward industrialized building. The part played by traditional crafts in urban construction thus tends to diminish as each of them, in turn, reaches its peak of perfection. Beyond a certain point the craft approach to building is valid only to the extent that alternative industrial methods have not yet been invented or perfected and in the production of experimental prototypes for the eventual application of such methods. The best of contemporary custom-designed and custom-built architecture falls into this latter category even though its function as a formal or technical experiment is rarely acknowledged. (Figure 41.)

figure 41   *Many examples of the best of contemporary architecture are in fact experimental prototypes for industrially produced buildings.*

The Industrialization of Building. The actual industrialization process introduces entirely new sets of constraints on the structural and formal conception of building. These directly affect both overall urban form and every smallest building detail. The place of the experienced craftsman's immediacy to problems of production is taken by the meticulously planned process which excludes all consideration of individuals beyond their value as productive units. The industrial process is essentially rigid and thoughtless and thus unnatural. In its basic form it cannot be adapted to the organic variations man demands from his environment; rather, the environment must be made to fit the process if it is to yield maximum economic benefits. And economic benefits are the very reason for the existence of the industrial process.

The constraints affecting the structure and form of industrially assembled buildings limit the materials, dimensions, modules, and finishes to those which are suited to the production, distribution, and assembly processes. Thus, traditional materials tend to be rejected in their natural form. If not completely ignored, they are at least suitably processed. Thus, tree trunks are sliced and the sheets laminated into standard grade and standard size plywood, or cut into small pieces to be glued into standard quality beams, or chopped up and processed into particle board, or at the very least sawed into pieces suitable for assembly into standard framing panels. Dimensions are similarly determined by processes, whether to fit industrial materials-handling and transport equipment, to suit merchandizing techniques, or, as in the case of bricks, to fit into an abstract modular coordination system rather than to suit the bricklayer's work rhythm or please the senses.

When standardized components are fitted together, modules are established. As industrialization takes over urban building, the human measure in which the relative significance of different individuals and institutions in the community might be reflected is sacrificed to the blind repetition of machine-derived modules—to a mindless modularity. The application of modular concepts to building design executed in the crafts tradition has proved that it is theoretically possible to reconcile industrial production with the satisfaction of basic human needs. (Figure 42.) However, this requires a great amount of thought and artistic ability in the design stage and is therefore expensive, whereas, in practice, economic considerations dominate all aspects of industrialized building. The practical success of building components, like that of any industrial product, is measured in terms of sales of identical units and the resulting length of production runs. As a consequence, the successful large-scale industrialization of building leads inevitably to urban monotony.

This monotony cannot be disguised convincingly by misleading surface textures and finishes. Aluminum and steel sheet may be shaped and colored to look like wood siding, and plastic may at first glance appear to be marble.

figure 42 *The industrial production of buildings can be reconciled with the satisfaction of basic human needs.*

Such visual disguises, however, readily yield their secret to the other senses—to hearing and smell, touch and taste. Sensory deception, moreover, succeeds only to the extent that man's sensory faculties are underdeveloped, a condition the advent of modern media of communication may well remedy.[10]

The Prospect of Automation. In contrast to the industrialization of urban construction, which implies an essentially thoughtless mass assembly of unvarying standard components, the concept of automation refers to a basically autonomous production process which can adapt itself to a great variety of outside stimuli. The product of the automated process need be of a kind only, rather than uniform, with the result that there need not be any demand on life to adapt to a rigidly planned industrial process. Automating a process means giving it artificial intelligence. The type and scope of the built-in brain determines the degree of the process's ability to adapt to life and thus to become organic in the same sense that the craft approach to building is organic.

Industrially produced urban structures, particularly housing, lack this organic quality. Hence, efforts to rationalize building have been doomed to defeat at the hands of a public which has refused to be fitted into grids and rigid spatial systems as long as there have been alternatives. Even in buildings for industry and commerce a noticeable trend away from the "grid-and-box" approach to design contrasts with its earlier enthusiastic acceptance. (Figure 43.) With automation the concept of mass production changes radically. An intelligent production process can be alerted to wide ranges of individual preferences permitting variations in size, proportion, and even in the form and detailing of building components within any predetermined parameter. The possibility of variations in component design simultaneously opens expanded choices in their assembly far beyond the traditional limitations imposed by stacking and lining up as sole alternatives.

figure 43 *Place Bonaventure in Montreal.*

The possibilities inherent in applying artificial intelligence to the design and mass production of building components have barely been tapped. This lag indicates that the major constraint on finding the best and most economical solution to building problems will shift from a shortage of manpower to one of the brainpower required to create, apply, and direct such intelligence. As the eventual automation of routine design and production tasks releases human energy and creativity, a great part of it can be expected to be applied once more to crafts and result in a linking of craft with mass production. At that point, the constraints on urban building inherent in production methods would again become negligible.

Resources and Processes

Raw Materials and Production. The process of building is sufficiently basic to human survival that even the oldest existing dwellings and structures are adapted relatively easily to the most modern concepts of living. At the same time, many building materials and methods originating in prehistoric times have remained viable to the present. The main constraints exercised on the use of natural building materials are inherent in their properties: their strength, weight, insulating value, available sizes, etc. As building materials are processed, however, and adapted to specific applications in the construction process, these constraints shift increasingly away from the technical to the economic aspects of building: vast dimensions and rapid erection are both possible as long as their costs can be justified.

Once traditional methods are replaced by sophisticated production techniques, the determination of the true cost of construction becomes an extremely complex task. The application of technology extends the building process far beyond the boundaries of the construction site. The use of factory-made bricks, of concrete, structural steel, aluminum, glass, plastics, not to mention lighting fixtures, internal communications equipment, or automatic elevators, depends on the existence of industrial plants closely linked by road, rail, or waterway to the place of building, and they in turn can only operate if sufficient energy and adequate trained manpower are available. Neither of these conditions are likely to be met in the absence of a well-developed service industry.[11]

figure 44   *Habitat 67 under construction.*

The establishment of industry to produce building components is thus a far from simple investment decision. Its future must be assured well beyond any foreseeable changes in trends. An industry, for instance, that is entirely dependent on a particular manner of architectural expression is doomed to failure. Adequate flexibility of the production process is obviously best achieved if building components constitute only a part of an industry's output. This, however, presupposes a higher degree of industrialization than exists in all but a few of the world's regions, and the complete and successful industrialization of building is only conceivable at a stage of development not yet reached anywhere.

Transportation.   The industrialization of construction cannot be divorced from the problem of transportation. To be assembled at the site, components and materials must be transported there from the plant. The means of transport employed determines maximum size, weight, and to a considerable extent the installed cost of all components. Locating fabricating facilities on the site, as was done at Habitat 67 in Montreal, still requires the shipment of materials and equipment to the place of construction which, when combined with the need to write off the cost of setting up a special plant, can result in severe economic constraints on the scope of new building. (Figure 44.)

Urban development that depends on the industrial prefabrication of building components is thus obviously tied closely to existing transportation systems. Indeed, the nature of the transportation system and its capacity may dictate the character of urban architecture: established rail-, road-, and waterways permit the use of heavy, large-scale components, while remote location and rugged terrain will naturally favor the use of light and small components that can be transported by air.

The considerations that will determine the location of future urban centers can be expected to deviate increasingly from those that were responsible for the establishment of cities in the past. As defense long ago lost its relevance as a factor, so will the presence of natural physical resources become an unimportant attraction. Natural resources of another order, however, such as attractive scenery and climate, particularly when their location ties easily into the existing global transportation network, can be expected to grow in importance as determinants of urban development.[12]

The transportation revolution has not only loosened industry's traditional close ties to the sources of raw materials but it has also permitted the urban working population to free itself from the necessity of settling in close proximity to places of employment. And the ease of transporting energy in the form of electric power, oil, or natural gas has made direct access to the earlier sources of energy—coal and water power—unnecessary. Finally, the harnessing of atomic power offers the promise of extending the existing distribution system of cheap electric power to all parts of the globe.

Organization and Communication. Every increase in industrial production requires simultaneous growth in a multiplicity of supply, distribution, servicing, and administrative systems. As a result, any substantial addition to productive capacity leads automatically to a multiplication of organizational complexity and a correspondingly greater need for communication. The modern city has reached the stage at which communications functions far outweigh those of production in importance. Thus the latter are being pushed to the fringes of the urban environment, while its centers have been taken over by the communications functions of industry, commerce, and government.

Organizations are in part systems of communications channels which become institutionalized and rigid as they are being perfected. Unadaptable to changing conditions, they tend gradually to turn inward and become closed and self-feeding. Once organizations have reached this stage they can hinder meaningful communications between individuals as effectively as they can perpetuate the futile interchange of internally generated information. To the extent that the city, or parts of it, operates as a communications system, this "hardening of the arteries" can similarly affect urban life and bring development to a standstill. An example is the continuing decay of central business districts in most North American cities which, despite desperate attempts at revival, continue to be deserted by their working populations as soon as they are released from captivity. At roughly the same rate as commercial communications activities are losing relevance in the urban environment, those related to education, research, and leisure are gaining in importance. The university is thus gradually replacing industry and commerce as a dominant generator of urban activity and growth.

Complex self-feeding communications systems become bureaucracies and eventually take on a more than superficial resemblance to megamachines.[13] The greater their perfection, the more their members are forced to act as cogs rather than autonomous individuals. Much of the form, if not the content, of the urban environment continues to be dominated by the bureaucracies of government, business, and labor through the control of urban planning and design processes. Once different departments or *machines* are assembled to process the planning and design of housing, schools, office buildings, factories, universities, etc., it can become almost impossible to interrelate these different categories: student residences may not be built over university facilities; nursery schools and shopping facilities may not be incorporated into the housing projects they serve; restaurants and hotels may not span public highways—simply because the rules governing the different building categories are of different domains and their administrators are unable or unwilling to adapt old rules to new needs. In addition, fear for the safety of investment capital and jobs usually unites capital and labor in hostility against any deviation from established practice.

The natural limitations inherent in the available traditional materials and techniques which once dominated urban building and which were supplemented by a collective concern for visual harmony have thus been superseded by a maze of rules, fears, and prejudices, very few of which can be rationally justified. Most of them were established outside the domains of urban planning and design, and only the absence of links between different organizations has permitted their obduracy.

The Human Element

Aptitude and Labor. The ultimate responsibility for a great many of the constraints exercised on urban development lies with people's inability or unwillingness to change them. Any such change demands individual effort which, when fruitful, leads to invention and improvement. The individual, however, can only be expected to expend personal effort when there is an incentive, be it to ensure personal survival or satisfaction, public acclaim, or monetary gain.

Basic human motivation in improving the environment tends to stop once the survival of individual and community seems assured. Further rises in standards of living are not the result of any prime motivation but rather a consequence of basic drives channeled toward secondary goals. Man's basic motive for action is to find individual fulfillment within a community; its secondary expression may be in the accumulation of goods, power, and glory, either in fact, or symbolically in the form of money. If the individual is to have a continuing incentive to improve his habitat, he must believe that there is a role for him to play within the urban community.

Urbanization has led both to the rapid growth of populations and to their increasing freedom from drudgery, thanks firstly to the mechanization of purely repetitive acts, and now to the automation of all systematic work. Human energy thus freed may, of course, be reemployed in the invention, production, and consumption of additional goods or be dissipated in idle amusement, but it may also be directed toward the creation of an improved environment.

Yet as potential pools of labor are forming, problems are arising in the employment of new men, new skills, and new ideas. Tradesmen who have found seemingly secure roles in the conventional process of urban building, thanks to aptitude and training, naturally resist attempts to change this process and permit men of different or no training to compete. In places where, on the other hand, no status quo has yet been established, the basic disciplines and skills necessary for large-scale urban undertakings are obviously still lacking. Not surprisingly, radically new building techniques have been developed furthest in "socialist" and "welfare" states where the individual is secure economically and the state has the power and determination to override objections from disgruntled craftsmen and to revoke their work rules.

The individual naturally resists any change in his role once he identifies with it. If the playing out of such roles becomes a part of every process of urban development, occupational structures may solidify and acquire the potential to block any deviation from established work practices and norms. This is what happens when unions are allowed to veto the site assembly of prefabricated building elements or the use of new materials-handling equipment and if the enforced continuation of traditional trades rules out the creation of new composite job categories. For example, the site assembly of a conventional apartment kitchen or bathroom now involves no less than six different and highly specialized trades, whereas industry can produce completely assembled units for easy installation on the site by one quickly trained crew. (Figure 45.)

In the past, thorough training in a craft assured the individual a secure occupational role in any mature community. At some stage of development, however, the value of these roles to the community must be reassessed and a decision made as to whether the personal security of the few merits the imposition of additional constraints on the creation of an improved urban environment. The value of skilled trades can be exaggerated; it was, after all, the very lack of carpentry and masonry traditions in North America that led to the development of the balloon frame in housing construction and of the suspension bridge, both of which proved vastly more efficient than the traditional prototypes they replaced.

figure 45 *Completely prefabricated bathroom being lifted into position at Habitat 67 in Montreal.*

Intelligence and Expertise.   New processes of design, construction, and administration do not evolve organically from traditional practices. They result from the application of creative thought to the problem of how to achieve optimum living conditions with minimum effort. Although the quality of the urban environment is linked to communal value scales, the relations between the two are anything but direct. Not only is there little agreement in the modern multicommunity on what constitutes quality or on the priorities of values, but available resources may simply be inadequate to meet expectations. Furthermore, the complex of administrative, productive, and consulting bodies involved in any change to the existing habitat is so vast and its parts so disjointed, that the relationships among communal values, individual motives, and the resulting environment are obscure indeed. A true and thorough understanding of the multiple interlinkage of all factors involved is quite beyond the grasp of individual intelligence. Only the emerging possibility of its electronic extension offers a hope that the global expansion of the urban environment can be brought once more under communal control.

In the meantime, any achievement is limited by its terms of reference. A new computerized traffic control system may be highly successful and permit cars to enter an urban core area at double the previous rate, but if this should mean a proportionate increase in air pollution, the improvement is obviously open to question. Similarly, the widening of an urban street obviously increases its capacity and the speed of traffic. However, if the new traffic lanes have been added at the expense of needed sidewalks or by cutting down rows of mature trees and have thus reduced the livability of the neighborhood, the improvement may exist purely in the limited imagination of a traffic engineer. A virtually unlimited number of additional examples could be cited illustrating how the free reign of short-term profit motives can devastate the urban environment, or how urban life arteries can become blocked by obsolete historical structures which remain standing because the emotions of a few members of the community cannot be countered by sufficiently strong, rational arguments. Urban development motivated by only a partial understanding of aims, resources, and constraints will necessarily lead to dubious results.

The determination of all factors affecting the modern urban environment and their relative importance in different locations and at different times obviously demands the application of vastly more intelligence than has ever been the case before. Only with the advance of research can expertise in a narrow discipline be assigned its proper place in the total system of values. Without an overview, immediate objectives such as a faster car trip to work or a quick profit in a real estate transaction may override long-term considerations, and stupidity, ignorance, and greed can gain free reign.

If value systems are dynamically conceived and are adaptable to change, they establish a framework within which human ingenuity can be applied to overcome the constraints arising from lack of resources and conflict of needs. The lack of expertise in solving these problems is most apparent in underdeveloped areas, the lack of intelligence applied to their solution more so in the clearly overdeveloped parts of the world. At the lower end of the economic scale, people suffer because they are unable to use available physical and human resources to their advantage. At the other extreme, human control of the urban environment is in danger of being lost because of a lack of intelligence in applying ample expertise and because of the resulting disastrous waste of developed resources.

Enterprise and Capital. Any undertaking designed to bring future, rather than immediate, benefits must be based on a prior accumulation of goods to assure the survival of those engaged in it. In free enterprise systems the task of accumulation is assigned to individuals or to the corporations they control; in socialist systems such accumulation is handled by the state and its agencies. The accumulation is essentially one of goods, a fact somewhat obscured by the convenience of money exchange. Capital is thus equivalent to goods accumulated for future use or consumption, and interest rates reflect the price that must be paid for its use.

Cities derive their origin from the citadel of prehistoric times where, in Mumford's words, "the chieftain's booty, mainly grain and possibly women, would be safe against purely local depredation."[14] With the food supply controlled by its leaders during most of the year, a community could be forced to partake in joint enterprises, be they the building of temples, cities, irrigation systems, or tombs. Conditions are quite similar today when a developer, because he has access to pools of capital, can exhort others to contribute their expertise and labor to the design and construction of apartment and office buildings. Even if the developer is a government functionary, the essential relationship remains the same.

The detailed aspects of the relationship between enterprise and capital are, however, entirely different and vastly more complex than they were even a few generations ago. Then, little more than the storage of staple goods, and possibly some simple tools, provided an adequate basis for major enterprises. Today, under modern economic conditions, basic industries, transportation networks, educational systems, and complex administrative bureaucracies are essential prerequisites to any undertaking directly benefiting society. Moreover, these subsystems require highly capable and experienced people in positions of control, and as each subsystem grows in complexity, the demands made on its managers increase at an even faster rate. For this reason the educational system has become the crucial institution in the advanced stages of capital accumulation. Knowledge stored in the form of interrelated data has become the most important form of communal capital.

In the economic context, knowledge thus becomes largely synonymous with goods, since capital can take either form. In addition, the principles of automation can be applied to the production of goods as well as of data to create an ultimate stage of automatic capital accumulation in which constant or even declining human effort can produce rapidly rising standards of living. For this reason, lack of capital can be expected to diminish as a constraint on urban development. Its application, however, will continue to depend on human enterprise which, in all its various forms, will likely remain the essential contribution to be made by individuals to urban development.

CHAPTER FIVE

FORM AND

HABITAT

FROM FUNCTION TO FORM

The Evolution of Form

In the discussion of human needs, their conflicts, and the constraints inherent in the environment, form determinants, so far, have been assumed to be essentially rational forces which sooner or later will prove measurable. But urban form rarely derives from the orderly interaction of rational forces. The generators of form that are dominant in the urban environment have always been irrational—they have been expressions of human feelings and of the human will rather than the result of logic and computation.

The Sum of Functions. To fit human life, the urban habitat must satisfy the basic needs of individual and community. These are surprisingly few, once they are isolated from the infinite number of possible transitory needs which an urban environment attempts to meet (Table 1). In the basic community of the traditional agricultural village, the features of the man-made habitat are clearly determined by the means that have been devised to satisfy these physical needs. At the primitive stage of economic development, the production of food is everyone's primary concern. What time remains available to meet the need for shelter is applied to the use of readily available materials and skills according to established, and thus safe, traditions.

TABLE 1   Basic Needs Reflected in the Urban Environment

Basic needs	Public domain	Private domain
Metabolism	Distribution systems	Food preparation facilities
Reproduction	Meeting places	Privacy
Growth	Educational facilities	Living space
Health	Recreational facilities	Facilities for hygiene
Safety	Intraurban boundaries	Isolation
Movement	Transportation systems	Living space
Comfort	Containment in collective space	Containment within shelter
Stimulation	Complexity of collective form	Complexity of unit form
Identity	Clarity of collective form	Clarity of unit form

Source: Bronislaw Malinowski, *A Scientific Theory of Culture,* Oxford University Press, paperbacked. New York, 1960, p. 91.

But, primitive village life remains viable only so long as a relentless fight for bare physical survival rules out any choice. As soon as a village community expands, the drastic improvements in work processes that are required to guarantee its survival inevitably lead to a specialization of individual functions within the community and slowly change its character from rural to urban. The resulting increased productivity increases wealth, but this new wealth spawns new needs which cannot always be satisfied within the framework of existing institutions. The reasons may be unresolved conflict among diverging interests, or constraints inherent in, or built into, the environment. To the extent that urban building helps satisfy constituent and transitory needs in specific combinations, every artifact placed in urban space therefore represents the satisfaction of some needs, achieved at the cost of frustrating the satisfaction of others. The sum of all artifacts at no time satisfies the sum of all functions.

Artifacts do not happen; they are deliberately conceived and put in place. Their creation derives from the expression of a dominant will. As a result, urban form is, of necessity, basically arbitrary, even if the expression of values held by individuals and subcommunities is strongly contained by the forces of tradition, by communal reaction, and by physical constraints. In symbolizing a public statement, the form of any artifact inevitably invites reaction, be it direct or indirect, positive or negative. Depending on the form givers' intent, urban artifacts may be assertive or unassuming, defiant or alluring; in all cases, their character helps determine the direction of new urban needs. Changing needs, however, create new functions which must be served by the urban habitat and which in turn lead to new forms. Urban form can therefore not be regarded as a separate static entity, but has to be recognized as being one aspect of a continuing evolutionary process.

Form as Function.   If form follows function, it does so with discrimination. The form-function relationship is never a direct one; the link between the two concepts is man. Every artifact is the result of human decisions induced by specific needs. The shapes that artifacts take, therefore, are a result of only those functions that are recognized in the building program. They in turn represent a deliberate selection from all of the functions that could conceivably influence form. In favoring some functions and neglecting others, and in establishing priorities on the basis of individual and communal value judgments, a strongly biased functional structure is established in every building program.

This functional structure is the more universal the more elements it connects; and the stronger their interlinkages, the more the resulting form is predetermined. In a primitive culture the universe of functional elements is limited and relatively small: transitory needs are nonexistent, materials and skills limited, environmental factors and the communal structure known and unchanging. Consequently, the form of its artifacts is fully predetermined and remains constant.

However, the introduction of new factors destroys this functional structure and, with it, its formal expression. The urban environment is characterized by a vastly expanded universe of functional elements, only a limited number of which remain constant for any length of time. Society continually regroups itself; subcommunities are formed and dissolved; individuals move freely; transitory needs arise and disappear; new materials are created and new skills developed. The functional structures that underlie the creation of artifacts change constantly as values shift. Form can no longer follow all the functions.

Yet by selecting a limited set of functional elements, and by structuring it, a clear bias is established. Depending on the number and kinds of elements and the pattern of their interlinkage, form is now more or less predetermined. The set may even be specifically composed to fully predetermine urban form, for example, by making the reduction of construction costs an overriding functional consideration. Urban form that is functional in this limited sense is too narrowly defined, too simple, and therefore never truly adequate.

For form to satisfy, the functional consideration must leave it indeterminate. The result is random form, which may be ordered and completed in the imagination of each individual who is confronted with it,[1] or which, alternatively, may be shaped by a designer who superimposes his artistic conception on the functional considerations. (Figure 46.) But an artifact may also be a collection of formally fully determined, self-contained components, each of which is designed independently of the others; or the inclusion of specific stylistic elements in an artifact may be a functional requirement, in which case a designer incorporates predetermined form elements into his artistic conception. (Figure 47.)

Any attempt to clearly separate function from form is futile. Consciously or unconsciously, a formal bias is built into the very selection of the func-

figure 46 *Functional considerations form the basis on which the designer superimposes his artistic conception.*

figure 47 *Form may be generated through the repetition of functional elements.*

tions an artifact is to satisfy. The same bias is apparent again in the shape of components, be they bricks, windows, or prefabricated apartment units, and once more in the range of possible methods of their assembly. This all-pervading formal bias automatically fills every gap in the functional structure and can be as much a determinant as a constraint of form. In either case, the form bias itself becomes a function which in turn leads to the artifact's final form.

The Determination of Form

Form-determining Forces. Artifacts satisfy needs through their forms which in turn are shaped by the forces generated by human needs. These form-determining forces are amplified and directed by the power of the will and thwarted or deflected by environmental constraints. Neither ever acts singly.

Urban needs are never constant for long; their structure is clearly dynamic. Underlying them, however, is the constancy of basic physiological and psychological needs. In their duality they tie man to nature but simultaneously drive him to express his distinctive awareness of the precariousness of individual human life. As soon as a community rises above the subsistence level, its primary efforts are thus directed toward establishing a symbolic transcendence of life's natural limitations—in the creation of artifacts and art: "Pyramids and skyscrapers suggest how much of the world's economic activity also is really a flight from death."[2] In the final analysis, the drives which create and shape the environment originate in the subconscious; cities are built essentially for the same reason that man engages in religious activity, wars, and space exploration. Basic drives find their conscious expression in the urban environment through the many facets of the human will to form.

At the level of bare economic subsistence of a community, physiological needs are clearly more urgent than psychological needs, and the will to form has little scope to express itself in communal enterprises. Only when physical survival appears assured does the priority of physiological over psychological needs begin to reverse itself until, in the age of abundance, the will to form takes primacy. City building becomes pure monument building and ceases to be rationally motivated, except in the sense that the legitimacy of the expression of subconscious drives is recognized by the community. The forms of urban artifacts take on sexual characteristics as they are designed to penetrate space or to shape spaces that invite penetration. (Figure 48.) Not surprisingly, the genders in those languages which differentiate nouns in this manner suggest specific communal attitudes to different urban artifacts. Thus in German the words "city," "street," and "church" are feminine; "tower," "fountain," and "palace," masculine; and "house," "monastery," and "village," neuter.[3]

Communal attitudes partly predetermine the essential character of urban artifacts, even if basic drives originate in individuals and die with them. To be effective in shaping urban form, individuals must thus be in tune with their community or with dominant subcommunities; and in a democracy, the individual will to form must be in harmony with the latent collective will to form.

This latent form determinant is not necessarily based on the will of the community as a whole. More likely is the emergence of subcommunities that are directly concerned with the forms of specific artifacts. The residents of a particular locality will take an active interest in the design of an expressway cutting through their territory without any reference to the aesthetics of highway design per se, while designers are interested in the forms of vehicular paths without necessarily thinking of specific applications. The exercise of the will to form within closed subcommunities is occasionally documented, as in the party line on principles of housing design which reportedly permeated the London County Council after World War II[4] and, half a century earlier, in the change in architectural style brought about, and apparently deliberately planned, by the designers of the Columbian Exposition in Chicago.[5]

As different individuals gain and lose positions of influence, communal attitudes change, and with them the collective will to form and the direction it takes as a form-determining force. Such changes are basic to human nature and unpredictable: "the historical process is sustained by man's desire to become other than what he is. And man's desire to become something different is essentially an unconscious desire. The actual change in history neither results from nor corresponds to the conscious desires of the human agents who bring them about."[6] In the form of urban artifacts both the constancy and continual change of human existence find lasting reflection.

The Fit of Form.   Urban form is determined by the simultaneous action of dynamic and constraining forces that result from the needs and demands of the moment. For this reason total urban form is collective form in the sense that it is an accumulation of components over a long period of time: of buildings, roads, canals, bridges, etc. Each such artifact is shaped to satisfy specific functions. To the extent that it accomplishes this, its form can be said to fit. A collection of fitting components does not, however, add up to a fitting urban environment unless every component has been clearly defined in its relationship to the total urban form, or unless the total form is left deliberately indeterminate and permits the addition of new artifacts to compensate for the inadequacies arising from the use of those already existing.

The distinction between component and total urban form was quite adequate in the era of the traditional city. For this reason both planned cities, in which every part was conceived as a predetermined component, and

figure 48   *Urban form dominated by vertical elements which penetrate space without shaping it.*

unplanned urban centers, in which growth was accommodated in a practical rather than in a principled way, could develop successfully. In the megalo-politan age, however, the concept of fitness can no longer be applied only at the scales of total form and of its components. "Total form" has become a meaningless term when applied in its traditional sense to conurbations that stretch across whole regions and become increasingly interlinked to span continents. The word "components," similarly, may refer to a building or to its parts of assembly or subassembly; but in the contemporary urban context it may also refer to the collective form of a cluster of buildings, to a clearly defined complex of clusters, to urban subcenters, or even to a part of a metropolitan area accommodating hundreds of thousands, and in some cases millions, of people. In considering the fitness of the urban environment, the term must therefore be applied not only at the global scale but also at every conceivable component level; from the fitness of the form of a metropolis within the regional pattern of a continent to the fitness of the form of an entranceway that leads to a residence.

The difference between the traditional city and an international network of regional conurbations is not simply one of scale. The functioning of the former could be understood by everyone engaged in its creation, and the individual's contribution stood in direct relationship to the city's total form; the specifications for its components, be they buildings or any of their parts, were clearly implied in it. This direct relationship between the collective urban form and the form of its parts has been lost and replaced by relation-ships of a vastly more complex nature. Not only has it become physically impossible for any single individual to understand all of the relationships between components and their contribution to urban form, but also the number of people involved in the determination of form has become so great that meaningful communication between them is no longer feasible.

In the absence of valid alternative criteria, the form of urban artifacts has tended to be fitted to simple sets of functional requirements. Hilber-seimer's definition of the city architect's goal "to achieve an optical order adequate to the city's physical order"[7] suggests the nature of the compro-mise: it ignores the relevance of all but one of the human senses; it avoids consideration of the ways in which form and function influence one another; it assumes the physical order of the city to be fixed and disregards its de-pendence on constantly changing individual and social needs. This kind of oversimplified conception of urban form-function relationships becomes dangerous if, as a result, form is fitted too closely to an insufficiently broad range of urban functions. The determination of urban form is essentially a long-range decision; if it is made on the basis of expediency, quick obso-lescence is inevitable. And urban obsolescence ushers in urban decay. Since cities are conceived as permanent artifacts, urban forms must fit functions both spatially and in time. For this reason, the fit of form must necessarily be loose in respect to either. The only conceivable alternative would be forms that adapt automatically to changes in the functions they are expected to fit.

Adaptability to change affects different components of the total urban artifact differently: whole cities may decay for lack of adaptability, or only parts of their structure, such as the transportation network; individual buildings may become obsolete, or any of their parts. The more massive the scale of an urban enterprise, however, and the greater the scope of any single form-determining decision, the more disastrous the potential consequences if changing conditions render the resulting artifacts unfit for further use.

The Function of Form

Communication through Form. All form becomes a medium of communication the instant it is perceived. It may be charged with, or void of, content; in either case, it communicates the fact. Ruskin's careful distinction "between Architecture and Building," in which architecture is "that art which . . . impresses on the building certain characters venerable or beautiful, but otherwise unnecessary" and "concerns itself only with those characters of any edifice which are above and beyond its common use,"[8] hints at the different degrees to which buildings may be used to transmit information. At the same time it betrays a value bias which raises the function of communication above all other common functions a building might serve. Their information content and the quality of its expression, then, determine the value of artifacts within the urban environment: "In its simplest form architecture is rooted in entirely functional considerations, but it can reach up through all degrees of value to the highest sphere of spiritual existence, into the realm of pure art."[9]

Every urban artifact is a constant transmitter of signals. From some the emission is controlled and the signals unified to constitute a clear and coherent message. From others the signals may be weak, or strong but incoherent. In general, the signal strength seems to be adapted to the sensitivity of the receiver—urban man. In times past, when individual and community were uniformly attuned to the symbolism of urban form, signals could be precise and messages subtle. But as the number of media grew and the competition between them sharpened, forms had to become crass and messages shrill. Moreover, in the modern city the authority to transmit messages has passed from the select few to anyone who insists on being heard, with the result that, instead of containing sequences of modulated messages, the urban environment is echoing with the unremitting din of high-pitched random noise.

The art of communication through the forms of buildings and their arrangement in space, all but lost in the process, offers opportunities for sensory involvement in an increasingly artificial environment. Explicit forms, packaged and labeled, repel the senses, and urban centers conceived as collections of trim concrete, glass, and metal boxes isolate man from contact with his environment and from the people who inhabit it. Form can introduce social cohesion into the urban environment by inviting mutual involvement between its occupants—not as hot medium[10] through the sharp formal definition of geometrically clear building shapes which appeal to the pure intellect, but through a richness of form that helps relate urban artifacts to the human senses.

The relationship of man to urban form introduces the question of the human scale of artifacts. At its simplest, this relationship is between the dimensions of the human body and those dominating the various parts of the urban environment. Even a purely visual concept of scale, however, must allow for a variation in the color of objects and in the relative speed of viewer and object when in motion. In addition, the concept of human scale may also be applied to the nonvisual senses—hearing, smell, touch, and taste.

Thus the question of human scale merges into that of how man perceives and controls his environment, and the considerations of scale cease to be merely a matter of aesthetics. Scale becomes one aspect of the fit of forms, and thus of the fitness of the total urban environment which is only rendered tangible through its form. By manipulating urban form, man, in a sense, exercises his control over the environment. To the extent that he loses his prerogative to mold the space surrounding him, he is alienated from his environment. And, to the extent that his senses fail to establish direct links with his environment—to the extent that the urban environment is, in other words, out of scale—man's sense of orientation within the environment is lost.

Feedback through Form.   The dual function served by urban form to provide a malleable medium for the expression of individual and collective values and to bring the environment into sensory focus implies a complex feedback relationship between the habitat on the one hand, and human motivation and the will to form on the other. These three basic form-determining forces are ever present in the urban environment.

Any of these forces may be positive or negative, or weak or strong. The simultaneous absence of distinguishing features of the landscape, of collective concern for urban form, and of a dominant will to form, for example, results logically in the formlessness that characterizes great parts of North American cities. (Figure 32.) Only at their natural boundaries, or at artificial ones such as expressways, does urban form under these conditions become defined (Figure 49), or, alternatively, in places where a distinct will to form has been exercised. (Figure 50.) Examples where all three forces are acting simultaneously, positively, and harmoniously can unfortunately only be

figure 50 Urban form crystallizes at the points where a distinct will to form has been exercised.

found in cities built in the distant past, memorable for the coherence of their form. (Figure 3 and Figure 39.)

In other combinations, the positive or negative manifestations of the basic form determinants have resulted in, for example, Brasilia, where an individual's will to form acted in a social vacuum and on a site that lacked dominant features, or in Le Corbusier's visionary *plan voisin,* referred to previously, which could not possibly have been realized if only because it proposed the superimposition of a dominant will to form on an environment which, by contrast to that of Brasilia, already served as habitat for a population clearly in favor of the preservation of its essential features.

The urban space-time continuum provides the universe within which the form determinants interact; where function may influence form and form in turn redefine function. The mutual feedback process is necessarily slow, the span of a human generation being the approximate unit of time. Within such a time span, form determinants may reverse their direction. This happens most obviously when an urban environment is created where none existed before, with its form inevitably becoming a positive force affecting all further development. The long-term feedback process acts in other, more subtle ways, however. People who are satisfied with their environment will develop a collective motive to retain its qualities, whereas others, dissatisfied with their habitat, may relocate or demand specific improvements. In either case, an urban population may take a positive attitude toward urban form where it was unconcerned before. The major difference between the attitude of the European and that of the North American toward urban form may indeed lie in the fact that, to the former, the urban way of life is inevitable as well as desirable, while the latter has traditionally considered it an inferior substitute for a way of life in close contact with nature.[11] Even the ease with which urban North Americans move from place to place may betray a basic dissatisfaction with an environment considered to be beyond redemption. Under these circumstances, every urban defect is too readily accepted as a confirmation of the collective opinion that any urban habitat is necessarily inadequate.

This feeling of confirmation is a form of feedback from the urban environment as is its opposite: a sense of proof that under certain conditions urban life can be highly rewarding. Thus the fit or misfit of urban form can have its aftermath one or more generations later. Fitting form will tend to generate more of the same, while nonfitting urban form may induce either attempts to escape from it or an experimentation with alternatives. Both are essential to balanced, long-term urban development, since without occasional misfits the quality of the fit of other form elements would be hard to evaluate. In this sense, the feedback from urban form pinpoints nonfitting form elements and invites a reexamination of the validity of apparent needs and of the eventual effects of the constraints imposed on environment-shaping forces. Urban form, and the success of the environment it defines, is, after all, the conclusive criterion of the processes that shape it.

THE HIERARCHY OF FORM ELEMENTS

The Hierarchy of Scale

Megascale. Form is perceived through an imperfect instrument, the eye, which can cover only a narrow field at any one moment, and that with only a limited degree of accuracy. With an angle of vision of less than 30 degrees on the horizontal and about half that much vertically above it, the human eye can perceive clearly, at a glance, only objects whose largest dimensions are less than half their distance from the viewer. Furthermore, it cannot discern differences over an angle smaller than one minute.[12] The largest dimension of an object that the stationary eye can still perceive whole, therefore, can measure not more than 1,500 to 2,000 times its smallest discernable part. An urban element seen from a distance of 1 mile, at which distance the presence of a human figure is still distinguishable, thus can be taken in at one glance only if its maximum dimension is less than ½ mile. For this reason the form of most medieval cities could be readily perceived as single entities, the total size of which remained in direct visual relation to that of the human body. (Figure 51.)

figure 51 *Even important traditional cities could be perceived as entities whose total form was seen in direct relation to the size of the human body.*

Beyond this direct human scale, the perception of urban form depends on gaining ever greater distance from the city. From a mountaintop or an airplane, one glance at an oblique angle can disclose the form of a city spread over many square miles, and from a space capsule even regional conurbations disclose their extent and form. But as distance increases, urban form gradually loses all human meaning and becomes an abstract pattern. Total urban form can no longer be conceived except in the mind; its perception through sensory organs is impossible. As the city loses its form it becomes total environment and, in the minds of its inhabitants, its image replaces the memory of its actual form.

This image is a mental construct made up of sets of visual associations supplemented by known facts about the urban environment. The individual makes a personal selection from the data available to him and, in the process, defines his own environment. Depending on inclination and opportunities, he may restrict his orientation to a minute part of a city, as the child orients himself in his immediate neighborhood, or he may form simultaneous images of many cities known to him in different parts of the world and thus develop a global orientation. In either case, urban images are formed, not by observing cities as closed forms from without, but while being enfolded in continuous urban space. The image is no longer evoked by looking at a city, but rather through involvement—no matter how superficial—in the urban environment.

The sensuous form of the regional metropolis is necessarily of another order than that of the closed traditional city; the difference is not only one of scale but also one of essence. Total urban form is no longer within the reach of objective evaluation but is perceived differently by individuals of, for example, different economic status, different ways of life, different backgrounds, etc. Only a few, if any, positive elements of the total form are recognized by all inhabitants as being a part of their image of the city. These few elements are the formal common denominators which define the public image of an urban environment, and the greater their number, the greater is the probability of social cohesion based on civic pride.[13]

The elements that determine the image of the urban habitat comprise the centers of human activity, the natural and artificial landmarks and physical boundaries, and the simultaneous movement system[14] that connects these various elements to the individual residences to which they all are related. With mechanization, the traditional pace of urban movement which was limited to pedestrian speed has multiplied over and over and, with the eventual development of hypersonic passenger planes, may eventually shrink the surface area of the globe, in terms of traveling speed, to that of a traditional city region of less than 20 square miles, comparable to the scale of eighteenth-century London or Paris, or the area of Manhattan.

Within megalopolis, and between world capitals, air travel has been integrated with surface and underground routes in a more or less continuous system. Individuals habitually using these air routes for intra- and interurban movement will read urban form differently and will therefore select elements to build up their image of cities that differ from those selected by people tied to one small locality. Environmental images are formed to enable the individual to orient himself in the physical world.[15] With the world perceived at different scales by different individuals, urban form will need to become increasingly differentiated if it is to remain legible form to everyone seeking orientation in the urban habitat.

Human Scale.   Urban form at the macroscale is beyond direct, simultaneous sensory perception. The scale of the total urban habitat, like that of mountain ranges, jungles, and the sea, is extrahuman:[16] accessible to the human senses only in parts that never add up to the whole. Total urban form may be conceptually defined in terms of images, pattern, and systems, but its sensory definition is limited to incomplete sequences of spatial impressions that are received at a range of less than 1 mile. Only at this distance can isolated elements of the urban landscape be measured against the size of the human figure and clear sensory relationships be established between objects and man.

Thus the individual's sensory environment lies within a spherical space 1 mile in radius of which he is the center, and his urban orientation depends on the number and the nature of the stimuli which he receives from the objects so contained. Yet this part of the urban environment is extended both in time, through movement, and in space, through electronic media. As long as movement was limited to walking speed, the urban environment could be considered as viewed from a series of stationary points and conceived as conventional compositional form.[17] But the perception from fast-moving vehicles and planes results in rapid sequences of images which give the illusion of objects seen simultaneously from different angles, a type of perception related to the media of film and television in the same way that static vision is related to paintings and photographs.

Compositional form is irrelevant not only at the extrahuman scale of the metropolis and beyond, but wherever elements of urban form are perceived from moving vehicles and through electronic media. Only at the personal and intimate scales, dominated by pedestrian movement and by individuals, does the compositional arrangement of spaces and artifacts retain its traditional importance. (Figure 52.)

The limiting dimension of the personal scale in the urban environment is the distance at which people are within range of kinetic communication and recognize each other as acquaintances or strangers. Individuals remain in direct sensory contact; parents recognize their children and can call to them; acquaintances are able to interpret each other's movements and actions; strangers may be judged by their behavior, physiognomy, and cloth-

ing.[18] Dimensions of this order governed the layout of medieval and Renaissance squares, the boulevards of Paris, London's major avenues, etc. (Figure 53.)

Contained within the personal scale is the intimate human scale, based on the distance at which people's facial characteristics can be clearly perceived.[19] This scale establishes the spatial intimacy of many of the public spaces that date from medieval times. (Figure 54.) But it is also the scale of slums, where escape from intimacy becomes impossible due to plain overcrowding, and that of another kind of urban space, the interiors of moving trains, buses, elevators, and aircraft, where the public scale is compressed into the dimensions of the intimate scale.

The intimate human scale represents a zone of transition in the conception of the urban habitat where the feeling of intimacy with one's surroundings can turn into the sensation of being crowded and result in abrasive hostility to the same environment. But within the intimate scale further ranges of distances may be defined. Edward T. Hall, for example, has distinguished personal, social, and public distances, all well contained within the intimate urban scale.[20] He has demonstrated, moreover, that such dimension ranges can and must be defined in more than visual terms and that their definitions may vary from culture to culture. A habitat designed to force everyone into intimate relations with his neighbors is thus as inhuman as its opposite: complete individual isolation in an environment conceived entirely in the extrahuman scale of the machine.

The Hierarchy of Values

Unit Form.   An image may be established at the megascale of the urban environment, but the experience of physical form is ultimately limited by

the nature of the human body's sensory receptor system. To make sense, form must be accessible to the ears, the nose, and to touch, as well as to the eye, and even, if only through association, to the sense of taste. But at best, urban form is under direct individual control only at the smallest scale of the urban environment—at the level of unit form.

The units whose total aggregate is urban form may be spaces or components, or spaces made up of components. When components are handmade and hand assembled, all aspects of unit form are naturally in human scale. (Figure 55.) But because of its potential repetitiveness, unit form is the natural focus of attention by industry, with the result that the environment is gradually becoming an assemblage of machine-produced components and subcomponents. In that case, however, their form is no longer determined primarily by human needs, but by considerations of industrial production and assembly.

When building components are designed for industrial production, the constraints inherent in the production process determine their form. Yet the final form of components is rarely fully predetermined by functional considerations. To a widely varying degree a will to form is exercised by industrial managers, sales engineers, industrial designers, etc. These technicians are the anonymous artists and artisans of the industrial age whose contribution to urban form compares, at least quantitatively, with that of the anonymous stone masons and master craftsmen of an earlier age. While the latter's competence arose out of their mastery of manual skills, however, the technicians' control is due to their understanding of industrial processes of production and distribution.

They should thus, in a sense, be the true folk artists of their time. Yet, firmly rooted in technological methodology, they rarely sense the connection between their work and the artistic potential of urban form. In the real world of technology there is no scope for pleasure and dreams. As Jacques Ellul has pointed out, "when the artist tries to enter the sphere of technology in order to integrate art into the universe of men it implies that, for his part, he is bowing to the law of technology," in which case "he will find himself caught between the two jaws of a vice created by our society's technology—on one side the utilitarian, on the other the superfluous."[21]

But industrially determined form may be softened through the use of adaptive components to result in an environment that is habitable. Elements of nature, furniture, and furnishings combine to lessen the impact of machine forms both in the public and private domains. With progressive industrialization of construction, the individual gradually loses the option of creating unit form; but simultaneously he gains a wider choice among prefabricated alternatives, both of dwelling spaces and of components that permit their adaptation to personal needs. As custom-built dwellings are superseded by mass-produced housing, the choice grows among different models of cars, of pleasure boats, and of furniture styles; and so does the

figure 54 *The intimate scale dominates most medieval spaces.*

TABLE 2   Urban Form and Scale

Urban form	Intimate scale	Personal scale	Public scale	Macroscale
Limiting dimension	60 feet	200 feet	1 mile	Unlimited
Form category	Unit form	Unit form	Collective form	Urban image
Dominant form determinant	Individual needs	Group needs	Collective needs	Human needs

choice between alternative locations of residence. The narrower the opportunities to fit environments to individual needs, the greater therefore is the urgency to incorporate multiple choices into the urban environment at the public scale. Demands that can no longer be met at the intimate scale of man's habitat are in this manner transferred to the realm of collective form.

Collective Form.   When urban boundaries enclosed unified communities, the collective form of their buildings was itself unit form. (Figure 56.) But the unity of collective purpose is lost, and collective urban form must reflect a communal structure that is characterized not by its unity but by its regional and global continuity. And since the continuity of communal interaction is dependent largely on random encounters between individuals, the continuity of collective urban form is essentially of a random nature.

The individual who projects his needs beyond the immediacy of his personal environment thus encounters a random assemblage of form elements. This part of his habitat, still in human scale, is the zone of transition from the intimate and personal scales to the macroscale of the total environment. Whether he feels confined to his *place* or drawn out to become involved in the larger environment beyond depends on the collective character of the urban form that surrounds him.

But if man is to move with confidence in an ever-changing environment, urban form at the scale of collective form must be an extension of form at the personal scale; and form at the macroscale—that distant world of vague patterns, shapes, and silhouettes—must in turn be continuous with collective form as it is perceived from any one point in the urban habitat. (Figure 57.) An environment composed entirely of self-contained private domains lined up endlessly along meandering suburban streets would deny individuals the opportunity to establish direct sensory links to the urban environment beyond the personal scale. If such links are desired, individual wants must be subordinated to collective needs, which are satisfied in collective form (Table 2). The nature of this subordination of individual wants may vary, however. In the presence of an assertive individual will to form, collective form may remain compositional in character, and the elements of unit form may be fitted into preconceived shapes and positions on the basis of artistic considerations. (Figure 58.) Alternatively, unit forms, if of one kind and clustered in a simple order, may constitute the subsidiary

figure 55   *Even in modern architecture, form remains naturally in human scale so long as all components are hand-assembled.*

figure 56 *United urban communities created unified collective form.*

figure 57   Urban form unmistakable regardless of the time of day or night and of the scale of the context in which it is seen. Views of Toronto City Hall from the air (left), from passing car (below), and from a pedestrian walkway (bottom).

figure 58 *Elements of unit form fitted into an artistic composition.*

figure 59   *Group form.*

figure 60   *Megaform.*

elements of group form—or of megaform if different unit forms are incorporated in more complex artifacts.[22]

Group form is essentially additive in character. (Figure 59.) Its structure is inherent in the pattern in which its elements are clustered. Megaform, by contrast, is generated by a structure that integrates divergent elements. (Figure 60.) In an urban environment composed of elements of collective form, group form may appear to grow out of megaform as one passes through it, only to congeal again into other configurations of megaform, and shaping in the process continuous sequences of interrelated urban spaces.

In earlier eras of city building, urban space and form were integrated in this manner, but scaled to the speed of pedestrian movement only. The coming task will be to reintroduce this same wealth of sensory stimulation into urban form at the personal scale while simultaneously enriching vehicular movement in a similar manner at the scale of collective form. (Figure 61.)

CHAPTER SIX

URBAN FORM, TIME

AND THE HUMAN WILL

THE GRIP OF THE PAST

Habitat and Tradition

The determinants of urban form have so far been assumed to reflect the needs and wants of autonomous individuals. Yet human wants, and all but the most basic needs, are themselves shaped by the urban environment both in its present form and in its past manifestations. The will to form, moreover, may be a will to dominate in disguise and may also be applied in the attempt to manipulate human motives. Official architecture in Nazi Germany, Stalinist Russia, and, at times, Washington, D.C., demonstrates the consequences of such efforts. In general, however, the forces that shape urban needs and wants act more subtly; their influence on urban form must now be examined.

Roots and Ruts. Every human decision grows out of past experience. Thus the sum of urban artifacts represents an accumulation of individual decisions and acts, sanctioned at one time or another by the urban community; it symbolizes the community's tradition. In removing any part of the built environment, an element of this tradition is publicly discarded. The deliberate retention of urban artifacts, on the other hand, particularly in the face of newly emerging forces, symbolizes a reaffirmation of traditional values—symbolizes an assertion of the continuing relevance of earlier generations' beliefs, opinions, and customs.

Urban symbolism is inherent in the major communal structures in which a collective will to form has found valid expression. In such buildings widely different subcommunities may recognize their common roots, and dominant artifacts may continue to condition the urban environment and, through it, collective attitudes. This relationship roots individuals in the past, permits them to draw on the collective values of former times, and offers them orientation in time.

The presence of elements of the past invites comparison with the present. However, in so doing, it ties the present to the past, and by giving direction to the present, it restricts the freedom of urban development decisions.

When the symbolism of urban forms was universally understood, the constraints imposed by tradition resulted in the continuity of form throughout the city. For some individuals and a few urban subcommunities, traditional building forms may remain significant today and may sometimes even be charged with meaning. As far as the great megalopolitan majority is concerned, however, the function of single dominant structures is reduced to that of signals in the urban environment. As landmarks they may help the passing automobile driver to orient himself in space and contribute to the composite urban image; but as urban form they are irrelevant. When the constraints of tradition act in the vacuum of a nonexistent collective will to form, the inevitable result is sterility of urban form.

Devoid of meaning, urban form comes to serve accessory functions in place of the primary ones it lost. The degree to which form elements are put to use has been indicated by Kevin Lynch. In spite of the fact that long-term residents were interviewed in the cities under investigation in his study,[1] the reaction to the urban image suggested an almost complete lack of involvement in form; the urban habitat invariably appears as a nondescript maze of paths which happen to be traversed in the process of commuting between place of residence and place of work. Along the way, the positions and shapes of convenient artifacts are committed to memory solely to mark frequently traveled paths.

Such use of urban form is not restricted to elements at the scale of the total environment. The orientation in the three dimensions of urban space requires the establishment of anchor points at all levels of the hierarchy of scales: the individual must determine ways of finding his dwelling unit or office cubicle, and within his intimate space enclosure he will need to relate himself to the environment beyond. When urban form is debased to serve as mere prop to gain spatial orientation, a purely intellectual relationship is established between man and his habitat. No longer rooted in his environment through sensory involvement in its form, man uses form to provide a convenient network of grooves which, deepened with time into ruts, force the form character of all urban form elements toward the explicit. Building form is reduced to the banality of a billboard.

For the individual who is rooted in his environment, the distinction between landmark and background is meaningless; all form elements merge into one total environment. Orientation is based on the composite of unconsciously memorized sense impressions.[2] His relation to the environment is sensory rather than intellectual, with building forms inviting involvement rather than demanding attention. Young children seem to experience their habitat in this manner. The sensuous urban forms of preliterate times indicate a similar involvement of whole communities in their habitat, a condition no longer found except perhaps in small enclaves untouched by modern developments. (Figure 62.) Elsewhere, a deadeningly rational approach to city building has resulted in an artificial environment often hostile to sensory involvement, thus precluding any possibility of individuals or subcommunities taking root.

The Urban Mix. Environmental conditions favorable to collective root taking appear tied to the presence of stable communities whose members are inclined to seek sensory involvement in their habitat. These conditions are met in the preliterate, preindustrial stages of development, and possibly where postliterate, postindustrial communities are emerging; only where they prevail can people truly be rooted in the environment. But preliterate enclaves are isolated parts of the world—urban slums or remote villages and towns—and the postliterate stage is represented by minute subcommunities in elite positions similarly isolated, if by virtue of wealth and education rather than of ignorance. And while traditional roots are local, theirs are global.

Yet the great urban majority everywhere is without roots. The modern city is inhabited by people who have come from somewhere else. Traditionally, the roots cut in the process have been of the kind that tied individuals to a rural community, tradition, and place. However, the same now happens within the urban habitat. An individual may change jobs, simultaneously move from one part of the city to another, and cut all ties to his past in the process. But the anonymity that permeates urban life and its pattern of interlocking subcommunities also permits individuals to cut roots selectively. The individual is free to leave his church community, to ignore his neighbors, or to cut all ties to his family: options the traditional city decidedly did not offer.

While the traditional urban community was closed, homogeneous, and of a single tradition, its modern counterpart is characterized by the plurality of its roots. Not only is the choice any one individual may make as to which of his ties to the past he cares to retain dependent on his social and cultural background, but it is based equally on the level of his education, on personal needs and desires, and on any number of other factors. The continuing divergence of different educational objectives and the variety of resulting personal aims and qualifications, in addition to an increasing global mobility,

figure 62 *The joint involvement of whole urban communities in their environment was, in preliterate times, reflected in the townscape.*

a growing ease of worldwide communications, and the gradual merging of individual cities and city regions, combine to make it extremely unlikely that the homogeneity of populations found in traditional cities will ever be achieved again. More probably, even the few major cities, such as Stockholm and Zurich, whose populations have remained culturally and racially homogeneous, will tend toward wider divergence in values and attitudes.

As people move from country to city and from region to region, the urban environment continues to absorb living traditions. Some of them survive, new traditions emerge, and old ones die with the generation that brought them into the city. Seemingly incompatible traditions may clash when first brought into close contact, but thanks to enforced propinquity, they come to merge and enrich each other. The result is a multiple overlay of traditions continually changing their relative force, position, and direction. The kaleidoscopic nature of urban values is reflected in the form mix of the modern metropolis. (Figure 63.) Not surprisingly, this blend of urban forms is richest where widely divergent traditions are permitted to clash freely—in New York, Hong Kong, Rio de Janeiro, etc.—and least noticeable where an official tradition remains dominant, as in Moscow and Paris. Significantly, the latter cities' image is defined by the important structures of the past, the former cities' image by the artifacts of the present.

The Urban Time Continuum

Rural Traditions in Urban Life. Ever since the medieval city broke out of its encircling walls, the progressive urbanization of regions and whole continents has depended on the continuing migration of people from rural to urban areas at a steadily growing rate. Immigrants may seek the city by free choice or because they were forced off their land; in either case, their roots in the rural past are irretrievably cut. A considerable proportion of city dwellers have been uprooted in this way during their lifetime, and in most parts of the world the adults whose urban roots go beyond their parents' generation are in a distinct minority. This steady invasion of the urban environment is not simply a movement of people from the provinces to the cities. The immigrants bring with them habits, attitudes, beliefs, and dreams rooted in the rural tradition. Individuals will cling to them even when inappropriate and attempt to pass them on to following generations. Under the surface of integration in the new environment, rural and urban values thus continue to clash.

Man's orientation in the natural environment of rural communities is based almost entirely on sense impressions. By contrast, orientation in urban space and time is primarily an intellectual process. Artificial space is a

measurable quantity that is subjected to the rules of geometry, and time becomes a mere series of uniform seconds, minutes, and hours, weeks and months. As a result, survival in the urban environment depends on the individual's ability to adapt and relate himself to abstract units of space and time.

In nature, space and time are not defined by the laws of geometry, astronomy, and mathematics. (Figure 64.) The day starts with the rising of the sun rather than the ringing of the alarm clock. Time is measured in seasonal cycles, and human activity is adapted to the life cycles of domestic animals, the weather, and the growth cycles of crops. Natural space is defined by orientation to the sun and the stars, the features of the land, the properties of the soil, the location of trees and forests, the direction of winds, and the formations of passing clouds. Rural buildings are designed and placed to fit into an order beyond man's control, understanding of which is gained through constant contact with nature. This sensory order contrasts with the intellectual order which dominates man's urban environment.

While urban man's orientation in space is predominantly intellectual, the rural immigrant thus depends largely on sensory data to orient himself. When in the city, he does not systematically define a place in terms of numbers of blocks, floor levels, and door counts, but continues to base his thinking on sense impressions. As a consequence, the artificial world created by

figure 64 *Traditional building forms respect nature's preeminence.*

people steeped in the intellectual tradition tends to elude his grasp. Wherever rural background and inclination come to dominate, a sensory reorientation is thus forced on the urban environment, be it in the form of South American squatter settlements[3,4] or North American suburbs and parkways.

Not surprisingly, the layout of early Greek cities was quite irregular until the purely intellectual orientation gained its first complete victory in the rebuilding of Miletus on a modified chessboard pattern in the fifth century B.C. The colonial cities founded by Imperial Rome expressed a similar clearly urban tradition. But after the collapse of Rome, the newly founded cities of Europe once more grew out of the sensory order that underlies rural tradition. Venice evolved this way, and the centers of Moscow, London, and Paris, not to mention scores of other cities, are still reflecting the same rural origin.[5]

It appears that whenever urban development reaches the stage at which an intellectual tradition becomes established as a dominant force, simple geometric patterns return to dominate the urban environment. The role of the intellectual is clear in the creation of plans for new cities such as Chandigarh,[6] Brasilia,[7] Islamabad,[8] and Hook.[9] His value bias is sometimes candidly expressed: "Implanted upon the formerly disciplined plans of classical Rome are the confused forms of the medieval city . . . ."[10] But if intellectual-geometric orders and sensory-organic orders are mutually incompatible, then urban development must obviously be planned to accommodate both modes of orientation simultaneously side by side.

Sense of Time and Sense of Place. E. H. Gombrich has made the observation that the will to form, due to the tendency of individual artists to assimilate new shapes to familiar patterns, is rather a "will-to-make-conform."[11] This statement is valid beyond the context in which it was made. It applies with particular pungency when urban, and thus public, form is concerned, where, in Blumenfeld's words, "beauty is in the memory of the beholder."[12] Because new shapes disturb man's need for orientation in his environment, the collective will naturally tends to favor new artifacts that conform to what exists. Nonconforming structures are tolerated only where existing ones have failed to offer such orientation; in other words, where a sufficiently large number of individuals feel alien in their surroundings. Indeed, the very acceptance of unfamiliar forms may indicate the degree to which a community has become estranged from its physical environment.

Urban form can give each individual a sense of involvement in time beyond his life-span and in space beyond his immediate grasp. (Figure 65.) The city, however, has long ceased to be the sole medium through which individual awareness can be extended. Both print and electronic media are able to relate the individual to the infinity of space and time. The urban environment, however, through its works of art and architecture, is the only

figure 65   *Urban form can give man a sense of involvement in time beyond his own life-span and in space beyond his immediate grasp.*

medium through which the awareness of both space and time can be conveyed simultaneously to the senses and the intellect, to people individually and collectively. Urban form thus defines the relationship of man to his community, and beyond to infinite time and space.

The term "city" has come to refer to the traditional core only of metropolitan areas. Where regions have grown economically and in size of population, the traditional urban artifacts have progressively lost meaning for the modern multicommunity. The efforts of past elites to overcome death "by accumulating time-defying monuments"[13] are increasingly ignored, if not resented. But the new society is still in its formative stage and will require an urban environment appropriate to its structure and scale. And the forms of artifacts will have to reflect the vastly expanded knowledge about universal space and time which are, for the first time, accessible to every individual.

New urban forms must thus be sophisticated to be viable. But beyond that, the search for a sense of place must permit individuals to relate spatially to the aspects of urban life they specifically choose to identify with. For example, one may wish to be near, or far removed from, the arteries of urban circulation, the centers of culture or intellectual activity, the focal points of social life, or the places of work or leisure activities. Sense of place in a pluralistic society must be based on multiple spatial relationships whereas a simple orientation toward cathedral, palace, or place of work[14] would have been considered sufficient definition in earlier societies.

Traditional urban form conveyed a sense of time in a similar manner through the sequence in which buildings were placed and in which collective form evolved. Gaining a sense of place means in essence that the individual can orient himself in his environment by what he sees, feels, hears, smells, and tastes. The sequence in which he perceives artifacts, and the elements of nature surrounding him, come into being and grow, similarly extending his sense of place in a sense of time. Neither is limited to the local time expressed in one place. Both sense of place and sense of time can refer to a composite environment made up of diverse parts of five continents just as well as to one small town. The sense of place may link one individual to a composite environment that is made up of diverse parts of five continents, while it ties another to a single small town. And one's sense of time in a similar way can be limited to the local history of a hamlet or be expanded to unite global sets of historical images that correspond to modern man's multiple urban roots.

CONSTRAINING THE FUTURE
The Future's Predictable Features

Concurrent Stages of Urban Development.   The grip of the past is not an unrelenting force; far from being constant, its strength varies widely. At times a negligible factor, it can on other occasions become a dominant urban form determinant. Its strength depends on social conditions which change with time and place. Even within the multicommunal structure of a single metropolis, tradition affects the many facets of urban development differently. There will thus always be groups opposed to the removal of old buildings regardless of their use value, as there are invariably those whose touching faith in the shiny and new is exceeded only by their contempt for anything old. Between these extreme attitudes a whole spectrum of individual and collective attitudes centers on the values that dominate life in the community.

Throughout the world, urban development has proceeded along rather similar paths regardless of local conditions. What has varied greatly is the timing and duration of trends rather than their direction. Global migration and specific historical events offer at best partial explanations for the different rates at which urbanization proceeded in different periods and places. The balance of reasons for the periodic acceleration and retardation of basic trends must lie in the social conditions prevailing at the local and regional levels. Until quite recently, such differences between civilizations and continents would develop in mutual isolation. The advent of instant global communication, however, has made the comparison between cities everywhere inevitable, even if the bias of the communications media available for this purpose has encouraged the comparison of easily measurable quantities rather than the evaluation of qualitative differences between urban life in different parts of the world.

As a result, local development anywhere may now be measured by global standards, and urban growth correlated on a global scale. New trends in one part of the world cannot help but influence development everywhere else, and the consequences of decisions in one metropolis can be measured and the results interpolated in the light of known data elsewhere.

The relative uniformity of global trends is of course not restricted to urban development, but is related to developments in the fields of science, industry, commerce, and the arts that disregard geographic boundaries. Thus the global flight from rural areas is an indirect result of scientific and technological advances. Similarly, the universal problem of urban sprawl arises from the decentralization of production and administration made possible by modern transportation and communications techniques and encouraged by shrinking workdays and workweeks. The new conurbations that blossom in the world's resort areas are a consequence of the increased freedom from local ties enjoyed both by industry and by growing numbers of individuals.[15] The return to city living, finally, may be largely motivated by people's search for cultural and social amenities—a search reflecting the higher educational qualifications required by increasingly sophisticated industries. The global trends in urban development are thus essentially determined by the continuing advances made in transportation, in communications, and in automation.

Even the forms that cities and new buildings take are influenced by aesthetic theories which confirm these same forces. What regional differences survive are based on secondary trends. These may be purely defensive and based on local political decisions which prop up declining traditions by means of obsolete building codes. Or secondary trends that represent pioneering attempts to solve specific problems may branch off from the mainstream to be watched by decision makers elsewhere and, if promising, find gradual global acceptance. But regionalism per se is doomed.

Predictable Obsolescence. Obsolescence, the passing out of use of elements of the environment, is an inevitable by-product of change. Change, however, is an integral aspect of life, and obsolescence thus a necessary aspect of urban growth. Among the elements affected, traditional dwellings and other artifacts which were never meant to fit narrowly defined purposes suffer relatively little from change. They pass out of use only after they have fully served their purpose: theirs is an organic obsolescence. The process of obsolescence accumulates momentum, however, as technology comes to dominate the creation of artifacts and fits them tightly to specific needs. It culminates in the concept of forced obsolescence, the fashioning of objects that are deliberately fitted to passing moods, which in turn are artificially created through the manipulation of mass media.

Artifacts may pass out of use for any of a number of reasons. They may have been designed to serve social, economic, or technical functions that have been superseded; better design solutions may have displaced earlier ones that served the same function; artifacts or some of their vital parts may have decayed physically and require replacement even though their design is still up-to-date. Obsolescence can thus refer to an object's physical structure, its design, or the function it serves. The term "artifact" need not refer to individual buildings either. Whole urban systems may become obsolete even though their individual elements perform adequately by themselves. The evolution of modern urban traffic systems provides obvious examples. Once such a system fails to fulfill its function, at least some of the buildings it serves become in turn obsolete, just as the channeling of fast traffic through a residential cluster renders dwellings useless to their occupants. (Figure 66.)

One difficulty of predicting trends in the urban environment arises from the fact that the needs it satisfies are predominantly transitory. Except for the decay of a building to the point of imminent collapse, the obsolescence of urban structures is related to changes in demand rather than in basic needs. A second difficulty springs from the first: with transitory needs depending on value judgments, the concepts of obsolescence vary from individual to individual and from subcommunity to subcommunity. Only a clear consensus, therefore, results in clear trends in the first place.

But urban development often reflects not so much a trend as, rather, an individual will to form consistent with the dominant communal values on

figure 66   *When a modern traffic system is superimposed on a traditional urban environment, the latter is inevitably rendered obsolete.*

the one hand, and with the absence of strong counter trends on the other. That the resulting buildings can be obsolete in terms different from those within which they were conceived is easily demonstrated in the case of any number of public housing projects which, while new in economic terms, were obsolete in social terms before they were occupied. The same concurrence of novelty and obsolescence is common to all narrowly specialized approaches to urban development. An undertaking may represent the ultimate in organizational and economic thinking, such as that applied to the creation of cultural centers, yet fail socially and architecturally; or a structure may be a full success as far as the implementation of industrial building techniques is concerned, yet become obsolete in architectural terms almost immediately. Even specialization in artistic terms is doomed to the same fate: "hot" architecture does not cool with time but goes stale instead.

The rejection of specialized forms and specialized functions marks the contrast between present trends and those dominating the times following the Renaissance and Baroque periods when the urban environment was itself treated as a sharply defined, specialized form. (Figure 67.) The obvious discrepancy between the two approaches betrays the fundamental change that has occurred in the basic trends which underlie urban development. Specialization, symptomatic of fragmented thinking and feeling, is one aspect of a historical trend that has run its course.

figure 67 *"Hot" urban form of the traditional kind.*

Paths Blocked to Change. In periods of transition, when there is a shift in the basic trends that shape the thought and feeling of different eras, the secondary trends which directly affect urban form can be thrown into utter confusion. During such times, frantic and tumultuous change results in correspondingly high rates of obsolescence, and parts of the urban environment can conceivably become so cluttered with suddenly obsolete permanent structures that they may well pass out of use as a whole and be bypassed by later development.

Obsolescence is a largely unpredictable process. Plainly speculative ventures, aiming no higher than for a continuing return on investment capital, can result in lasting contributions to the urban scene, while enterprises inspired by the loftiest ideals may go astray in short order. Every major city has examples of both. Place Vendôme in Paris and the Crescents of Bath are celebrated examples of the former (Figure 68), while most prewar examples of modern architecture, by contrast, have been victimized beyond redemption within one generation.[16]

In urban design, the difference between success and failure is ultimately between artifacts that adapt to change and those that resist it. The traditional builder's anonymous contribution to urban form is of low definition. In the case of the French and British examples mentioned, the definition of form is confined to the front elevations of buildings. Shapes and spaces as a result

figure 68 *Plainly speculative ventures have, at times, resulted in lasting contributions to the urban scene.*

permit multiple interpretation and give the user every option of further personal elaboration; form is malleable and indeterminate. By contrast, buildings that are conceived as monumental form—definitive, hard, and self-contained—leave their users no alternative but to fit into the form giver's dream. This may have been a fitting relationship at the times of medieval cathedrals and of Renaissance palaces, but in the modern metropolis, it remains valid only in exceedingly few instances.

In democratic societies, an individual architect's attempt to impose his personal values permanently on the urban habitat is not readily tolerated. No matter how exalted its aims, all idealizing architecture is specialized and explicit and permits only one formal interpretation.[17] Being right, it does not tolerate change and therefore does not tolerate life. The lesser the degree of their specialization, the easier fixed, man-made structures accommodate new life.

The specialization of an artifact is of a multidimensional nature, however. A structure such as a modern office building which superficially serves a single purpose accommodates great varieties of internal traffic functions, human activities, communications needs, and mechanical equipment. Indeed, its downtown setting in the typical North American city falls far short of the potential flexibility provided within the building itself. There, an obsolete street system reduces all movement to a pedestrian pace along single-purpose channels, simultaneously denying the excitement of speed to the driver and spatial enjoyment to the pedestrian. Thus the central business districts, together with the parts of the urban environment dominated by industry in what Mumford refers to as the "paleotechnic paradise,"[18] may well be beyond revitalization, regardless of the flexibility built into individual structures. Only in major centers where the use of irreplaceable natural assets or the fate of exceptionally large capital assets are tied to the fate of the core may the cost of drastic urban restructuring be economically justified.

In a pluralistic society, singleness of purpose expressed in urban form and structure leads directly and inevitably to urban blight, regardless of the aim pursued. Even intentions laudable by themselves, such as large-scale attempts to fit the poor into sanitary housing or to allow millions of private cars to enter and pass through population centers, end in urban disaster if the multiplicity of interlinkages between urban problems is ignored or only partially recognized.

Massive interventions in the urban habitat are the natural result of the machine operations that dominate much of the thinking in government and business. Both bureaucratic megamachines and computers can produce decisions with equal ease whether the data at their disposal reflect true human needs or not. Since any lack of valid reasons to support a decision is usually balanced by a corresponding absence of irrefutable counterevidence, machine-directed urban action is not easily opposed. Fortunately, computer systems offer the potential of permitting direct personal intervention at any point in the decision-making process in a manner unthinkable in a bureaucratic system. Alternatively, however, the rigidity of thought patterns governing the operation of bureaucracies could easily become oppressive once they are endowed with the precision of electronic brains.[19] The ultimate consequence of such a development could conceivably be the blocking of all paths to change with a dehumanized urban habitat gradually taking on all the attributes of a hive.

The Future beyond Prognosis

Facing the Unknown. Among the vast numbers of variable determinants and constraints which, in continuous multiple interaction, shape the form and structure of the urban environment, there are some factors which are constant or whose variations can be predicted with a fair degree of accuracy. Each foreseeable development, however, is accompanied by unforeseen circumstances. While a general global population growth can be predicted for the immediate future without much chance of error, the actual size of the increase remains in serious doubt. Similarly, inequities between different individuals and groups appear to be basic to human nature and can be expected to persist in any society, but the relative positions of such individuals and groups in the social framework need not remain constant and can indeed be suddenly reversed.

As long as basic human motivation is little understood, any long-term prognosis must assume the continuation of specific trends, and the trends naturally considered most likely to serve this purpose are those that have persisted longer than others in the past. Not surprisingly, the present trend most taken for granted is that of technological progress. Technology's two main characteristics are its rationality and artificiality;[20] it is a method of applying reason to systematically extract the resources of nature for purposes invented by man. The only values it recognizes are those that are measurable and consequently fully understood in physical terms.

Thus, as Giedion put it: "The one-way street of logic has landed us in the slum of materialism."[21] The blind belief in technological progress has put economic goals near the top of communal value scales, with the consequent emphasis on man's productive functions. It has changed time into money and forced the redesigning of urban movement systems to minimize the loss of either. It has justified large-scale environmental pollution in the interest of paltry economies in industrial processes. But, curiously, a naïve trust in technological progress persists and pervades much of the thinking about the urban future. Admittedly, technology has developed increasing respect for human needs as more of them have become measurable. The rapid advances expected in the life sciences will without doubt further mitigate the more destructive aspects of technology. In essence, however, its progress remains by definition antinatural and therefore antihuman.

There are indications that, at its present speed, technological progress is fast approaching its ultimate limits. To quote Ellul: "Since techniques, proportionally to their development, exhaust the resources of nature, it is indispensable to fill the vacuum so created by a more rapid technical progress. Only inventions perpetually more numerous and automatically increasing can make good the unheard-of expenditures and irremediable consumption of raw materials such as wood, coal, petroleum, and even water."[22] But as the world is feverishly engaged in attempts to equal the steadily rising consumption records set in North America, basic raw materials will gradually become scarce.

The concept of progress will obviously require radical redefinition. The linearity of technological advances which permitted reasonably accurate forecasting of at least one dominant aspect of urban development can no longer be taken for granted. No comparably clear trend has emerged in its place, and only increased leisure and a general rise in sensory awareness offer any promise of eventually achieving similar predominance. These tendencies, however, are in many ways incompatible with the conventional patterns of urban growth which persist even though they are based entirely on the unquestioned acceptance of the myth of the machine.

When buildings or roads or any other urban artifacts are planned, their constraining function is projected forward beyond the present. In predetermining the physical features of the urban environment, the constraints which the past exercises over the present through its artifacts are extended into the future. Master plans become the past's hold on the future. They are in essence conservative, even when they attempt to preserve progressive ideals. Planning for the future can be as much an exercise in will to form as the placing of concrete monuments—and equally stultifying for subsequent urban development.

Dreams, Visions, and Utopias.   For an artifact to be created, it must be preceded by its design, which in turn represents the materialization of a dream. All form is thus ultimately determined by dreams, as all conscious action is in the end governed by ideas. Dreams and ideas grow out of the constancy of the human condition. They reflect man's aspirations to rise above mere animal existence toward the timelessness of the divine. But while thus constant in one sense, the content of dreams and ideas varies continually in response to changes in the environment. These changes are reflected in the differences between the forms of artifacts created at different times in history and in different places. In the realm of dreams and ideas, the past is alive and, in the eternal present, directly linked to the future. Through them, man catches an occasional glimpse of the ultimate reality of human existence.

figure 69   *A vision of future urban form: floating geodesic spheres over one mile in diameter—the air within heated by solar radiation—could each accommodate thousands of people.*

When sequences of dreams and ideas are consciously interrelated, they can become the elements of a vision. The visionary thus sees reality in depth, time being the added dimension, while the realist perceives the world around him only in unrelated sequences of flat reality, without concern for the links between present, past, and future. Any narrowly realistic policy is therefore by definition aimless. Given the unavoidable time gap between conception and execution of urban development, the inherent aimlessness of the realistic engineering approach is moreover dangerous: by binding the morrow's reality to that of today, urban growth is constricted in all but physical terms. Instead of growing organically, urban form bulges and sprawls.

Visions exist only in the minds of individuals. To gain substance and be transferred into the public domain, they require translation into a medium of communication, such as language or image. (Figure 69.) In being forced to fit a medium, however, the vision undergoes a process of rationalization; to quote the architect Louis Kahn, "the dream becomes less." Thus utopias are rationalized visions, as dystopias are rationalized nightmares. Both give orientation to urban development: not directly as form determinants or constraints, but indirectly by influencing their direction and strength. In utopian thought motives for subsequent action take their initial shape.

The classical utopias, like those of Plato and Sir Thomas More, were narrowly place-related, referring to a self-contained city, island, or country, often completely isolated from the rest of the world and dominating every aspect of the life of every inhabitant. They were conceived as closed social, economic, and physical entities. This genre has survived only on the outer fringes of escapist literature, in science fiction. The mainstream of utopian thought has meanwhile become divided into a multitude of branches reflecting the specialization and fragmentation of modern knowledge. The all-encompassing utopia has lost its general relevance, but its place has been taken by the partial visions of specialists. Utopian views are thus offered on the moral-psychological plane (e.g., by Norman O. Brown[23]) or on the scientific-technological plane (by R. Buckminster Fuller[24]); on the economic-sociological plane (by Kenneth E. Boulding[25]) or on the architectural-environmental plane (by Leonardo Ricci[26])—to mention but a few. As varied as their different points of view may be, they are all directly relevant to the urban future. Since all modern utopias are dynamic in concept and can therefore be developed beyond the set of initial assumptions, their open ends invite the possibility of eventual mergers. And if the urban environment is too complex to remain within any one man's mental grasp, then electronic technology must be enlisted to help coordinate and integrate the diverse visions and communicate the resulting composite overview.

CHAPTER SEVEN

BEYOND THE

STATUS QUO

Symptoms and Trends

Glimpses of the Invisible.   To the extent that it is taken for granted—that life is totally immersed in it—the urban environment is invisible. Awareness is limited to those aspects of man's habitat that change: to movement, un-expected views and events, surprising combinations and contrasts. This kind of variety is built into nature in the antithesis of day and night, in the yearly seasons, in the changes in wind and weather. But the people that fully experience these changes become fewer the farther nature recedes from the centers of urban activity.

In a predominantly artificial habitat, nature plays at best a supporting role, adding a touch of ambiguity to forms that would otherwise be painfully harsh. (Figure 70.) But to remain consciously aware of their artificial urban environment, those fully enclosed in it become dependent on artificially produced anti-environments. None of these are total in scope, however, and none illuminate more than an insignificantly small part of man's total en-vironment. Scientific concepts and works of art, news stories, and television images offer the occasional fleeting glimpses of urban reality. The compound anti-environmental image that results, fragmentary as it is, defines the indi-vidual's vision of his real environment.

At times and in places where changes are few and far between, this vision is static. In the evolving urban environment, however, reality changes rapidly and continuously; and unless growing numbers of people are to become isolated from the stream of contemporary life, anti-environments must be created at a matching pace.

Once he has lost touch with the realities of urban life, the individual can no longer interpret the feedback he receives from his environment. And if enough such individuals occupy positions of social responsibility, as everyone does to some extent in a democratic society, urban affairs become progressively less manageable. The dangers of gradual alienation from reality are the more acute since those thus estranged may be quite unaware of the fact. Worse still, specialists' understanding of problems within their disciplines may deepen while their ties to the reality of urban existence simultaneously deteriorate. Individuals may thus find more and more manifestations of daily life incomprehensible: new trends in arts and sciences, new patterns of behavior, new tastes and fashions, or new popular reactions to established facts. When such incomprehension becomes sufficiently widespread for public policy to be based on it—when the conscious shaping and reshaping of collective values yields to a dual tendency of either blind repression of anything new or helpless surrender to it—then urban civilization is in danger.

Much of the contemporary reaction to urban ills is of this nature.[1] Rising crime, the physical decay of city centers, increasing use of hallucinatory drugs, corruption in municipal government, environmental pollution, growing mental health problems, race riots, the financial difficulties of municipalities, etc., are all coped with separately. If attempts are made to find their patterns of interlinkage, these tend to be sought in the dead, or dying, values and institutions of the past. But even if the roots of urban evils are thus unearthed, their cure must be accomplished in the present and the future. The relevance of previous generations' morality to crime, drug addiction, and corruption today is doubtful at best.

The links between urban ills lie in the present, possibly in the gradual disintegration of underlying collective values. The myths of perpetual technological progress, of the intrinsic value of work, and of the sanctity of national objectives are dying—developments made plainly visible in the work of artists, the most perceptive observers of the human condition, who have turned from admiration of the machine to its caricature in one short generation. (Figure 71.) Indeed, the fact that the values of technology can be, and are, seriously and widely discussed and questioned[2] indicates that we may be emerging from an age that has been unwittingly dominated by the machine.

The Urban Potential. Urban problems are essentially those of unsatisfied needs at the levels of the individual, the subcommunity, and the urban

figure 70 *Nature adds an element of ambiguity to urban form which otherwise would be painfully harsh.*

community. Such needs may not have been dealt with because they are newly emerging or newly recognized, or, alternatively, because physical and social constraints blocked earlier relief attempts, or rendered them ineffective. However, both the act of recognition and the effort to overcome constraints must be motivated. The one prerequisite for urban renewal that overrides all others is thus for a collective sense of purpose. Without it the urban environment has meaning only to the extent that it provides the arena for the fight for survival of the fittest—an objective that contains the seeds of collective suicide.

Sense of purpose was in the past instilled in individuals as members of local communities which were loosely linked in nation states. But the once autonomous centers are gradually dissolving in an emerging world community whose constituent parts are subcommunities without geographic definition. As a result it is becoming increasingly difficult to find any purpose in actions that do not transcend local boundaries.

The restructuring of the urban habitat from the concentric groupings of homogeneous populations to that of dynamically interlinked and constantly changing subcommunities calls for objective quantitative and qualitative measuring techniques that were unnecessary in the past. The quantitative analysis of the urban environment has been relatively well served by statisticians. Even if incomplete and often lacking in uniformity, the data have been shown to be readily transferable into graphic form and made directly applicable to the study of urban problems.[3] Qualitative data, in the form of environmental indices, by contrast, are totally inadequate. Performance data in terms of productivity and profitability, and environmental information concerning climate and the degree and kind of air and water pollution, give little indication of the rate at which the human organism and particularly the senses are assaulted in a given environment, or of the intensity of the assaults.

The standard of living can thus as yet not be expressed in human terms. Tied to standards of production and consumption, its figures obscure the paradoxical fact that standards of living can rise while those of production and consumption simultaneously drop.[4] The prospect of supersonic flight before all associated noise problems are solved provides a prime example of how a substantial accretion to the gross national product can be accompanied by a sharp drop in the livability of the total environment.

The obsession with production and the corresponding dominance of the profit motive has severely limited the scope of urban development, particularly in the fields of housing, commerce, industry, and entertainment, but indirectly also in every other use of urban land, including that for public purposes. The prospect of profit as reward for individual and corporate initiative can without doubt be a powerful stimulant to urban improvement. But the fiscal constraints affecting such development need the most careful

figure 71 *The machine seen as a self-destroying device.*

manipulation by governments if lasting improvements are to be achieved. The growth of urban populations everywhere has obscured the fact that much of what has been built is quite unfit for human habitation and use. The automatic expansion of demand for enclosed, serviced space has made it impossible for supply to catch up and denies any meaningful choice of urban accommodation to all but the fortunate few whose needs happen to fit the supply.

Private enterprise is ultimately given its direction by the bias inherent in the scale of collective values. This bias expresses itself in the manner in which public investments are applied to the channeling of economic growth and in the use of legal and fiscal constraints. The control of urban development through the deliberate manipulation of incentives and curbs naturally presupposes a clear understanding of their interaction with the existing habitat. In the absence of dependable measuring techniques, the consequences of such intervention can be evaluated qualitatively at best. An indication of the unpredictability of urban development is implied in the difference between the rates of interest applied to mortgages and those paid on bonds and corporate stocks. Money loaned on urban real estate is clearly considered a high-risk investment and sometimes an outright speculation. This risk element tends to be increased by policies of individual and corporate taxation which entirely disregard the difference between extractive real estate operations and investments that add value to the urban environment and therefore to human life.

Emerging Tools

Communication and Transportation. If a sense of purpose is a prerequisite to the creation of a viable urban habitat, then communications systems that interlink the members of the community are in turn necessary to permit the continuing redefinition of aims. For a time the new media of communications furnished by technology—print, telephone, radio, television—appeared to fulfill their role so well that the dominant traditional media, including architecture, appeared to be dispensable. Misunderstanding of the nature of the new media, however, and particularly the absence of feedback, obscured widening rifts within the urban community. While elite subcommunities established communications links with their counterparts around the globe they lost all ties with population groups in their immediate proximity. The consequence is a social delamination process that threatens the urban community. Existing media of communications that might be applied to the reestablishment of communal bonds have been largely preempted by commercial users, at least in the United States. What is worse, their utilization tends to be socially divisive, since they are used to stimulate needs which the community may be unwilling or unable to satisfy.

When channels of communications are becoming clogged, the transfer of messages and information is not necessarily stopped. To a large extent, communications systems and transportation systems can substitute for each other, and any given communications load can be processed through either. Different messages are, however, suited to different media. While overloading an urban communications system need not lead to a breakdown of communications, it definitely impedes the flow of information and therefore reduces the fitness of the environment for urban life. Except in the rare instances where an urban transportation system has ample capacity, the transfer of communications functions simply transfers congestion from one system to the other.

Where communications and transportation functions are interchangeable, the comparative cost of operating either kind of system ultimately determines the loads they are assigned. A fair distribution requires, however, that investments in the public sector are fully reflected in such a cost analysis. The use of radio and television for educational purposes might thus reduce investments in educational buildings, as the use of telephone connections obviates some travel and lessens the need for roads. But even among the different communications and transportation systems, efficiency varies widely depending on equipment used and on energy costs.[5] Any substantial future change in either can therefore be expected to have serious repercussions on the location of urban centers as well as on their internal organization.

Similar dislocation will result from new construction techniques that affect transportation. The concept of rapid excavation, for instance, promises to open up economic ways of tunneling and the creation of complex high-speed underground transportation networks.[6] Such transportation systems will have to depend on the perfection of control devices permitting automated automotion of the type under development by leading automobile manufacturers. But once in operation they may well entice all purely functional movement as well as some urban activities permanently underground. (Figure 72.)

Methods and Materials.   New rapid-excavation techniques, however, are but one aspect of a maturing materials-handling technology. Its evolution may indeed have a more profound and more immediate effect on the urban environment than the development of new building materials and products. Metals of greater strength, for instance, and expanding ranges of plastics may marginally alter the economic feasibility of new forms but are not likely to affect their conception.

The constraints imposed on form by the limitations inherent in construction materials have gradually become negligible, and the technical and economic feasibility of large-scale urban undertakings depends increasingly on the effectiveness of time- and laborsaving processes or, in other words,

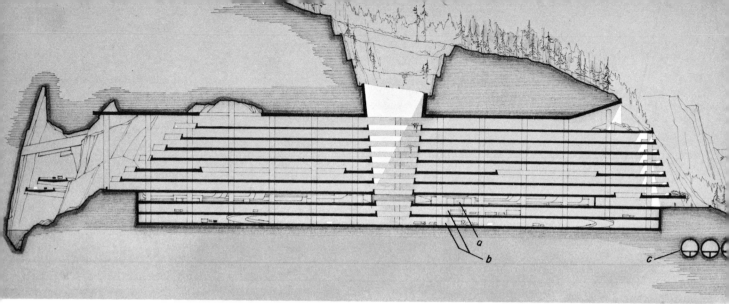

figure 72 *The potential for urban development underground is as yet little explored. Housing at sunlit walls circled by commerce, recreation, government, and industry. (a) Power, cooling, and ventilation; (b) two parking levels; (c) transcontinental freight tubes.*

on the perfection of sophisticated techniques of project management and materials handling. They in turn help transfer new concepts of urban form from the realm of dreams into that of reality, a transition noticeable simultaneously on four fronts:

1. The ease and speeds achieved in global communications and travel permit the concentration of worldwide resources of capital, expertise, and talent on large-scale urban projects anywhere and at any time.

2. Engineering science has reached a degree of sophistication where virtually any conceivable urban form can be realized anywhere on the globe and on any desired scale.

3. Earth-moving equipment has been perfected to the point where urban development need no longer follow the physical features of the earth surface but can itself determine them.

4. Industrial production techniques, endowed with artificial intelligence, can be applied to the building process without imposing a deadening pattern of mindless modularity on urban form.

Such is the potential of technology when applied directly to the methods of molding the urban habitat. But its promise remains unkept. The bulk of the world's resources in money or brains continues from force of habit to be wasted or applied locally in minute doses. The art of deliberately shaping features of the landscape and their integration with building elements is rarely practiced (Figure 73), and then usually only under the compulsion of engineering considerations. Industry, finally, has as yet to make a concerted effort to become involved in urban building.

The constraints built up and codified over generations too often combine to defeat new approaches to urban form. These constraints find their primary expression in the small scale they impose on the urban environment. The fragmentation of the ownership and use of urban land forces planners, developers, and designers to think small, and the same thinking tends then to be transferred to the planning, design, and development of the parts of the urban habitat where these constraints do not apply. Only on rare occasions do fresh visions prevail.

The limitations imposed by traditional land-use patterns have been successfully overcome in the planning and construction of urban expressways. Serving a single, well-defined public purpose, their value relative to other collective needs is comparatively easy to determine. In applying the same scale of thinking to urban development in general, however, the conflict is no longer only between individual and collective needs but between the needs of those owning and occupying existing property and the requirements of others who would take their places. The large-scale use of existing urban land for such redevelopment is obviously only feasible in areas declining in both use value and population density, or where high-density development is planned to replace existing low-density land use, or where society is determined to supplant what is existing without regard to costs, as in conventional slum clearance operations.

figure 73 *Building form deliberately integrated with the landscape.*

The first of the three alternatives is obviously the most desirable, but as long as urban populations grow, there is little scope for a redevelopment policy based on the existence of surplus land in urban centers. However, by reducing the desirability of areas in physical decline through appropriate tax measures, and by simultaneously applying all public land resources to the relief of population pressure, surplus land can be created artificially. The wasted air space over roads and railways and parking and docking facilities becomes thus habitable. Alternatives are the creation of new land through fill operations, and beyond that, perhaps, the creation of new urban cores over open water. (Figure 74.)

The integration of public with private spaces in the same building, and of transportation, housing, commercial, educational, and recreational functions on the same property, obviously requires the restructuring of old problems. Besides coping with what is established practice in a multitude of government, business, and labor bureaucracies, any new departure will require a much closer collaboration between them. The financing and maintenance of mixed-use structures has to depend on the highly sophisticated management and control techniques made possible by computers. The complexity inherent in the planning, design, and realization of such integrated structures requires that they be conceived on a scale transcending local boundaries. Urban megastructures thus require the support of corresponding organizational megastructures in government as well as in finance, design, development, and construction.[7]

CHANGING NEEDS

The New Awareness

Global Expectations. As urban communities have broken out of their local isolation and have linked up in an ever-tightening global communal network, disparities of living standards and opportunities have become increasingly apparent. Media of instant communications force the painful comparison between ages of abundance and of subsistence prevailing side by side. Television has brought people living in dire need face-to-face with those enjoying affluence, and jet travel has established direct contact between them. Virtually every metropolis, moreover, contains the full spectrum of living standards from affluence to abject poverty. In the technologically advanced parts of the world, social policy tends toward easing the harshness of the lot of those most in need. Where industrial development is lagging, however, the proportion of urban populations living near or in destitution rises drastically, and the means at society's disposal are simply not adequate to lift them out of poverty to any significant degree.

While urban development in the technologically advanced parts of the

figure 74 *Future urban development need not take place on land only.*

world can be directed away from its purely economic aspects toward the enrichment of life, the prime concern elsewhere is to barely sustain the rapidly growing urban population. The concept of what Gerald Breese has called "subsistence urbanization"[8] thus dominates many of the major population centers of Africa, Asia, and South America. Overpopulation, lack of educational and job opportunities, and lack of capital—in addition to the often stubborn adherence to obsolete social systems, ways of thinking, and institutions—combine to impede efforts to bring about evolutionary change.

The problems of urban growth are thus quite different in the technologically underdeveloped parts of the world and in the cities of North America and Europe. And neither the North American nor the European city provides relevant models for urbanization on the scale and at the rate needed in newly developing countries. In North America and Europe, the arrest of population growth is for one thing at least a possibility for the foreseeable future, particularly if it is assumed that the maximum human life expectancy cannot be extended substantially beyond present limits and that the massive movement from rural to urban areas has, similarly, about run its course. Urban populations on these two continents will thus, at worst, have doubled by the end of the century. However, using the same set of assumptions, the urban populations in Asia, Africa, and South America will grow at least sixfold in the same period.[9] And since the bulk of the present housing stock on these continents is inadequate by any standards, the traditional approach to urban planning and housing production will obviously not satisfy the exploding need for shelter.

It appears that for the great masses of urban dwellers, basic shelter can, under the circumstances, only be provided by marshaling all available initiative, and, in particular, through the self-help of the individuals concerned.[10] But even with a supply of technical and economic help, the allocation of land and building materials and the provision of basic municipal services can pose considerable organizational problems. Their solution and the simultaneous coordination of local efforts with wide planning objectives may well come to depend on the judicious application of computers to such tasks.

Their use depends, of course, on the presence of a highly technically trained elite. The people belonging to it, however, are globally mobile by virtue of this very training. Therefore, they can be expected to remain in economically backward population centers only if the facilities for working and living are at least comparable with those offered elsewhere. The image of progress created through the display of modern office buildings, housing, hotels, and airports in underdeveloped countries thus not only symbolizes the very real ties such new cities have established with other population centers, but serves the practical purpose of accommodating the people and processes needed to support further advances. The social structure in the urban centers of developing countries appears not to be too dissimilar from that in other parts of the world. Subcommunities at the ghetto level may be far more numerous since they reflect extended family and tribal ties, and the subcommunal interactions between masses and elite correspondingly fewer and less complex. But the elite's orientation, there as elsewhere, is predominantly global.

Housing Urban Nomads.   In contrast to animals, who are tied to limited territories which also define the scope of their social activities, man's territory is the world. If mature individuals limit their interests to specific places, they do so by choice, and if a majority of people choose to remain in familiar surroundings, their reason is convenience reinforced by tradition. While the animal's built-in territoriality determines the patterns of its social life, man, due to an almost unlimited adaptability to changing environmental conditions, does not need a sense of territory unless it is imposed on him by the society he lives in. (Figure 75.)

Technology has given man the option to follow his natural inclination to move about on the globe unencumbered by the practical considerations that once tied him to one place. In medieval Europe, the same end was achieved by reducing personal possessions to an easily transportable minimum.[11] The global urban environment, however, no longer even extracts a noticeable price in terms of personal comfort from those opting for a nomadic existence. As a result, the functional need for the mobility of urban populations—a requirement of industry and commerce[12]—has been supplemented by voluntary moves in response to personal needs. Such moves may be extended vacation trips, seasonal journeys inspired by the climate, or voluntary relocation for any of an unlimited number of personal reasons.

Whether an individual chooses confinement to one place or freedom from territorial ties is essentially a matter of choice—collective in the traditional community or tribe, individual in the urban environment. To accommodate both requires a social structure adjusted to the continuing movement of individuals and family groups, a physical environment similarly adapted or adaptable, and facilities to transport people and their belongings comfortably, quickly, and safely. These purposes are served in a variety of ways. Social adjustment is eased through appropriate habits and styles of living. Physical adaptation, at least in advanced countries, is accomplished through the simplicity of the procedures by which the ownership or tenure of property is transferred.[13] The transportation problem, finally, has been solved mainly through the efficient use of existing multipurpose facilities: airlines, roads, railways, and waterways.

Migration has become a central urban issue. The number of people attracted to, or forced into, a nomadic existence at least during part of their lives will increase, and patterns of urban activity and the character of urban building will evolve accordingly. And the fact of urban mobility will demand expression in new kinds of artifacts. The organic integration of mobile housing units into the urban habitat thus represents one of the obvious challenges in which the new way of life confronts traditional urban form. If the desire and need of modern man to relocate freely are superimposed on his constituent and traditional needs, the functional performance specifications for a truly contemporary dwelling call for an easily movable, multicellular cluster of private spaces to which units can be added or from which they can be detached as needs change.

Permanent structures that provide universal spaces easily adapted to the demands of changing tenants are an alternative. Neutral spaces would in this case be adapted to individual needs through the free arrangement of movable elements—be they complete prefabricated rooms, partitions,

figure 75 *Man has always had the option of creating his own movable territory. (Photograph courtesy of the National Geographic Society)*

figure 76 *Modern technology has made it possible to conceive of universal space at the public scale of urban form and beyond. The United States Pavilion at Expo 67 in Montreal may represent but a tentative step in the construction of even larger space enclosures.*

plants, or conventional furniture—placed to create a landscape on an intimate scale. The possibilities of either approach are unlimited. (Figure 76.)

Dissolving Boundaries and Dying Centers. In spreading out and merging at their edges, cities have lost their physical definition as focal points of human life. And with instant global communications, even the remaining boundaries between the growing conurbations are losing their significance as one metropolis becomes the suburb of another.

Boundaries impede freedom, but in doing so they offer protection. Thus is security bought at the price of liberty. When physical and communal boundaries coincide, communal sets of values are physically reinforced, a fact visibly expressed in the harmony of traditional urban form. Technology has conquered the defensive walls, the natural borders, and the distances between dwellings that once meant safety. But in the process it has created boundaries of its own: canals, railways, highways, parking garages, pipelines, electric power transmission lines, etc. Yet despite their obvious potential, and often in a deliberate and perverse preference for the expedient, such boundaries are applied rarely, if ever, to the definition of the urban environment in human terms.

The need for social orientation and security found in the identification with places and groups appears to be universal. When traditional boundaries became ineffective, they were promptly replaced by new legal and economic boundaries, which in turn define such makeshift residential communities as suburban neighborhoods, racial ghettos, self-contained apartment projects, and their counterparts in other spheres of urban life whose sole organizing principle is social and economic homogeneity. In the quest for security, the freedom of social mobility within the total community has been compromised. Social mobility has come to depend on the ease with which individuals break out of their subcommunities and fit themselves into others. Meanwhile, a fake territoriality confines the large majority within limits imposed by the fear of individual isolation.

The subdivision of urban space into socially and economically homogeneous territories implies a gradual disintegration of urban society. Since the beginning of this fragmentation followed the demise of traditional urban boundaries, it is at least conceivable that the two developments are linked in a cause-and-effect relationship. This would in turn suggest that a drastic restructuring of urban form might lead to greater social integration rather than result from it.

The enclosing quality of traditional cities resulted not only from the presence of encircling walls, but from a design approach that was directed toward the shaping of spaces rather than of buildings. The architectural treatment accorded the present urban environment, by contrast, fosters the expression of identity, not its enjoyment. Hence an urban environment fraught with symbols and thrusting forms, but devoid of enfolding spaces. Yet the return to the traditional approaches to planning and design is barred; urban communities that have no spatial definition cannot be spatially enclosed. And the dream of truly dynamic urban space, in which attention has shifted from the appearance of space to its nature, is as yet unfulfilled.[14]

figure 77 *". . . where aims are well defined, activities are predictable, and clear form results."*

Objectives and Integrities

The Nature of Urban Activities. Human activities, their motives, and the environment are locked in mutual interdependence. Thus, where aims are well defined, activities are predictable, and clear form results. (Figure 77.) Clear aims, however, are not natural to human existence; they are imposed by circumstances. At the subsistence level, the objective is survival, and the same aim pervades life in the isolated citadel. Man's urges to play, to create, to discover, are all made subservient to the one all-important purpose. It is hoped that the functional city may be the historically last manifestation of the large-scale subordination of individuals to the collective goals of survival. With man the producer superseded by the machine, and with the associated communications functions served by electronic equipment, there is no longer either any necessity nor any justification for the forced integration of people into production processes, megamachines, or technostructures. For the first time, individual autonomy is conceivable as a choice open to everyone.

The greater the number of people who are free to opt out of the coercive type of social system that characterizes functional organization, the more human the urban environment becomes and the more unpredictable its development. What makes the planning of the conventional city's functional components possible is the fact that the behavior of its inhabitants is controlled: people are forced to work for a living; therefore they must live within commuting distance from the available places of work; and on this basis housing and commercial developments, road and rail transportation, and recreational and educational facilities can then be planned with reasonable accuracy. Take away the compulsion to work, or even the compulsion to work during fixed hours, and one set of foundations is pulled from under the conventional planning approach.

If, however, urban planning is deprived of the solid base that the control of demand has provided, then its very function changes. Instead of following and accommodating trends, the act of planning becomes one of deliberately charting the course of urban trends. In this case the responsibility for the urban future comes to rest solely with the planning profession, in the same sense that the management of a business corporation cannot blame the failure of the products it planned on the lack of cooperation by its customers. But while corporate management has the relatively easy task of producing and supplying specific items for the market, the planner's product is the urban environment itself. Like the manager, he must learn to estimate correctly the changes in customer reaction, and one measure of such reaction is the quality and quantity of urban activity. The environment structures the human community; it assigns places to individuals and channels their communications, movements, and all other activities. The higher the density of activity, the more pronounced the structure's definition becomes, and the greater the need for urban organizing principles carefully adapted to the community's nature.

In contrast to the multiple choices provided for in a lived-in, organic urban habitat, theory of urban design is dominated by the notion that hierarchical principles underlie all urban structure.[15] This idea has found its possibly best known expression in Le Corbusier's theories on urban planning, where not only the traffic patterns, but those of land use and even residence, are interrelated to clearly express the dominance of a simple hierarchical order. By separating different aspects of urban life and fitting them into neat categories, the field of planning thus has been fitted conveniently to conjunctive patterns of thought. Yet urban problems are essentially of a disjunctive nature, and any attempt at translating them into conjunctive (or relational) terms tends to result in dangerously oversimplified solutions: "The problem-solver faced with the task of discovering the defining attributes of a disjunctive class of objects must . . . abandon the conventional strategies of attempting to isolate those features that are common to all members of the class. For in a disjunctive class, there are no such universal common features."[16]

Urban movement systems, for instance, may be isolated by classing the people within buildings as stationary and by defining the street system as the area of their interaction in motion. Such a strategy may yield valuable results if the distinction is conceptual only and made in full awareness of its irrelevance to reality. Real people are moving all the time as they constantly reorient themselves to changes in their environment. Except while asleep, and during short periods of mental concentration, man's natural state is motion, and if confined to a stationary position, at a desk or in the back seat of a car, he invariably seeks compensation by visually relating to other moving objects. Movement is central to all aspects of urban design.

A conceptual path-place dichotomy pervades the conventional approach to urban planning and design. It finds expression in the very separation of, for instance, office buildings from apartment structures; in the static internal organization of both: lobby—elevator cab—corridor—cubicle; finally, in the attention lavished on the technical perfection of the paths connecting the two. Significantly, the sensory experience of movement, both from the essentially static position of driver or train passenger and that of the office and apartment occupant—in other words the view both *from* the path and *of* the path—are entirely neglected. The conventional urban habitat *contains* a movement system when it should *be* a movement system.

But the environment must be other things as well, and simultaneously. Urban movement, to stay with the same example, is not and never was primarily a functional activity. (Figure 78.) Automobiles and airplanes are

figure 78 *"Urban movement . . . is not and never was primarily a functional activity."*

not simply conveyances; they are the realization of age-old dreams. "The mere fact that there are things in nature that do fly, and that there are animals in creation that run faster than you, makes that part of your brain and your motivation want to do so."[17] Movement systems are amenities serving man's leisure needs, potentially helping him maintain his health. This conceptual link suggests, moreover, that health problems in turn are not solved conjunctively by the creation of a class of buildings called hospitals, but must be regarded as total environmental problems. Nor are the needs for education, popular assembly, work, etc., served adequately by the construction of isolated buildings.

Integrated Concepts. The functional city is modeled on the hive, in which the environment is perfectly matched to its inhabitants' needs. But then, hive-building animals are genetically programmed to create specific social environments for themselves. Human needs, by contrast, vary constantly, with the result that man's social environment requires continuous adaptation to change. And since the direction of such changes is unpredictable, people must reinvent their environment all the time. Invention is thus not so much a cause of progress as a way in which changing needs can be adapted to a stable environment; and design is the method by which invention is applied to urban form. In other words, invention shapes intervention through design.

But if the design process is the intermediary between invention, the form-conceiving process, and intervention—the process of construction— then it is also the medium of control through which the realization of dreams may be impelled or blocked. And since form directs activity, all planning of urban development must ultimately focus on the design process. Urban activity may thus be integrated to any desired degree through the corresponding integration of urban form; and the function of the design process then becomes that of realizing the form potential of activity integration.

Form has always served an activity-integrating function: the medieval city, the large convention hotel, and the ocean liner are examples of artifacts in which a multitude of activities have been fused together. Yet characteristically, they exist in isolation. In all their multiplexity, each is essentially self-contained; and the activities each accommodates are severed from the larger environment. This is true even of modern architecture's prototype of an integrated urban structure: Le Corbusier's unité d'habitation in Marseille, completed in 1952, which in one crystalline shape unites several hundred dwellings of various sizes, hotel rooms, stores, a children's nursery, a club, and other social amenities.[18] (Figure 79.) But the isolation of the building and what would be an arbitrary fragmentation of a population housed uniformly in such blocks denies all social structure except that imposed by the pattern of elevators, corridors, and connecting roads. Le Corbusier's urban forms are predicated on the existence of a homogeneous mass society

figure 79 *Unitée d'habitation in Marseille, designed by Le Corbusier.*

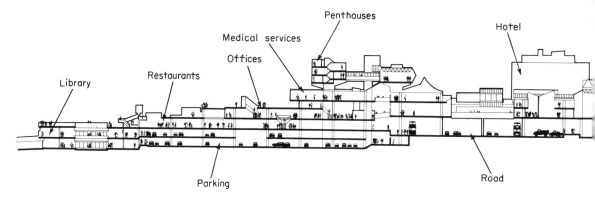

willingly packaged to fit a grand design; the integration is achieved only in terms of pure form.

To be relevant, urban form must integrate a wider range of functions, as was attempted in the project for the Cumbernauld New Town central area in Great Britain.[19] (Figure 80.) The vastly greater variety of activities and accommodations provided for is reflected in an overall form of appropriately lower geometric definition. The building does not presume to be a declaration on the equality of men. But it does venture to integrate multidirectional pedestrian and vehicular movement with a variety of residential, commercial, and administrative building functions.

Neither Le Corbusier nor the architects of Cumbernauld had to face the added difficulties which high urban densities inevitably impose. The integration of urban travel at greatly varying speeds, of multitudes forced into propinquity despite individually different backgrounds and aspirations, and of constantly changing institutions competing for urban space is probably beyond human design ability. But if the conventional design approach has failed, computer-aided processes may yet prove adequate to the challenge of urban complexity.

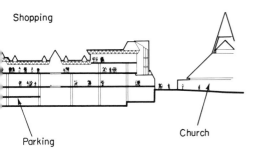

Shopping

Parking

Church

figure 80 (above) *Section through the multilevel central area of Cumbernauld New Town in Scotland. (below) View of the central area from a nearby residential cluster.*

CHAPTER EIGHT

SYSTEMS APPROACH

AND COMPUTER APPLICATION

THE PROBLEM STRUCTURE

Coping with Urban Problems

The Growth of Complexity. Life in the modern city is probably no more complex for the average individual than it was in earlier periods of history. By submitting to rigid routines in their day-to-day existence, people isolate themselves from unwanted stimuli. They cope with the latent complexities of urban life by establishing predictable patterns that fit readily into the overall rhythm of urban activity. Thus each individual, in evolving his own life-style, scales his awareness of the metropolis down as near as possible to his own mental, emotional, physiological, and economic level. The greater the divergence of such individual life-styles, the greater is the complexity of the resulting urban environment.

This complexity, however, is not solely a function of the multiplicity of individual life-styles which the environment must accommodate. The effective interaction of individuals and the maintenance of their standard of living depend on the unfailing performances of machines and of the personnel serving and controlling them. Together they form interlocking systems of production, administration, and distribution, each directed from different centers. As a result, a simple job such as the baking and distribution of bread, traditionally carried out within the confines of small neighborhood shops, now involves the operation of factories, fleets of trucks, and chains of supermarkets, and therefore the cooperation of thousands of people.

Similarly, the construction of a simple dwelling, which traditionally involved the owner, perhaps a moneylender, and a team of craftsmen and laborers, has become a task that depends for its success on the smooth interaction of large organizations—the megamachines of business, labor, and government—concerned with matters of finance, of law, of engineering and design, and with the manufacturing and supply of countless items for site assembly by numerous teams of specialized tradesmen. Any increase of efficiency in production, administration, and distribution, when sought through mechanization, appears inevitably to be accompanied by a corresponding increase in urban complexity.

The growing complexity both of purely human and of man-machine relationships is moreover superimposed on an already existing urban environment which rigidly constrains all development. The existing features of a site, be they artifacts or elements of nature, cannot be ignored, nor can established institutions, laws, labor practices, etc. The natural consequence is that new development invariably tends to be conceived as an extension to what is already there rather than to follow its own inherent logic.

Urban problems are in essence multidimensional and, for that reason, cannot be visualized in all their ramifications simultaneously. The painstaking analysis of every interaction possible within a set of form determinants may in the end result in intelligent planning and design decisions. But urban planning problems arise out of dynamic processes, and their solution does not usually bear postponing. Complex urban problems can therefore only be coped with successfully under one of three conditions:

1. Urban development is slowed down to suit the conventional decision-making processes.

2. Urban development is restricted in scope and kind to that familiar to decision makers to permit the acceleration of conventional processes without changing their structure.

3. The decision-making process is adapted to the pace of urban development.

To give clear priority to the first alternative is obviously unthinkable except when the growth of the population has been arrested and if expectations are largely met in the existing environment—a policy that is only conceivable in an atmosphere of stagnation. The results of the second alternative are apparent in every modern city in the form of endlessly repeated buildings whose lack of identity is only thinly disguised by cosmetic treatment—in unvarying street widths, constant building setbacks, etc. This leaves the third alternative.

Rather than accommodate physical processes to the accustomed speed of what are essentially mental processes, this third approach to the direction of urban development presumes the possibility that intellectual processes can be substantially accelerated. To complete an intellectual task in less time obviously requires an increase in brainpower, an accomplishment theoretically possible either by putting more human brains to work or by automating mental processes. In practice, however, the latter choice, which involves electronic computers in the problem-solving process, proves to be the only one. Not only is it doubtful whether additional trained human brainpower required to keep up with the pace of global urbanization could be made available in time, but the very notion of thousands of men equaling the work of a computer ignores the problems of their effective intercommunication. Only the computers, used as extensions of the human brain, promise to be capable of assuming full control over the machines—the mindless extensions of man's body. In the process, the crudity of the modern urban environment which was brought about by the unrestrained application of brute machine power may be supplanted by a new refinement of urban form as mechanical power is matched with mechanical intelligence, and as human imagination is freed from its bondage to technology.

Real and Conceptual Structures.   Man orients himself in his environment by classifying all objects he encounters and thus structures the reality he perceives. In other words, he orders his sense impressions to fit his preconceptions, a process elaborated through education: "Science and common-sense inquiry alike do not discover the ways in which events are grouped in the world; they invent ways of grouping."[1]

Depending on his preconceptions, an observer of the urban scene may thus see a random collection of shapes, some moving, some stationary; or he may relate the people he sees conceptually to the surrounding artifacts and elements of nature; or his interest in architecture may lead him to speculate on the quality of the urban space and its effects on the life it contains. In all cases, he retains the impression of an environment structured in space and time. While the environment itself remains "invisible,"[2] its reality is perceived in the conceptual structure which the human mind has imposed on it.

The perception of reality is thus directly related to the individual's conception of it. If, for example, a planner has conceived a city as broken up into different zones of human activity and isolated neighborhoods that are interconnected by highways, he will be strongly inclined to search for solutions to environmental deficiencies within the framework of these preconceptions. He will tend to redefine the zones, improve the neighborhoods, and ease the traffic flow, but without sacrificing any of the essential categories that define the problem structure he knows.

To superimpose a conceptual structure on reality appears to be a reaction natural to man when forced to cope with the unknown. But since urban reality is artificial, its structure is conceptual in essence; its very creation represents the transfer of a concept into the realm of reality. Thus the structure of urban reality will always tend to adapt itself to the conceptual structure prevalent in the community.

When, during periods of tranquility, this condition of coincidence between real and conceptual structure is established, the two inevitably continue to reinforce each other. If finance, roads, parks, public works, welfare, and housing are established as administrative departments, all subsequent physical planning must be based on the premise that there will be little enthusiasm for development proposals that do not fit or are readily divisible into these categories. In addition, such coinciding structures tend to perpetuate each other: new buildings are placed in locations favored by existing roads; the resulting added traffic then justifies improving (meaning widening) these same roads, which in turn invites more building of the same kind in an unending self-feeding process.

Urban development becomes in this case a closed process which tends to run an established course long after its validity in philosophical and social terms is exhausted. Indeed, the self-perpetuating aspects of urban development are in the long run also self-defeating. To come back to the example mentioned above, continuing construction along an ever-widening highway can only lead to eventual total congestion and an environment unfit for life of any kind.

The process of urban development must thus be one in which structural changes can be introduced at any time. This was accomplished with relative ease in the traditional city whose structure was still simple enough to be comprehensible in its entirety. The modern metropolis, by contrast, is characterized by the loss of such conceptual unity, and by a conceptual structure complex beyond the grasp of the unaided human intellect. The first role of the computer must thus be that of helping reestablish an understanding of all the forces which interact in the urban environment. Only on the basis of total comprehension is there a hope of exercising environmental control.

Dynamic Structures, Processes, and Systems. The structures discussed so far have been essentially static. Conceptual structures rarely involve relations between elements that are of a dynamic nature. Rather, they tend to substitute static concepts for actual dynamic processes whenever possible. The very building of cities and of the monuments they contain represents in part an irrational attempt to substitute unchanging permanence for the inevitability of change.

However, all life is process rather than state, and urban life differs only to the extent that it is tied to the environment's fixed physical elements. Man's purpose in consciously structuring his conception of the urban environment is to be able to cope with it successfully. When, in times past, the social structure was fixed and individuals were assigned unchanging roles in it, it was possible to think of cities in terms of static entities. By contrast, few aspects of today's metropolis can be understood except in terms of dynamic structures in which the relationship between elements changes constantly. As a result, the urban environment must be conceived as a field of interaction of dynamic processes, and its fixed elements as processes that are temporarily frozen.

Processes are frozen as artifacts are shaped to fit them. They are those of decision making, of urban orientation and image building, of the evolution of urban circulation patterns, of land use, of capital investments, etc. As these processes are arrested, however, new ones are generated: new subcommunities are formed, new visual patterns emerge in the environment, new problems are created, and, hence, new decision-making processes initiated. They are the results of feedback.

Whenever a dynamic process is constrained, secondary, reverse processes are set in motion which impel an adjustment of the forces causing the conflict. These secondary processes feed back information, whether through a nervous system, the use of natural media of communications, or through the channels of modern urban communications. Such feedback is an important factor in the evaluation of urban processes; indeed, it is often the only factor. If processes are to be controlled, their direction and strength must be known.

At its most primitive level the exercise of control is based on a closed community's collective and unquestioning conformity with patterns established in the past. In this case traditions direct the dominant urban processes: those that determine the social structure, major activities, and urban development. However, accumulated experience has in most places been superseded by conventional wisdom as the ultimate authority. This is the kind of wisdom that is expressed in a master plan: a fixed model against which all real processes that affect the urban environment are measured. And only when the resulting reality does not meet expectations are adjustments made in the master plan.

The procedure corresponds to archaic industrial processes in which production machinery is only adjusted when permissible tolerances are clearly exceeded. Rather than depend on such incidental feedback, modern industry has been using adaptive control processes to regulate production. Modern control techniques, employing computers whenever complex decisions must be reached quickly, have made continuous production processes possible. The evolution of new approaches to urban planning and design which can parallel these achievements depends on the successful application of control theory to urban problems.[3]

Processes of planning and design are essentially multistage decision processes in which decisions are made on the basis of partial understanding and incomplete information. Since the decisions are made in sequence rather than simultaneously, however, errors in judgment can be compensated for during the process if feedback information from the preceding stages is correctly interpreted. Feedback is in this case obviously no longer incidental to the process but becomes an integral part of it.

In concentrating on processes, however, the discussion has gradually shifted away from the structure of urban reality to focus on the interaction of urban elements within systems.

Urban Systems and the Systems Approach

Systems are structured groups of elements organized for a common purpose, or to use a somewhat more rigorous definition: A system is a set of objects with relationships between the objects and between their attributes.[4] Such objects may be the urban form determinants and constraints discussed in earlier chapters; they may be separate processes or the stages of processes; they may be sets of interlinked data; they may be urban artifacts; or for that matter any other component part of urban reality.

The value of the systems approach lies in its demand for a clear definition of all objects, their attributes, and their relationships. But urban problems are of such a magnitude that insistence on meeting all these conditions simultaneously and from the very beginning would reduce the applicability of the method to trivial subsystems and, moreover, deny any assurance that they could later be successfully fitted into larger subsystems. Systems concepts must thus be of a kind that can be gradually introduced into the fields of urban planning and design.

The Hierarchy of Systems.   The systems approach has been highly successful whenever a clear aim could be pursued with means known to be available. Problems associated with cost accounting, the control of industrial processes, and the planning of space probes come immediately to mind. Urban problems, however, are of an entirely different nature. Far from being clearly defined, objectives differ with every member of the urban community and are furthermore constantly changing and in continuous conflict. Even if the sum total of available resources may conceivably be measured, their allocation to divergent aims remains ultimately arbitrary.

The term "systems approach" in the context of this book implies the application of the scientific method to the analysis, design, and control of urban processes. Any systems approach to urban problems will therefore tend to concentrate on their readily quantifiable aspects. For a number of urban variables, numerical values are indeed easily obtained. Thus, the volume of traffic that streets can accommodate is obviously a linear function of their width and the permissible speed of movement. The capacity of other means of transportation is determined with similar ease, as is the maximum number of potential users of a mass transportation system when it is placed in a known environment.

Movement systems would thus appear ideally suited to the application of the systems approach. Unfortunately, the scientific method has a built-in bias which tends to exclude those aspects of the problem from consideration that do not lend themselves to accurate measurement. Automobile traffic on a certain network may be regulated to maximize speed or to minimize accidents, but not to maximize the driving pleasure of its users, nor to maximize its positive and minimize its negative side effects on the total environment.

As long as no more than a minute part of the environment yields to quantitative measurement, a rigorously followed systems approach thus leads to meaningful results only when restricted to minute aspects of urban problems. Examples of urban microsystems are computerized elevator control systems, local traffic control systems, systems of scheduling the operations on construction projects, or the occupancy of space in schools or hospitals, etc.[5] In these instances, value judgments obviously do not enter the decision-making process to any noticeable degree.

Urban microsystems are only precariously linked to the macrosystem of the total urban environment. But as they become interconnected to form larger subsystems, their relations to the whole change qualitatively as well as quantitatively. Microsystems may by themselves be irrelevant in the urban context and their secondary linkages to the environment therefore disregarded—if they can be traced at all. But the strength of a tenuous link multiplied many times ceases to be negligible.

For subsystems to be related to the total environment, the latter must in turn be conceived as a system. The aggregation and expansion of subsystems does not in the end necessarily add up to a complete macrosystem. Due to the bias inherent in scientific systems building, some important elements will tend to be permanently ignored and remain unconnected, while others will assume an importance out of all proportion to their actual relevance. To avoid this contingency, a conceptual macrosystem must first be established within which subsystems can then be related to each other as well as to a coherent whole.

The Conceptual Macrosystem.   To serve as universe of all possible urban systems, the conceptual macrosystem must meet four basic conditions:

1. All known elements of the urban environment and their attributes must be included.

2. Every possible link between any two elements must be defined.

3. The system must be open, i.e., permit the addition of new elements at any time.

4. The system must be adaptable; i.e., the links between elements must permit rearrangement and redefinition at any time.

In such a system, known facts concerning the urban environment can be fully interrelated and linked to a range of probable and possible facts, thus permitting the building of valid conjectural models. When evaluating potential urban development in terms of environmental pollution, for example, the planner would automatically be able to anticipate alternative results of current medical research on the effects of pollution on human health or to anticipate the perfection of anti-pollution devices. Should such information be linked simultaneously to economic data, the planner could moreover predict the wider implications of any one decision under any number of assumptions. He might even be in a position to relate planning decisions to the eventual effects on the physical and mental health of the people served. Similarly, if noise sources were related to statistical data concerning the known and suspected susceptibility of people to noise, the planner could obviously draw convincing conclusions on the effects of highways and flight paths on people's lives, particularly if both activity patterns and the projected noise distribution were readily available in graphic form.[6]

The assembly of an urban macrosystem, like that of a dictionary or encyclopedia, obviously has to be a long-range project and may involve the collaboration of experts on an international scale. Definitions of elements and the nature of their linkage, initially loose and qualitative only, can then be translated into quantitative terms gradually as hard data become available and the elements expand to form blocks of data in an urban data bank. But even in its early phases of development, the macrosystem can serve two functions: it makes it hard if not impossible to think of any urban phenomenon as isolated fact, and it permits the determination of indirect links between apparently unrelated facts. In addition, the establishment of an urban macrosystem represents part of the first phase of a systems approach whose aim is the gradual improvement of environmental control.

The Systems Approach.   Whenever the systems approach is applied to a problem, a sequential pattern can be discerned which appears to be common to all its applications. It is reasonable to suppose that the same pattern will prove applicable when urban problems are approached with the same method, even if the terminology used in engineering applications may not be entirely suitable.[7] The approach is thus assumed to pass through five distinct phases:

> Systems study
> Systems planning
> Systems formulation
> Design and development
> Feedback analysis

The systems study phase focuses on the formulation of general systems environments which are defined as the set of all objects outside the system, a change in whose attributes affects the system and whose attributes are changed by the behavior of the system.[8] Should a problem thus be of a legal nature, its immediate environments are the legal and political systems. But if the law is in any way related to, for example, the use of urban land, its environment extends obviously also into other parts of the urban macrosystem. Problems might similarly be defined within combinations of philosophical, social, economic, administrative, and educational systems. The systems study phase is thus characterized by the broad investigation of all environmental factors potentially related to the specific field of inquiry; in a sense the bulk of this book may be regarded as an outline for an urban systems study.

In the systems planning phase, interest shifts to specific problems and their possible solutions. To define a problem, relevant elements are isolated and the relations between them and their environment quantified wherever possible. With the problem thus defined, concrete objectives can be selected; this in turn permits the assembly of alternative systems within which these objectives can be met. Of these the system best suited is finally selected following a detailed analysis of all alternatives.

The process then enters the systems formulation phase. The system previously selected is now adapted to existing constraints, such as those of time, cost, and manpower limitations. In the urban context, the role of existing artifacts may be considered in detail at this stage. The system is in other words translated into a detailed plan for action.

These first three phases of the systems approach are essentially interdisciplinary. Even when applied to relatively simple industrial production processes, they may simultaneously involve the management, research, engineering, and sales aspects of a company's operations. And most urban problems are vastly more complex. Once a system is formulated, however, the direction of the process is set, and the remaining detail problems of design and development and of feedback analysis correspond once more to conventional approaches (except to the extent that they in turn lend themselves to the application of the systems approach).

The crucial decisions that affect the process are obviously made in its systems study and systems planning phases. The approach is biased from these early stages on because of the natural tendency, already mentioned, to favor the measurable attributes and relationships of objects when compiling the macrosystem and again when planning the process. Knowingly or not, personal bias will moreover influence the selection of elements, their definition, and their ultimate linkage pattern. A final bias is deliberately introduced when the objectives of the systems approach are stated.

This systems bias can often be safely ignored. For example, in a system designed to determine the best warehouse locations for a distributing firm, the bias is obviously pecuniary, and everybody involved in the creation and use of the system is fully aware of the fact. In large urban systems, however, this clarity of purpose is absent, and safeguards against domination by individual preference must be built into such systems. The means to achieve such control lies in the maximum use of feedback both within and from outside the system, in a manner best explained with the help of an example.

A process determining urban development policy is assumed to be divisible into the following six stages:

Stage A—Population projections and projection of available resources
Stage B—Projection of collective and individual needs
Stage C—Projected distribution of the population in urban space
Stage D—Projected range and distribution of urban activity
Stage E—Projected conflicts
Stage F—Formulation of development policy

It is furthermore assumed that each stage is assigned an equal unit of time, and that immediately after completion of any one operational stage the process is repeated on the basis of revised input. The initial Stage A_1 is thus followed by revision stages $A_2, A_3, A_4, \ldots, A_n$, as well as by the serial stages $B_1, C_1, D_1, E_1,$ and F_1. It follows that stages A_2 and B_1, or in general form $A_n, B_{n-1}, C_{n-2}, \ldots, F_{n-5}$ are concurrent stages of the process.

When this process is presented in graphic form (Figure 81), both internal

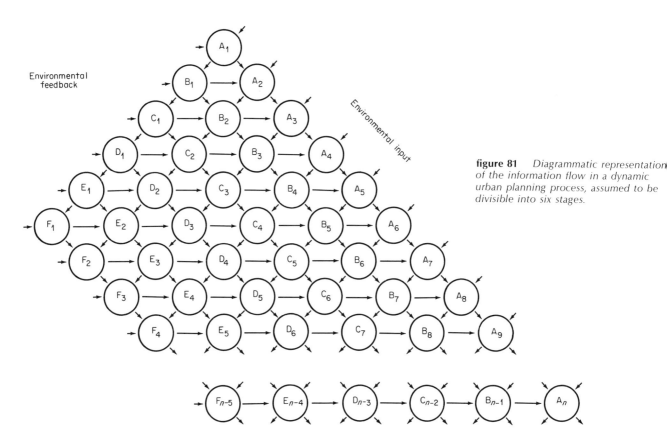

figure 81 *Diagrammatic representation of the information flow in a dynamic urban planning process, assumed to be divisible into six stages.*

and environmental feedback relations can be indicated diagrammatically. The projection of needs, population and activity distributions, and conflicts obviously invites the continuing comparison of facts with theory and permits the correction of the latter before it affects public policy. Internal feedback, similarly, ensures the successive adaptation of the process to social and physical reality.

From System to Form. Urban form is the residue of past decision-making processes. Artifacts being the lasting result of development policy, the processes determining it must be analyzed with particular attention to the stages at which form-determining decisions are introduced. In the case of the process outlined above, the major decisions on future urban form are clearly made in Stage C, when projected needs are interpreted in terms of the probable population distribution in urban space.

By isolating the element denoting this crucial stage and its immediate systems environment (Figure 82), the focus is placed on the basic form-determining forces latent in the process. These are shown to arise out of the needs determined in the immediately preceding stage (B_n), but also from revisions to the previous method of their interpretation (C_{n-1}) and from the experience gained concurrently while applying previous decisions to the next stage, the evaluation of urban activities that result from the assumed population distribution (D_{n-1}). The diagram also indicates the flow of information from the operation under study (C_n) to a simultaneously reviewed needs analysis (B_{n+1}), its subsequent interpretation in spatial terms (C_{n+1}), and of course to the next sequential stage of the process, the projection of activity distribution (D_n).

Evidently, the process outlined admits only a small proportion of the forces that actually determine urban form. The reason for the limitation is that the system as presented is essentially two-dimensional, the parameters being on the one hand the six stages listed and on the other hand their elaboration in time. However, as these diagrams indicate, even a primitive system presents considerable communications problems. The necessary extension of such a process in three and more dimensions, assigning specific roles to, for example, the will to form, is clearly impossible without the help of faster data processing and communications facilities than the unaided human brain can provide.

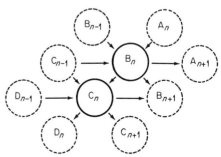

figure 82 *Analysis of the information flow at the stage where the will to form intervenes in the urban planning process.*

THE SCOPE OF COMPUTER APPLICATION

Computer Uses

The Total Problem and Its Solution. In essence, urban development is the concrete result of man's continuing effort to superimpose his concept of reality on the environment. But how can the widely differing personal and collective concepts of individuals and subcommunities be reconciled in a limited and, in fact, shrinking space? In other words, urban development poses a combinatorial problem made exceedingly complex by the vast number of elements involved, their intricate patterns of interdependence, the constant changes both in the elements' attributes and in the nature and degree of their interlinkage, and by the fact that combinations are possible in four dimensions—the three dimensions of space extended by that of time.

There is obviously not one single solution. Rather, solutions are infinite in number and partial by nature, which means that for a limited number of individuals, parts of the urban environment fit their needs and aspirations some of the time. And in an age of abundance the precedence of these needs is anything but clear: the need for roads, public housing projects, shopping centers, and golf courses is ultimately no more essential than that for royal palaces, zoos, and art galleries; preference for one or the other simply reflects a personal or collective bias.

In the absence of compelling reasons for specific policies, the temptation to base urban development decisions on uninformed popular opinion is too often irresistible. The resulting political decisions may prove shortsighted, but as long as planning expertise is only loosely defined and permits, for example, highway planners under certain conditions to make what are in fact social planning decisions, urban planning may be too important to be left to the planners. The alternative is the establishment of a multidisciplinary decision-making process which confines expertise to well-defined areas. The urban macrosystem proposed earlier suggests a framework for such a process: if the relevance of each discipline within the planning profession were clearly defined in relation to specific urban phenomena, then the links between these disciplines would become that much clearer. As a result, every aspect of every step in the planning process would be examined, as a matter of routine, within the total urban systems environment.

Urban problems, at least at the metropolitan scale and beyond, must be recognized generally to be complex beyond individual comprehension. Even if the macrosystem—once it is committed to a computer memory—becomes fully accessible, one difficulty remains: how to quantify important urban relations that cannot be expressed in terms of conventional utilities such as population counts, time intervals, scoring points, monetary units, numerical index figures, etc. In some instances the missing links may be found by measuring urban relations in terms of the information exchanged in urban interaction and possibly even in the information stored in the form content of urban artifacts. The quantitative analysis of this communications aspect of urban systems has again only become possible with the development of computers, and at this stage one can only speculate on the possible course and outcome of research in this field.[9] Nevertheless, there will always be an important value component in every decision-making process that cannot be expressed numerically. And to yield satisfactory results, even the most elaborately devised systems approach to the planning of a living city must allow for political intervention at every step.

Computers and Compartments.   In the absence of an urban macrosystem, subsystems tend to be limited by the boundaries of departmentalized authority and competence. A plan of action that affects the urban environment must thus inevitably be structured in accordance with the hierarchical order of government levels and departments, in accordance with political boundaries, in accordance with the special interests of existing financial, industrial, and marketing organizations, in accordance with existing land-use and traffic patterns, etc. Subsystems must, in other words, fit the status quo.

Under these conditions computers fulfill the encumbered role of an instrument, the use of which permits their operators to direct, control, or simulate automatic processes that might otherwise demand more human attention and consume a great deal more time. But computers are thus severely limited in their functions. They may facilitate and accelerate conventional processes of storing, retrieving, and handling data; simulate alternative uses of traffic facilities, the financial aspects of real estate transfers, or even the interaction of decision makers, etc.; and control some such processes.[10] Ultimately, however, electronic data processing equipment, when used in this manner, elaborates existing methods but does not contribute to the evolution of alternatives. Its only function, in such instances, is to fractionally improve the operations that underlie a basically unsatisfactory urban environment.

The application of computers is always preceded by what is in essence a systems approach to the problem, which involves the quantification of relationships within the system under study. Such relationships naturally tend to be clearly defined within single departments and narrow disciplines, permitting the programming of computers without great difficulty. Interdisciplinary and interdepartmental relationships, by contrast, are more likely to be vague and can thus form effective barriers to systems analysis, and consequently to computer application.

This tendency to systems fragmentation abates when computers cease to be looked upon as incidental tools and are accepted as participants in a joint process which they help to shape.[11] Joint action and the resulting man-machine symbiosis, however, depend on close man-machine communication, made increasingly possible by graphic input and output devices linked to real-time computer processes. The machine's weaknesses when faced with recognition problems or in game playing are in this manner compensated for by man's superiority in these realms, while the human brain's low level of accuracy in routine computations is balanced by the computer's dependability in straightforward computing tasks and in rapid repetitive symbol manipulation.

Once symbiotic man-machine relations are established, however, it becomes impossible to contain knowledge and thought processes in their traditional compartments. Computers can no longer be fitted to the needs of branches of existing organizations, but the whole organizational structure must at this point be adapted to the reality of the electronic age. The electronically extended capabilities of the human brain overflow the traditional containers and channels of information which were tailored to the limitations of man's unaided intellect.

The symbiotic man-machine relationship is represented graphically on this page. The human operator directs the machine's thought processes, guided by continuing feedback information which is based both on computation and on information directly available from a data bank. An expanded data bank, structured to serve as the core of an urban macrosystem, next permits a number of operators to interact. (Figure 83, right.) These might, for example, represent different urban form determinants. Traffic requirements would in this manner be linked via the urban data bank to housing needs, to the demands for municipal services, to capital requirements, etc. In other words, deterministic or stochastic processes built into the macrosystem have superseded the games that may be played between departments and special-interest groups when collective needs are interrelated in their traditional fashion.[12]

The human operators represent in this case the technostructure whose role it is to monitor the input and output of the urban macrosystem. With growing automation, however, the links to other macrosystems and the larger environment will gradually become more clearly defined and permit electronic links to take the place of the human interpretation of input and output data. Dependable weather forecasts might thus conceivably be translated automatically into traffic control and, in the case of storm warnings, into flood control measures; changes in the availability of capital into development policy; variations in population growth into housing policy; imbalance in the use of traffic facilities into changes in land-use policy; etc. At that stage of development (see Figure 83, far right) the technostructure has become largely automated. The remaining human control functions are reduced to their essence: the determination of policy in resolving conflicts between needs and constraints, and the exercise of the will to form.

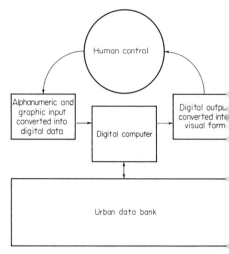

figure 83   *Diagrammatic representation of the potential of a symbiotic man-machine relationship. (Above) Human use of urban data via computer. (Right) The simultaneous access to an expanded urban data bank by different users. (Far right) Environmental control exercised directly on the basis of a computerized data bank with human control limited to essentials.*

Process, Form, and Automation

The Computer's Terms.   Two elements of the urban macrosystem have thus been found not to yield to rational analysis: the resolution of need conflict which invokes moral questions, and the expression of the will to form. These, however, are precisely the factors that ultimately give direction to urban planning and design processes. But while the personal bias remains hidden

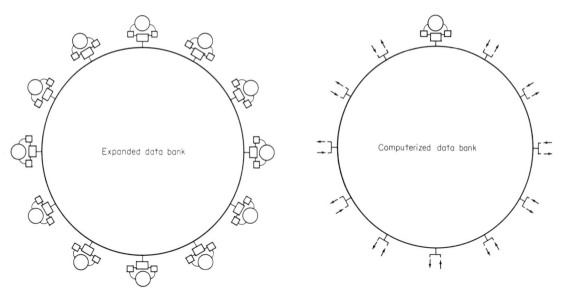

Expanded data bank

Computerized data bank

in the conventional approaches to planning and design, it becomes explicit when the process is automated.

Moral values lend themselves readily to verbal description and can therefore be introduced into logical processes with comparative ease. By contrast, the aesthetic bias is rooted in the psychology of individuals and is totally unrelated to the logical operation performed in a computer. Since, moreover, the urban environment fulfills the essential function of accommodating the expression of man's will to form, the processes that generate urban form can obviously not be purely logical.

One of the human brain's capabilities that is unmatched by the computer is to engage in different but interrelated thought processes simultaneously. Even if it were possible to isolate these processes in their full complexity, they could not be transferred directly into computer terms. Rather, they would have to be dissected and reassembled in a form suitable to the computer. But this would be an attempt to simulate the conventional design process with the help of electronic equipment obviously unequal to the task.

Alternatively, a different process can be developed to yield equivalent results, one which is conceived to fit the electronically extended human brain instead of its extension only. This approach will first of all demand the earlier-mentioned divorce of thought processes from the established association between words and the familiar images and concepts they stand for. Any discussion of the urban environment in terms of single and row houses, apartment and office buildings, hotels and shopping centers, streets and parks, inevitably invokes a mental picture of the city in its present state.

Only when urban design problems are stated as combinatorial problems in which individuals and groups are thought freely distributed in urban space depending on their functional relationships can the imagination break out of its accustomed confinement.

The overall urban form that results from the distribution of people in space and time is obviously dependent on the way in which functional relationships are defined. This becomes clear when the distribution pattern is assumed to represent a mathematical model of the urban environment which permits the optimization of the distribution in relation to a number of different factors. Even when all basic urban needs are assumed to be satisfied, a distribution that is governed by the requirement for maximum immediate return on investment capital would obviously be quite different from one devised to minimize potential conflict within the urban space.

In reality, such general optimizations are neither possible nor particularly desirable. A metropolis is, after all, never designed in one single step; its form evolves over generations from a vast number of minor decisions that are often unrelated. The problem is therefore not to plan and design an urban environment in its entirety. The problem is to plan and design the parts of such an environment—single building complexes, clusters of build-ings, movement systems, communications systems—in such a way that they are mutually compatible in every sense and that this compatibility is not disturbed by subsequent and possibly uneven growth of the component parts.

With this holistic concept in mind it is possible to consider any one project space within the urban environment as isolated from the total fabric so long as its boundaries are clearly defined. This definition must relate the project space to its environment in terms of its ecology, its movement sys-tems, its form and use, etc. The total urban environment, in other words, must be regarded as the systems environment of the project space.

The dominant functional form determinant within such a project space is almost invariably the dynamic distribution of people: the patterns in which individuals and groups position themselves horizontally and vertically at different times and their patterns of movement. Since human needs can be expressed in terms of man's sensory, intellectual, and functional links to an environment consisting of people, plants, inanimate nature, and artifacts, the patterns of this distribution reflect a projection of individual and collec-tive needs into urban space. Not all these links are of equal importance. Most service functions, such as bearing structures and mechanical systems, adapt to urban form rather than determine it. Their roles as form deter-minants are therefore secondary in comparison with the sensory and intel-lectual links that relate man to his environment.

A detailed investigation of these sensory and intellectual linkage patterns must start with an evaluation of the relative positions of all relevant objects in the project space. Thus, the people may be stationary or moving: if stationary, they may be contained in the privacy of intimate space, or they may be contained in an enclosed public space, or they may be out in open space; if moving, they may roam idly in the open, or they may follow predetermined paths—either as pedestrians or in vehicles at varying rates of speed.

This list could obviously be further elaborated. But even as presented, the positions of the people in the project space can be thought of as a hierarchically ordered set of at least ten elements, each of which represents in turn a collection of individuals—some of whom belong in the project space, while others pass through it. These individuals are linked to each other and their environment through their senses and their intellects. In a list of perceptual links (Table 3) the range of value of each is suggested by its possible positive and negative aspects. On this basis it is now possible to establish clear relations between the position of people and objects in and around the project space and the value of the resulting perceptual links. Depending on the number of individuals affected positively or negatively at different times by different conditions, various spatial distributions can thus be evaluated. Passing high-speed traffic will obviously have a negative effect on the senses of smell and hearing, while the same activity may provide visual stimulation and, to the extent that it eases communications, improve direct intellectual links beyond the project space. Similarly, trees and moderate exposure to sunlight will assure positive multisensory links to the environment.

It might appear to be feasible to optimize the population distribution within limited spaces if human response to form could be introduced into the value scale in statistical terms. But to achieve maximum values for the perceptual and, in particular, the visual links, the environment must be consciously shaped—given form both at the public and the personal scale: a task that is complicated by the many constraints inherent in the environ-

TABLE 3   Man's Perceptual Links to the Urban Environment

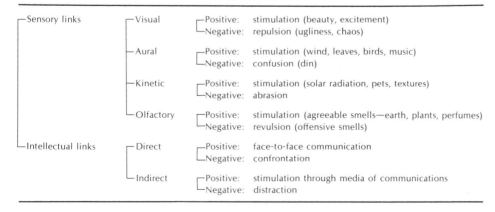

Sensory links	Visual	Positive:	stimulation (beauty, excitement)
		Negative:	repulsion (ugliness, chaos)
	Aural	Positive:	stimulation (wind, leaves, birds, music)
		Negative:	confusion (din)
	Kinetic	Positive:	stimulation (solar radiation, pets, textures)
		Negative:	abrasion
	Olfactory	Positive:	stimulation (agreeable smells—earth, plants, perfumes)
		Negative:	revulsion (offensive smells)
Intellectual links	Direct	Positive:	face-to-face communication
		Negative:	confrontation
	Indirect	Positive:	stimulation through media of communications
		Negative:	distraction

ment. The use of the computer in its present and foreseeable forms helps clarify and thus simplify the form giver's function; but if the machine is ever to take over the task in its entirety, it will have to reach a far higher level of artificial intelligence than the present experiments lead one to expect.[13]

The Automated Design Process.   The pattern of perceptual links, superimposed on the distribution of people in space, establishes the structure of urban form. The purely logical process on which this structure is based must now be integrated with a process of another kind which involves the free exercise of an often irrational will to form. And since this latter process depends on the visualization of spatial relationships, a recognition problem which computers are by their nature poor at solving, it must be planned to permit direct human intervention whenever crucial design decisions are made. To this end the logical and the irrational aspects of urban planning and design processes need to be linked in an element that lends itself to easy manipulation. The link here proposed is the concept of a design unit that can be defined in any way that suits the process.

Such design units are any of the numerous repetitive elements that make up the urban habitat—the multiples that represent the fill of the physical environment. The *soft* parts of cities throughout history have been visually dominated by such repetitive elements. The atrium houses that formed the residential parts of ancient cities, the rows of houses and shops that lined medieval streets, the multistory apartment and office buildings and the suburban bungalows of the modern metropolis: they all represent a repetition of standard elements, the forms of which differ only superficially from each other as they evolve with time and changing tastes. Design units are in essence the same: predesigned elements of urban form, be they whole dwelling units, space modules, structural modules, or conventional building components.

The possible spatial arrangement of these units is limited by combinatorial rules which define the mutual relationships that are possible between the design units and within the project space. But these combinatorial rules are in turn governed by, and are indeed the mathematical equivalents of, the perceptual links desired between the users of the design units and the project space and reflect previous planning decisions on the needs which the particular project should serve. The uses of this approach may become clearer when examined with a view to a specific application, in this case the problem of housing design.[14]

Until prefabrication of large-scale building components becomes a dominant design consideration, the design unit most obviously suited to the application of computers to housing design is the dwelling. The layouts of currently produced housing units fall into very few types, particularly if luxury units are disregarded for the present purpose. As indicated in Table 4, it might thus initially be possible to cover all basic layout requirements

TABLE 4   Minimum Number of Basic Housing Types

	Bachelor	One-bedroom	Two-bedroom	Three-bedroom	Four-bedroom	Five-bedroom
Ground access	1*	1*	1	1	1	1
Stair access			1	1	1	1
Elevator access	1	1	1	1		

*Refers to senior citizen units.

for mixed high-rise and low-rise developments with fourteen housing unit designs.

In addition to meeting the conventional housing design criteria, these units might, for example, possess the following attributes:

1. Their design must permit a maximum number of three-dimensional combinations.

2. Horizontal and vertical connecting links (corridors, staircases, elevator shafts) must be conceived as flexible, three-dimensional movement systems related to the pedestrian traffic pattern in the project space.

3. Car parking spaces should be thought of as separate design units linked to the vehicular movement system.

4. Controlled geometric transformation should permit the variation of specific room dimensions and possibly of angles without prejudice to the above-mentioned criteria.

5. Each of the design units as well as any of the possible combinations have to conform with all relevant code requirements.

With the combinatorial possibilities thus limited, any number of technical aspects of building design could be handled automatically as subroutines. Examples that come to mind are the design of bearing structures and foundations, the design of mechanical and electrical systems, the preparation of specifications, the compilation of lists of materials, the computation of construction costs, etc. The basic computer program governing the automatic design process, however, would contain mainly the following kinds of information: data on all the design units that form part of the program, in sufficient detail to allow the generation of visual displays; instructions on how each can be linked physically to any of the others; the range of possible geometric transformation of each unit; data on the type and number of occupants the units are designed for and their probable needs and preferences; etc.

The combinatorial possibilities would obviously require detailed definition. The criteria that govern the position of design units or any of their combinations may for instance simply limit the distances between buildings and their height or the population density. Alternatively, however, the criteria may be conceived as complex performance specifications requiring, for example, minimum amounts of sun exposure per dwelling unit, minimum privacy for residents, minimum distances from different sources of noise, etc. In recognition of variations in individual preferences, such conditions may be further elaborated by using statistical data in specifying certain percentages of units to have ground level access, or sun exposure, or a view.

There is obviously no limit to the number of variables that could conceivably be introduced into the design process. On the other hand, there is a practical limit to the number of variables a computer can handle, not only in terms of memory capacity and computing ability, but also in terms of cost. The reason why more attention has not been paid to such factors in the discussion is that the speed and capacity of computers are increasing rapidly and continuously while their costs are decreasing. It is thus not unreasonable for the systems study phase of any work on fully automated design programs to stay well ahead of what appears technically and economically feasible at the time.

The introduction of design units into the automated design process has made possible a first direct manifestation of a will to form, at least at the personal scale of the urban environment. Strong and sufficiently varied unit form, outwardly expressed, might even accidentally add up to satisfactory urban form. More likely, however, the ensuing form at the public scale would be trite. The artistic aspects of form, unfortunately, cannot be maximized mathematically. To obtain an optimum urban environment, further human interventions in the automatic process are required.

Architecture as art is basically the result of the manipulation of geometric elements in space which, through a variety of associations, convey sensual and intellectual values. There is no reason why computers cannot be applied as tools to ease such manipulations. Not only can computer output be in the form of graphic displays, but the same display equipment may permit direct input of graphic information. The visual consequences of the machine's logical operations can thus be presented to the human operator for his interpretation in terms of urban form while, inversely, visual input can be introduced for interpretation by the machine in terms of mathematical data.[15] In the field of urban design, graphic input and output equipment is essential to the establishment of a state of man-machine symbiosis.

The input for a specific design process would thus be in graphic form and supplemented by alphanumeric data:

Graphic input might consist of a detailed site plan, the geometric definition of the project space, and the operator's initial basic layout in graphic form.

Supplementary data would define the boundary conditions of the project space, such as obstructions to view, noise sources, sun orientation, climatic information, subsoil information, etc., as well as the number and type of expected occupants of the project space, their specific requirements, etc.

Provided that the input data are not contradictory, the computer could at this point produce a design that would meet all the conditions of program and input data. In the case sketched out, it would presumably satisfy the will to form, expressed both in the selection of the design unit and in their distribution on the site. If not, revised graphic input could generate alternative designs. Moreover, the criteria that govern the combinatorial options were previously defined to guarantee a satisfactory spatial distribution of people, as well as to meet minimum aesthetic and technical standards. Conceptual links between design units and project space have thus, in a sense, been substituted for the direct perceptual links that relate individuals to their environment.

The program outlined can obviously be brought to any desired degree of sophistication. Heating requirements can be related to heat loss for different building orientations and the resulting capital and operating costs evaluated against land and construction costs; maximum densities for any particular site can be determined and related to other requirements such as view, privacy, construction costs, potential revenues, etc. The basic scheduling of construction operations and lists of all materials required can be made part of the output. It would, finally, be a relatively easy task to adapt computers to the compilation of sets of construction drawings and specifications, to the extent that they will still be needed once construction operations are industrialized. But most important of all, any design generated by the process would of necessity meet all the needs considered in the planning of the program.

It should be obvious that the same process described to illustrate the application of computers to housing problems can serve other aspects of urban design. The design units for commercial and industrial space may be conventional modules defined by a geometric grid or complex structural modules designed for multiple infill options; the combinatorial problem remains essentially the same. Nor is there any limit to the possible combinations of different kinds of design units. A simple program may permit only the conventional stacking and lining up of conventional units, but with some ingenuity vastly more complex spatial combinations can be made equally easy to manipulate.

In all these applications, the automatic design process can be represented as shown in the diagram in Figure 84. Its essential features are the close interrelation of the three blocks of data and the corresponding separation of the human functions of design control, policy control, and technical control. This representation of the urban design process clearly reflects the earlier classification of the forces that jointly shape the environment into three sets of determinants, based respectively on individual and collective human needs and on physical constraints. Being relatively static, the latter, organized as an urban data bank, requires gradual elaboration rather than

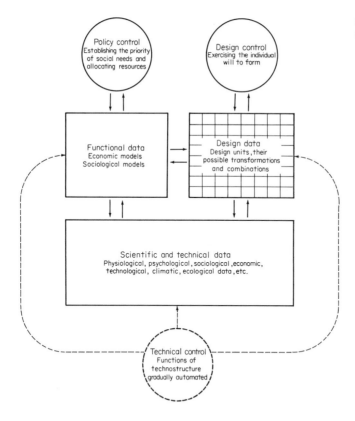

figure 84   *Diagrammatic representation of the automated urban design process.*

change. Needs, by contrast, contain an unchanging constituent component but otherwise fluctuate widely with time. Such change is introduced into the automatic design and control process as policy input in the case of collective needs and as visual input where individual needs are concerned.

The Limits of Design Automation

Beauty and the Brain.   In separating policy from design control, the automation of the urban design process helps clarify the roles of the various disciplines that are involved in shaping the forces which direct urban growth and development. This is of particular significance to the designer who can no longer impose his personal will to form on the environment, as has been his traditional prerogative as architect and master builder. Except for the unique instances where the form-giving function may be deliberately delegated to an exceptionally gifted artist, the exercise of the will to form must clearly be shared by many designers concerned either with the form of components or with that of design units and intimately scaled spaces, or with the shaping of collective form and the creation of public spaces. Moreover, the policy control aspect of the process through which resources are allocated and needs quantified further limits the exercise of the will to form by confronting it with the community's collective needs.

The clarification of the designer's role can help to increase his effectiveness when interventions in the physical environment are planned. In contrast to the conventional situation, the essential requirement for a careful consideration of form at every scale is not only spelled out but built into the decision-making process. The systematic approach to urban design, furthermore, need not only increase the speed and quantity of design decisions, but can be directed toward raising their quality. While the conventional design approach simplifies large-scale problems by reducing urban form to elements that are additive in character—such as identical housing units, identical space modules, identical floors and building blocks—the computer offers the option of modulating the form elements to enrich the total environment.

So far the discussion of the automated design process has concentrated on the creation of group form, which is a collective urban form of a relatively simple order. However, the complexity of computer-generated form may be vastly increased if several form-generating processes are interlinked, either in parallel or in series. Accordingly, group form may be made up of elements which represent in turn a subsidiary group form at a smaller scale. In the case of multiple-housing design, for example, dwelling units obviously can be conceived as design units which are themselves clusters of rooms, and a computer program may interrelate the clustering processes at the two scales simultaneously. Moreover, combinatorial problems involving equivalent classes of form elements may be solved simultaneously if they are related to each other; housing, commercial space, car parking, transportation, and recreational facilities may thus be combined to yield computer-generated megaform.

Needless to say, the resulting integrated design processes are far more complex than the automated design process as it was outlined in its basic form, and the design operator's control function is by no means an easy one. If the architectural quality of a project is to be high, all the details of its ultimate form must be consistent in their appeal to the senses, in the values they communicate, and in the language and the vernacular chosen as medium for such communication. In practical terms, this means that every smallest detail and every combination of details must be considered by the designer in their relations to both overall building form and to urban form. The visualization of these detail aspects, moreover, has to take place at the same rate at which the computer combines the design units. If these conditions are not met, design control is at best partial.

Clearly, no human operator can direct an automated design process simultaneously at the public scales of total form and collective form, and at the private scales of unit form and component form. A considerable portion of the design decisions must obviously be taken out of the operator's immediate control and be delegated to the computer. Urban form then comes to depend on the kinds of decisions that have been delegated to the computer, on the order in which design decisions are made, and on the pattern of their interaction both among each other and with the human decisions that are introduced into the process.

Automated design decisions fit most readily into the functional design process where it is difficult to separate the will to form from functional considerations in any case. The following three stages of the design process are particularly crucial in this regard:

> The selection of building materials and of building techniques to be used
>
> The role of the bearing structure and the mechanical services of buildings
>
> The determination of dimensions and the resulting proportions

The selection of the materials a building is constructed of and the techniques and skills applied in their assembly determine to a large extent its ultimate character and style. A decision in favor of one or other range of materials may thus equally well be an assertion of the will to form or one of the instances in which form is permitted to follow function. However, it is often impossible to distinguish clearly between the two sets of forces. The decision to use concrete throughout the Habitat 67 housing project in Montreal, for example, was based on the fact that no other material would permit the realization of its design concept, which required every housing unit to be a part of the load-bearing system.[16] The use of precast concrete was thus, at least superficially, functional. But a similar building form could have been created using a structural suspension system, in which case the prefabricated housing units would have had to be as light as possible. Metal framing and cladding would in that case have been the functional choice, and the character of the building complex would have been entirely different, even if its shape had remained essentially the same.

The role of the bearing structure as form determinant is illustrated by the same example. Again, the structural concept, and similarly the arrangement of mechanical services, may be organic parts of the total design concept, or they may be superimposed on form on the basis of functional considerations which in practice are mostly those of expediency. The same is finally true of the dimensions of buildings, which may be recognized as an essential aspect of form or left to expediency whether it be disguised as a universal 4-inch grid or manifest in the standard sizes of readily available building components.

Architectural quality depends on a deliberate choice of materials, a deliberate choice of engineering concepts, and a deliberate choice of dimensions which must be a part of the architectural concept that underlies the automated design process. Design units and their orders in space must be defined accordingly. Beyond this, however, additional mathematical tools may be applied to imbue the computer itself with a measure of discrimination in modulating and arranging the design units.

Mathematical considerations have served as form determinants since the very beginnings of civilization.[17] Geometry in particular has consistently played an important part in architectural theory: Euclidean geometry since ancient Greece, perspective techniques since the Renaissance, descriptive geometry and applications of the calculus since the time of the Baroque.[18] The introduction into the design process of the computer and the mathematical concepts underlying its operations thus brings a five-thousand-year-old trend up to date. At the same time, it permits the use of known design routines that are based on simple arithmetic but which have been too cumbersome to be applied to all but a few projects so far.

The outstanding example is Le Corbusier's *Modulor*,[19] which consists of two related series of dimensions, each representing a sequence in a Fibonacci progression. Being based on the measure of the human body, the modular series of dimensions extends this measure, and with it human proportions, into man's larger environment. If, in addition, the notion of human scale were quantified in the manner suggested earlier, and if the *Modulor* series were divided into ranges corresponding to the intimate, personal, and public scales of urban building, the task of proportioning and scaling of urban artifacts could conceivably be delegated to automated design processes.[20]

But scale and proportion refer to the elaboration of form only, and mathematical ordering principles can also be applied to the generation of form itself. Stacking and lining up are, after all, such principles at their most primitive, and a look at the structure of crystals suggests that vastly more complex formal configurations are possible.[21,22] Computer-generated graphical patterns hint at some of the possibilities, particularly where random variables are introduced into the form-generating process. The richness of such patterns gives hope that human idiosyncrasies can be accommodated to a far greater extent in an environment based on computer-generated geometry than has been possible in the eggcrate geometry that pervades existing urban cores. Still, the resulting form is in essence rigid and consistent, and therefore inhuman. The question of how far geometry, and mathematics in general, should be permitted to determine urban form remains unanswered.

Aims and Priorities. The applicability of mathematical thinking to the determination of urban form is ultimately limited by the aims which the urban environment is meant to serve. To the extent that any part of the urban habitat serves a known number of clearly defined functions, the scientific method will obviously yield an acceptable design for it. Out of a population of 100 million people inhabiting an urban region, there will always be thousands who are satisfied with a certain type of dwelling for a certain period of time. A thorough analysis of housing needs might even permit a reduction of the number of such dwelling types to a manageable order, with the result that all urban housing design and production could be rationalized and automated.

But of course, not every individual thus accommodated would be equally contented. The effort to adapt themselves to their home environment would in due course force a considerable number of the population to find compensating conditions outside their dwellings. To provide these, a great variety of amenities would have to be provided: new places to work, to move about, to play, to fight, to love. Some of these would inevitably detract from the value of previously adequate dwellings, resulting in another wave of new demands on the urban environment. The problem, in other words, is solved in one domain only by being transferred to another. The urban environment obviously can never reach a condition of static equilibrium, and no design approach directed toward this end can succeed.

But what if a dynamic balance is sought? Could motivational research predict the degree of dissatisfaction bred by the restriction of housing choice inevitable in an era of rationalized design and industrialized building? More important still may be the question of how many individuals would permit their motives to be manipulated by advertising. The building industry has so far lagged behind the producers of consumer goods in that it has made no concerted attempt to control the demand for its products through artificial stimulation.[23] The success of the advertising industry in other fields suggests, however, that once basic shelter needs are satisfied, the trends of urban development could be rendered predictable to a considerable degree through the deliberate creation of transitory needs.

But consumers may let themselves be led only on paths which they are not adverse to follow in the first place. Human behavior is by definition unpredictable, and for this reason alone the city of man, unlike the animal hive, is beyond the grasp of reason. This insight is echoed in mathematical theory. Thus Goedel's incompleteness theorem states that a system of mathematics that is without internal contradiction must be incomplete, and if it is complete it must be inconsistent.[24] If, however, only limited aspects of the urban environment can be represented in mathematical form, then human intuition is required to connect the resulting subsystems. To remain viable, therefore, the urban habitat depends on the direct involvement of human beings in its evolution.

The application of computers to the living field of urban design points up a danger not readily apparent in the realm of the physical sciences: that complete design automation would be equivalent to a total submission of urban life to the form will of the machine. But if the price of total automation is an environment stripped of all human values, then the boundaries must be drawn beyond which the value of further rationalization of the design process becomes doubtful. Wherever man chooses to exercise his will to form is one such boundary; where he asserts his needs as a human being is another. In a technological era, any such affirmation of human values inevitably defies established trends. But where mechanization is in command, the battle against technology's invasion of the living field may have to be fought with technology's own tools, and rather than attempt to slow the momentum of progress, the most effective defense of human values in the urban habitat may rest on man's ability to apply this very momentum to its own redirection.

REFERENCES

Chapter 1

[1] Lewis Mumford, *Techniques and Civilization*, Harcourt, Brace & World, Harbinger Books, New York, 1963, p. 30.

[2] Ibid.

[3] Lewis Mumford, *The Myth of the Machine*, Harcourt, Brace & World, New York, 1967, p. 189.

[4] Ferdinand Tönnies, *Community & Society*, Harper & Row, Torchbooks, New York, 1963, p. 59.

[5] Arnold J. Toynbee, *A Study of History*, Oxford University Press, London, 1961, vol. XII, p. 281.

[6] Marshall McLuhan, *Understanding Media*, McGraw-Hill, New York, 1964, p. 122.

[7] Harold A. Innes, *The Bias of Communication*, University of Toronto Press, Toronto, 1964, p. 191.

[8] The fact that people living in suburbs may be content with their lot as, for instance, Herbert Gans reports in his book *The Levittowners* means nothing more than that they are not aware of the potentially richer experiences a truly urban environment might offer.

[9] This number was arrived at on the basis of personal observation and found confirmed in Hans Blumenfeld, *The Modern Metropolis*, Paul D. Spreiregen (ed.), M.I.T., Cambridge, Mass., 1967, p. 177.

[10] Mumford, *The Myth of the Machine*, p. 192.

[11] The kinesthetic sense appears to contribute little to man's experience of his urban environment. (See Kevin Lynch, *The Image of the City*, M.I.T., paperback ed., Cambridge, Mass., 1964, pp. 54ff.) One reason for this fact may be the design of the typical North American automobile, which is conceived to isolate driver and passengers from sensing the road.

[12] Marshall McLuhan, *The Gutenberg Galaxy*, University of Toronto Press, Toronto, 1962, p. 3.

[13] Innes, *op. cit.*

[14] Norbert Wiener, *Cybernetics*, M.I.T., paperback ed., Cambridge, Mass., 1965, pp. 95-96.

[15] *Ibid.*, pp. 24ff.

[16] David Riesman, *The Lonely Crowd*, Yale, paperback ed., New Haven, Conn., 1961.

[17] Norbert Wiener, *The Human Use of Human Beings*, Doubleday, Anchor Books, Garden City, N.Y., 1954, p. 57.

Chapter 2

[1] Hans Selye, *The Stress of Life*, McGraw-Hill, New York, 1956, p. 118.

[2] *Ibid.*, p. 209.

[3] Philippe Ariès, *Centuries of Childhood*, Random House, Vintage Books, New York, 1962.

[4] *Ibid.*, p. 398.

[5] *Ibid.*, p. 398.

[6] Susanne Langer, *Philosophical Sketches*, Mentor Books, New York, 1964, p. 101.

[7] *Ibid.*, p. 101.

[8] Margaret Mead, *Continuities in Cultural Evolution*, Yale, New Haven, Conn., 1964.

[9] *Ibid.*, p. 302.

[10] Hans Blumenfeld, *The Modern Metropolis*, Paul D. Spreiregen (ed.), M.I.T., Cambridge, Mass., 1967, p. 42.

[11] Sigfried Giedion, *Mechanization Takes Command*, Oxford University Press, New York, 1948, pp. 46–50.

[12] From Anthony Storr, "Possible Substitutes for War," in J. D. Carthy and F. J. Ebling (eds.), *The Natural History of Aggression*, Academic Press, London, 1964, p. 140.

[13] Henry S. Stone, Jr., "Youth and Motorcycles," in Gyorgy Kepes (ed.), *The Man-made Object*, George Braziller, New York, 1966, pp. 172–191.

[14] Michael Polanyi, *Personal Knowledge*, University of Chicago Press, Chicago, 1958, p. 196.

[15] Morse Peckham, *Man's Rage for Chaos*, Chilton, Philadelphia, 1965.

[16] Hadley Cantril, *The Patterns of Human Concern*, Rutgers, New Brunswick, N.J., 1965, p. 10.

[17] Peckham. *op. cit.*, p. 314.

Chapter 3

[1] Policies of urban dispersal have often been postulated—in recent decades, for example, by Frank Lloyd Wright, *The Living City*, Horizon Press, New York, 1958; and by L. Hilberseimer, *The New Regional Pattern*, Paul Theobald, Chicago, 1949.

[2] Robert K. Merton, "Anomie, Anomia, and Social Interaction," in Marshall B. Clinard (ed.), *Anomie and Deviant Behaviour*, Free Press, New York, 1964, pp. 213–242.

[3] Nathan Glazer and Daniel P. Moynihan, *Beyond the Melting Pot*, M.I.T., Cambridge, Mass., 1963.

[4] An example of a defensive strategy in urban planning is proposed by Jane Jacobs, *The Death and Life of Great American Cities*, Random House, New York, 1961.

[5] For a discussion of the conflict between the aesthetic needs of the community and the economic goals of the technostructure, see John Kenneth Galbraith, *The New Industrial State*, Houghton Mifflin, Boston, 1967, pp. 343–353.

[6] For a detailed discussion of the stages of communications overload, see Richard L. Meier, *A Communications Theory of Urban Growth*, M.I.T., Cambridge, Mass., 1962.

[7] For a report on the situation, see William K. Stevens, "U.S. Running Short of Radio Waves for Urban Communications," *The New York Times*, July 28, 1968, p. 55.

[8] Thomas S. Langner and Stanley T. Michael, *Life Stress and Mental Health*, vol. II of The Midtown Manhattan Study, Free Press, New York, 1963.

[9] David Riesman, *The Lonely Crowd*, Yale, paperback ed., New Haven, Conn., 1961, pp. 11–13.

[10] Le Corbusier recounts in *Une Petite Maison*, Éditions Girsberger, Zürich, 1954, how after the completion of a small house he designed on the shore of Lake Geneva, the municipal council in a neighboring village forbade the erection of a similar *crime de lèse-nature* within its own boundaries.

Chapter 4

[1] William P. Lowry, "The Climate of Cities," *Scientific American*, vol. 217, no. 2, pp. 15–23, August, 1967.

[2] Pockets of this kind are described in detail in Jane Jacobs, *The Death and Life of Great American Cities*, Random House, New York, 1961, and in Herbert J. Gans, *The Urban Villagers: Group and Class in the Life of Italian-Americans*, Free Press, New York, 1962.

[3] L. Srole, T. S. Langner, S. T. Michael, M. K. Opler, and T. A. C. Rennie, *Mental Health in the Metropolis*, vol. I of The Midtown Manhattan Study, McGraw-Hill, 1961, p. 72.

[4] In practice, the value of a site for a potential new use rises substantially above its value established by the capitalization of profits derived from existing use; it then becomes profitable to demolish existing buildings to clear the site for another use.

[5] Le Corbusier, *Oeuvre Complète 1910–1929*, Éditions Girsberger, Zürich, 1937, pp. 109–117.

[6] Hans Blumenfeld, *The Modern Metropolis*, Paul D. Spreiregen (ed.), M.I.T., Cambridge, Mass., 1967, p. 41.

[7] David Riesman, *The Lonely Crowd*, Yale, paperback ed., New Haven, Conn., 1961, pp. 17–19.

[8] Jean Gottmann, *Megalopolis*, M.I.T., paperback ed., Cambridge, Mass., 1964, pp. 217-257.

[9] Charles Abrams, "Squatting and Squatters," *Man's Struggle for Shelter in an Urbanizing World,* M.I.T., Cambridge, Mass., 1964.

[10] Marshall McLuhan, *Understanding Media*, McGraw-Hill, New York, 1964.

[11] John Kenneth Galbraith, *The Underdeveloped Country,* Canadian Broadcasting, Toronto, 1965; see also Abrams, *op. cit.,* pp. 165-168.

[12] Jean Gottmann, "The Rising Demand for Urban Amenities," in Sam Bass Warner, Jr. (ed.), *Planning for a Nation of Cities,* M.I.T., paperback ed., Cambridge, Mass., 1966, pp. 163-178.

[13] Compare "Data Processing in a Bureau Drawer," in Elting E. Morison, *Men, Machines, and Modern Times,* M.I.T., Cambridge, Mass., 1966, pp. 45-66.

[14] Lewis Mumford, *The City in History,* Harcourt, Brace & World, New York, 1961, p. 36.

Chapter 5

[1] For examples, see Bernard Rudofsky, *Architecture without Architects,* Museum of Modern Art, New York, 1964.

[2] Norman O. Brown, *Life against Death,* Wesleyan, Middletown, Conn., 1959, p. 100.

[3] For a more general discussion of sexual aspects of form see Lewis Mumford, *The Myth of the Machine,* Harcourt, Brace & World, New York, 1967; in particular, pp. 139-141.

[4] Reyner Banham, *The New Brutalism,* Reinhold, New York, 1966, pp. 11ff.

[5] James Marston Fitch, *American Building: The Historical Forces That Shaped It,* 2d ed., Houghton Mifflin, Boston, 1966, pp. 207-211.

[6] Brown, *op. cit.,* pp. 15-16.

[7] L. Hilberseimer, *The Nature of Cities,* Paul Theobald, Chicago, 1955, p. 161.

[8] John Ruskin, *Collected Works,* John W. Lovell, New York, 1885, vol. III, p. 16.

[9] Quoted from Mies van der Rohe's Inaugural Address as Director of Architecture at the Armour Institute of Technology in Chicago; see Philip C. Johnson, *Mies van der Rohe,* 2d ed., Museum of Modern Art, New York, 1953, p. 197.

[10] Marshall McLuhan, *Understanding Media,* McGraw-Hill, New York, 1964, p. 45.

[11] In particular the intellectual; compare Morton and Lucia White, *The Intellectual Versus the City,* Mentor Books, New York, 1964, pp. 13-17.

[12] The data presented here are adequate for the purposes of this book; for more detailed information refer to G. M. Wyburn (ed.), *Human Senses and Perception,* University of Toronto Press, Toronto, 1964, pp. 89ff.

[13] Unfortunately, this relation acts in reverse as well; blighted parts of a city and ugly or otherwise repulsive artifacts may combine to dominate the image, resulting in civic shame.

[14] Edmund N. Bacon, *Design of Cities,* Viking, New York, 1967, pp. 240-241.

[15] Kevin Lynch, *The Image of the City,* M.I.T., paperback ed., Cambridge, Mass., 1964.

[16] Hans Blumenfeld, "Scale in Civic Design," *The Modern Metropolis,* Paul D. Spreiregen (ed.), M.I.T., Cambridge, Mass., 1967, pp. 216-234.

[17] Fumihiko Maki, *Investigations in Collective Form,* The School of Architecture, Washington University, St. Louis, Mo., 1964; Fumihiko Maki and Masato Ohtaka, "Some thoughts on Collective Form," in Gyorgy Kepes (ed.), *Structure in Art and in Science,* George Braziller, New York, 1965, pp. 116-127.

[18] Blumenfeld, *op cit.,* p. 222.

[19] *Ibid,* p. 218.

[20] Edward T. Hall, *The Hidden Dimension,* Doubleday, Garden City, N.Y., 1966, pp. 107ff.

[21] Jacques Ellul, "The Artist in the Technological Society," *The Structurist,* no. 6, 1966, pp. 40 and 41.

[22] Maki, *op. cit.*

Chapter 6

[1] Kevin Lynch, *The Image of the City,* M.I.T., paperback ed., Cambridge, Mass., 1964.

[2] *Ibid.,* Appendix A: "Some Reference to Orientation."

[3] John C. Turner, "Dwelling Resources in South America" (special issue), *Architectural Design,* vol. 33, no. 8, August, 1963.

[4] William Mangin, "Squatter Settlements," *Scientific American,* vol. 217, no. 4, October, 1967, pp. 21-29.

[5] Ernst Egli, *Geschichte des Staedtebaues,* 3 vols., Eugen Rentsch Verlag, Zürich, 1959, 1962, and 1967.

[6] Le Corbusier, *Oeuvre Complète 1946-1952,* 2d ed., Éditions Girsberger, Zürich, 1955, pp. 116-161.

[7] Edmund N. Bacon, *Design of Cities,* Viking, New York, 1967, pp. 220-227, 283.

[8] "Islamabad, the New Capital of Pakistan," *Ekistics,* November, 1964, pp. 331-334; Anthony Walmsley, "Planning the Landscape of Pakistan's Capital," *Landscape Architecture,* October, 1965, pp. 18-22.

[9] *The Planning of a New Town,* Greater London Council, London, 1961.

[10] Bacon, *op. cit.,* p. 147.

[11] E. H. Gombrich, *Art and Illusion,* 2d ed., Pantheon, New York, 1961, p. 77.

[12] Hans Blumenfeld, *The Modern Metropolis,* Paul D. Spreiregen (ed.), M.I.T., Cambridge, Mass., 1967, p. 269.

[13] Norman O. Brown, *Life against Death,* Wesleyan, Middletown, Conn., 1959, p. 286.

[14] Compare L. Hilberseimer, *The New Regional Pattern,* Paul Theobald, Chicago, 1949, appropriately subtitled *Industries and Gardens, Workshops and Farms,* for a proposal which would orient a continent-wide urban environment almost entirely toward its place of work. Le Corbusier's *plan voisin* of 1925 and his *cité linéaire industrielle* of 1943 show a similar if less extreme predilection for relating housing directly to the places of work.

[15] Jean Gottmann, "The Rising Demand for Urban Amenities," in Sam Bass Warner, Jr. (ed.), *Planning for a Nation of Cities,* M.I.T., paperback ed., Cambridge, Mass., 1966, pp. 163-178.

[16] For a detailed survey see "Heroic Relics" in *Architectural Design,* December, 1967, pp. 543-564.

[17] For lack of a better term, "idealizing" refers to an architecture that seeks to impose the designer's ideas, rather than only his dreams, on the building users, excluding any deviations or alternatives. Its opposite is a pragmatic approach which results in a use architecture that embraces as many diverse ideas and accommodates as many individual values as possible, i.e., an architecture that invites community-wide involvement.

[18] Lewis Mumford, *The City in History,* Harcourt, Brace & World, New York, 1961, pp. 446-481.

[19] For an inquiry into the workings of bureaucracies, see Elting E. Morison, *Men, Machines, and Modern Times,* M.I.T., Cambridge, Mass., 1966.

[20] Jacques Ellul in *The Technological Society,* Knopf, New York, 1964, pp. 79ff, lists additional characteristics as "technical automatism, self-augmentation, monism, universalism and autonomy." However, these may be considered secondary in the present context.

[21] Sigfried Giedion, *The Eternal Present: The Beginnings of Art,* Pantheon, New York, 1962, p. 81.

[22] Ellul, *op. cit.,* p. 90

[23] Brown, *op. cit.*

[24] R. Buckminster Fuller, *Ideas and Integrities,* Prentice-Hall, Englewood Cliffs, N.J., 1963.

[25] Kenneth E. Boulding, *The Meaning of the 20th Century,* Harper & Row, New York, 1964.

[26] Leonardo Ricci, *Anonymous (20th Century),* George Braziller, New York, 1962.

Chapter 7

[1] *Report of the National Advisory Commission on Civil Disorders,* Dutton, New York, 1968.

[2] In the work of Mumford, Giedion, McLuhan, Ellul, Galbraith, and numerous others.

[3] Joseph R. Passoneau and Richard Wurman, *Metropolitan Atlas: 20 American Cities,* M.I.T., Cambridge, Mass., 1966.

[4] Bertrand de Jouvenel, *Niveau de vie et volume de la consommation,* Bulletin S.E.I.D.E.S., no. 874, Paris, Jan. 10, 1964.

[5] Richard L. Meier, *Science and Economic Development,* M.I.T., paperback ed., Cambridge, Mass., 1966, pp. 130-131.

[6] Thomas E. Howard, "Rapid Excavation," *Scientific American,* vol. 217, no. 5, November, 1967, pp. 74-85.

[7] For a detailed discussion of one such alternative see Harold Kaplan, *Urban Political Systems: Functional Analysis of Metro Toronto,* Columbia, New York, 1967.

[8] Gerald Breese, *Urbanization in Newly Developing Countries,* Prentice-Hall, Englewood Cliffs, N.J., 1966.

[9] Homer Hoyt, *World Urbanization: Expanding Population in a Shrinking World,* Urban Land Institute Technical Bulletin, no. 43, Urban Land Institute, Washington, 1962.

[10] Charles Abrams, "Self-Help, Core Housing, and Installment Construction," *Man's Struggle for Shelter in an Urbanizing World,* M.I.T., Cambridge, Mass., 1964, pp. 164-181.

[11] Sigfried Giedion, "The Nomadic Furniture of the Middle Ages," *Mechanization Takes Command,* Oxford University Press, New York, 1948, pp. 270ff.

[12] Marc A. Fried, "The Role of Work in a Mobile Society," in Sam Bass Warner, Jr. (ed.), *Planning for a Nation of Cities,* M.I.T., paperback ed., Cambridge, Mass., 1966, pp. 81-104.

[13] Where the ownership of considerable parts of urban land is in doubt, as for example in squatter settlements, mobility is necessarily reduced. See Breese, *op. cit.,* pp. 121-122.

[14] Sigfried Giedion, *The Eternal Present: The Beginnings of Architecture,* Pantheon, New York, 1964, pp. 525ff.

[15] Christopher Alexander, in his well-known essay "A City Is Not a Tree" (*Design,* February, 1966, pp. 46-55), has analyzed a number of new town plans, such as that for Columbia, Md., Kenzo Tange's Tokyo Plan, Paolo Soleri's Mesa City, Lucio Costa's plan for Brasilia, and has demonstrated that they are all based essentially on the hierarchical tree principle.

[16] Jerome S. Bruner, J. J. Goodnow, G. A. Austin, *A Study of Thinking,* Wiley, Science Editions, New York, 1965, p. 157.

[17] Louis I. Kahn, "Design with the Automobile: The Animal World," *Canadian Art,* vol. 19, no. 1, January–February, 1962, p. 50.

[18] Le Corbusier, *Oeuvre Complète 1946-1952,* Édition Girsberger, Zürich, 1955, pp. 193-227.

[19] For a detailed presentation of the project, see *Architectural Design,* vol. 33, no. 5, May, 1963, pp. 209-225.

Chapter 8

[1] Jerome S. Bruner, J. J. Goodnow, G. A. Austin, *A Study of Thinking,* Wiley, Science Editions, New York, 1965, p. 7.

[2] Marshall McLuhan, "The Invisible Environment," *The Canadian Architect,* May and June, 1966, pp. 71-74 and 73-76, respectively.

[3] For a brief general introduction to the subject, see Richard Bellman, "Control Theory," *Scientific American,* vol. 211, no. 3, September, 1964, pp. 186-200.

[4] Arthur D. Hall, *A Methodology for Systems Engineering,* Van Nostrand, Princeton, N.J., 1962, p. 60.

[5] It may be significant that of the examples referring to urban problems discussed in P. M. Morse and L. W. Bacon (eds.), *Operations Research for Public Systems,* M.I.T., Cambridge, Mass., 1967, all those both operational and fully tested are of this kind.

[6] Prototypes of computer-based information systems for the storage and manipulation of map-based land data are already operational. Refer to R. F. Tomlinson, "A Geographic Information System for Regional Planning," in G. A. Stewart (ed.), *Land Evaluation,* Macmillan (Australia), 1968, pp. 200-210.

[7] Hall, *op. cit.,* pp. 7-11. Hall refers to the five phases as (1) systems study, (2) exploratory planning, (3) development planning, (4) studies during development, (5) current engineering.

[8] *Ibid.,* p. 61.

[9] Refer to Richard L. Meier, *A Communications Theory of Urban Growth,* M.I.T., Cambridge, Mass., 1962. For a general introduction to information theory and its applications see J. R. Pierce, *Symbols, Signals, and Noise,* Harper & Row, New York, 1961, and the special issue "Information" of *Scientific American,* September, 1966.

[10] A number of examples are discussed in detail in Morse and Bacon (eds.), *op. cit.*

[11] This concept is elaborated in Anthony G. Oettinger, "The Uses of Computers in Science," *Scientific American,* vol. 215, no. 3, September, 1966, pp. 160-172.

[12] Note the importance assigned to gaming simulation in the education of planners; see, for example, Richard L. Meier and Richard D. Duke, "Gaming Simulation for Urban Planning," *Journal of the American Institute of Planners,* vol. 32, January, 1966, pp. 3-17.

[13] For a variety of assessments of the potential of artificial intelligence, refer to Marvin L. Minsky, "Artificial Intelligence," *Scientific American,* vol. 215, no. 3, September, 1966, pp. 246-260; Martin Greenberger (ed.), *Computers and the World of the Future,* M.I.T., Cambridge, Mass., 1962; Mortimer Taube, *Computers and Common Sense,* Columbia, New York, 1961.

[14] Much of the following is based on an earlier study by the author, published in part under the title "The Computer and the Design of Multiple Housing," in *Architecture Canada,* vol. 43, no. 9, September, 1966, pp. 48-54.

[15] For more detailed information refer to Ivan E. Sutherland, "Computer Inputs and Outputs," and to Steven A. Coons, "The Uses of Computers in Technology," in *Scientific American,* vol. 215, no. 3, September, 1966, pp. 112-124 and 176-188, respectively.

[16] August E. Kommendant, "Post Mortem on Habitat," *Progressive Architecture,* March, 1968, pp. 138-147.

[17] Sigfried Giedion, *The Eternal Present: The Beginnings of Architecture,* Pantheon, New York, 1964, pp. 471-492.

[18] Albert Bush-Brown and Imre Halasz, "Notes toward a Basis for Criticism," *Architectural Record,* vol. 126, no. 10, October, 1959, pp. 183-194.

[19] Le Corbusier, *The Modulor,* Faber, London, 1951, and *Modulor 2,* Faber, London, 1958.

[20] Table 2.

[21] Arthur L. Loeb, "The Architecture of Crystals," in Gyorgy Kepes (ed.), *Module, Proportion, Symmetry, Rhythm,* George Braziller, New York, 1966, pp. 38-63.

[22] Stanislaw Ulam, "Patterns of Growth of Figures: Mathematical Aspects," *ibid,* pp. 64-74.

[23] For an explanation of the ways in which advertising is related to planning in industry, see John Kenneth Galbraith, *The New Industrial State,* Houghton Mifflin, Boston, 1967.

[24] Ernest Nagel and James R. Newman, "Goedel's Proof," in James R. Newman (ed.), *The World of Mathematics,* vol. III, Simon & Schuster, New York, 1956, pp. 1668-1695.

BIBLIOGRAPHY

Abrams, Charles: *Man's Struggle for Shelter in an Urbanizing World,* M.I.T., Cambridge, Mass., 1964.
———: "The Uses of Land in Cities," *Scientific American,* vol. 213, no. 3, September, 1965.
 Alexander, Christopher: "A City Is Not a Tree," *Design,* February, 1966.
———: *Notes on the Synthesis of Form,* Harvard, Cambridge, Mass., 1964.
———: "The Theory and Invention of Form," *Architectural Record,* vol. 137, April, 1965.
Appleyard, Donald, Kevin Lynch, and John R. Myer: *The View from the Road,* M.I.T., Cambridge, Mass., 1965.
Ariès, Philippe: *Centuries of Childhood: A Social History of Family Life,* Random House, Vintage Books, New York, 1962.
Arnheim, Rudolf: *The Dynamics of Shape,* complete issue of *Design Quarterly 64,* 1966.
Bacon, Edmund N.: *Design of Cities,* Viking, New York, 1967.
Banham, Reyner: *A Clip-on Architecture,* complete issue of *Design Quarterly 63,* 1965.
———: *The New Brutalism,* Reinhold, New York, 1966.
Banz, George: "The Computer and the Design of Multiple Housing," *Architecture Canada* (Journal of the Royal Architectural Institute of Canada), vol. 43, no. 9, September, 1966.
Bellman, Richard: "Control Theory," *Scientific American,* vol. 211, no. 3, September, 1964.
Bernoulli, Hans: *Die Stadt und ihr Boden,* Verlag für Architektur, Erlenbach-Zürich, 1946; 2d ed., 1949.
Blumenfeld, Hans: *The Modern Metropolis,* Paul D. Spreiregen (ed.), M.I.T., Cambridge, Mass., 1967.
Boissonnade, P.: *Life and Work in Medieval Europe,* Trench, Trubner & Co., London, 1927; Harper & Row, New York, 1964.
Bose, Nirmal Kumar: "Calcutta: A Premature Metropolis," *Scientific American,* vol. 213, no. 3, September, 1965.
Boulding, Kenneth E.: *The Meaning of the 20th Century,* Harper & Row, New York, 1964.
Breese, Gerald: *Urbanization in Newly Developing Countries,* Prentice-Hall, Englewood Cliffs, N.J., 1966.
Brehm, Jack W., and Arthur R. Cohen: *Explorations in Cognitive Dissonance,* Wiley, New York, 1962.
Brown, Norman O.: *Life against Death,* Wesleyan, Middletown, Conn., 1959.
Bruner, Jerome S., J. J. Goodnow, and G. A. Austin: *A Study of Thinking,* Wiley, New York, 1956; Science Editions, 1965.
Buchanen Report: *Traffic in Towns,* H. M. Stationery Office, London, 1963; Penguin (shortened ed.), Baltimore, 1964.

Bush-Brown, Albert, and Imre Halasz: "Notes toward a Basis for Criticism," *Architectural Record*, vol. 126, no. 10, October, 1959.

Cantrill, Hadley: *The Patterns of Human Concern*, Rutgers, New Brunswick, N.J., 1965.

Carthy, J. D., and F. J. Ebling (eds.): *The Natural History of Aggression*, Academic Press, London, 1964.

Carver, Humphrey: *Cities in the Suburbs*, University of Toronto Press, Toronto, 1962.

Clark, Samuel D.: *The Suburban Society*, University of Toronto Press, Toronto, 1966.

Clinard, Marshall B. (ed.): *Anomie and Deviant Behavior*, Free Press, New York, 1964.

Conrads, Ulrich, and Hans G. Sperlich: *Phantastische Architektur*, Verlag Gerd Hatje, Stuttgart, 1960.

Cook, Peter: *Architecture: Action and Plan*, Reinhold, New York, 1967.

Coons, Steven A.: "Computer-aided Design," *Design Quarterly 66/67*, 1966.

————:"The Uses of Computers in Technology," *Scientific American*, vol. 215, no. 3, September, 1966.

Doxiadis Associates: "Islamabad: The New Capital of Pakistan," *Ekistics*, vol. 18, no. 108, November, 1964.

Doxiadis, C. A.: *Urban Renewal and the Future of the American City*, Public Administration Service, Chicago, 1966.

Dubos, René: *Man Adapting*, Yale, New Haven, Conn., 1965.

Dyckman, John W.: "Transportation in Cities," *Scientific American*, vol. 213, no. 3, September, 1965.

Egli, Ernst: *Geschichte des Staedtebaues*, 3 vols., Eugen Rentsch Verlag, Zürich, 1959, 1962, and 1967.

Ellul, Jacques: "The Artist in the Technological Society," *The Structurist*, no. 6, 1966.

————: *The Technological Society*, Knopf, New York, 1964.

Erskine, Ralph: "The Challenge of the High Latitudes," *Journal of the Royal Architectural Institute of Canada*, vol. 41, no. 1, January, 1964.

————: "Community Design for Production, for Publication, or for the People?" *Journal of the Royal Architectural Institute of Canada*, vol. 41, no. l, January, 1964.

Van Ettinger, Jan: *Towards a Habitable World*, Elsevier, Amsterdam, 1960.

Ewald, William R., Jr. (ed.): *Environment for Man*, Indiana University Press, Bloomington, 1967.

Fetter, William A.: "Computer Graphics," *Design Quarterly 66/67*, 1966.

Fitch, James Marston: *American Building: The Historical Forces That Shaped It*, 2d ed., Houghton Mifflin, Boston, 1966.

Fuller, R. Buckminster: *Ideas and Integrities*, Prentice-Hall, Englewood Cliffs, N.J., 1963.

Galbraith, John Kenneth: *The Affluent Society*, Houghton Mifflin, Boston, 1958.

————: *The New Industrial State*, Houghton Mifflin, Boston, 1967.

————: *The Underdeveloped Country*, Canadian Broadcasting Corporation, Toronto, 1965.

Gans, Herbert J.: *The Levittowners*, Pantheon, New York, 1967.

————: *The Urban Villagers: Group and Class in the Life of Italian-Americans*, Free Press, New York, 1962.

————: "Urbanism and Suburbanism as Ways of Life: A Reevaluation of Definitions," in Arnold M. Rose (ed.), *Human Behavior and Social Processes*, Houghton Mifflin, Boston, 1962.

George, Patricia Conway: *Mass Transit: Problem and Promise*, complete issue of *Design Quarterly 71*, 1968.

Giedion, Sigfried: *The Eternal Present: The Beginnings of Architecture*, Pantheon, New York, 1964.

————: *The Eternal Present: The Beginnings of Art*, Pantheon, New York, 1962.

————: *Mechanization Takes Command*, Oxford University Press, New York, 1948.

————: *Time, Space, and Architecture*, 5th ed., Harvard, Cambridge, Mass., 1968.

Ginzberg, Eli (ed.): *Technology and Social Change*, Columbia, New York, 1965.

Glazer, Nathan, and Daniel P. Moynihan: *Beyond the Melting Pot*, M.I.T., Cambridge, Mass., 1963.

Gombrich, E. H.: *Art and Illusion*, 2d ed., Pantheon, New York, 1961.

Gottmann, Jean: *Megalopolis*, Twentieth Century Fund, New York, 1961; M.I.T., paperback ed., 1964.

de Grazia, Sebastian: *Of Time, Work, and Leisure*, Twentieth Century Fund, New York, 1962; Doubleday, Anchor Books, Garden City, N.Y., 1964.

Green, Peter M., and Ruth H. Cheney: "Urban Planning and Urban Revolt: A Case Study," *Progressive Architecture*, January, 1968, pp. 135–156.

Greenberger, Martin (ed.): *Computers and the World of the Future*, M.I.T., Cambridge, Mass., 1962.

Gropius, Walter: *Scope of Total Architecture*, Harper, New York, 1954.

Gutkind, E. A.: *The Twilight of Cities*, Free Press, New York, 1962.

Hall, Arthur D.: *A Methodology for Systems Engineering*, Van Nostrand, Princeton, N.J., 1962.

Hall, Edward T.: *The Hidden Dimension*, Doubleday, Garden City, N.Y., 1966.

————: *The Silent Language*, Doubleday, Garden City, N.Y., 1959; Fawcett, Premier Books, New York, 1966.

Hanlin, Oscar, and John Burchard (eds.): *The Historian and the City*, Harvard, Cambridge, Mass., 1963.

Hilberseimer, L.: *The Nature of Cities*, Paul Theobald, Chicago, 1955.

————: *The New Regional Pattern*, Paul Theobald, Chicago, 1949.

Hoffer, Eric: *The Temper of Our Time*, Harper & Row, New York, 1967.

Höhn, Heinrich (ed.): *Alte Deutsche Städte*, Karl Robert Langewiesche Verlag, Königstein/Ts, 1956.

Hoover, Edgar M.: *The Location of Economic Activity,* McGraw-Hill, 1948; paperback ed., 1963.

Horton, Donald, and R. Richard Wohl: "Mass Communication and Para-Social Interaction," *Psychiatry,* vol. 19, no. 3, August, 1956.

Howard, Thomas E.: "Rapid Excavation," *Scientific American,* vol. 217, no. 5, November, 1967.

Hoyt, Homer: *World Urbanization: Expanding Population in a Shrinking World,* Urban Land Institute Technical Bulletin, no. 43, Urban Land Institute, Washington, 1962.

Huizinga, J.: *The Waning of the Middle Ages,* St. Martin's, 1924; Doubleday, Anchor Books, Garden City, N.Y., 1954.

Huntington, Ellsworth: *Mainsprings of Civilization,* Wiley, New York, 1945; Mentor Books, New York, 1959.

Innes, Harold A.: *The Bias of Communication,* University of Toronto Press, Toronto, 1964.

Jacobs, Jane: *The Death and Life of Great American Cities,* Random House, New York, 1961.

Johnson, Philip C.: *Mies van der Rohe,* Museum of Modern Art, New York, 1947.

de Jouvenel, Bertrand: *The Art of Conjecture,* Basic Books, New York, 1967.

Kahn, Louis I.: "Design with the Automobile: The Animal World," *Canadian Art,* vol. 19, no. 1, January-February, 1962.

————: "Spaces, Order, and Architecture," *Journal of the Royal Architectural Institute of Canada,* vol. 34, no. 10, October, 1957.

Kaplan, Harold: *Urban Political Systems: Functional Analysis of Metro Toronto,* Columbia, New York, 1967.

Kaufmann, Edgar, and Ben Raeburn: *Frank Lloyd Wright: Writings and Buildings,* Horizon Press, 1960.

Kepes, Gyorgy (ed.): Vision & Value Series I: *Education of Vision; Structure in Art and in Science; The Nature and Art of Motion;* George Braziller, New York, 1965. Series II: *The Man-made Object; Sign, Image, Symbol; Module, Proportion, Symmetry, Rhythm;* George Braziller, New York, 1966.

Kommendant, August E.: "Post Mortem on Habitat," *Progressive Architecture,* March, 1968.

Lane, Barbara Miller: *Architecture and Politics in Germany 1918-1945,* Harvard, Cambridge, Mass., 1968.

Langer, Susanne: *Philosophical Sketches,* Johns Hopkins, Baltimore, 1962; Mentor Books, New York, 1964.

Langner, Thomas S., and Stanley T. Michael: *Life Stress and Mental Health,* vol. II of The Midtown Manhattan Study, Free Press, New York, 1963.

Le Corbusier: *Manière de penser l'urbanisme,* Éditions de l'architecture d'aujourd'hui, Paris, 1947.

————: *The Modulor,* Faber, London, 1951.

————: *Modulor 2,* Faber, London, 1958.

————: *Oeuvre complète 1910-1965,* 7 vols. Éditions de l'architecture, Zürich, 1937-1965.

————: *Une petite maison,* Éditions Girsberger, Zürich, 1954.

————: *The Radiant City,* original French ed., 1933; Orion Press, New York, 1964.

————: *Les trois établissements humains,* Éditions Denoël, Paris, 1944.

————: *Vers une architecture,* Éditions Vincent, Fréal & Cie, Paris, 1922; édition revue et augmentée, 1958.

Litz, Karl: "Städtebau in kulturmorphologischer Sicht," *Werk,* July, 1959, pp. 223-228.

Lorenz, Konrad: *On Aggression,* Harcourt, Brace, New York, 1966.

Lowry, William P.: "The Climate of Cities," *Scientific American,* vol. 217, no. 2, August, 1967.

Lynch, Kevin: *The Image of the City,* Harvard, Cambridge, Mass., 1960; M.I.T., paperback ed., Cambridge, Mass., 1964.

Lynes, Russell: *The Domesticated American,* Harper & Row, New York, 1963.

Maki, Fumihiko: *Investigations in Collective Form,* School of Architecture, Washington University, St. Louis, Mo., 1964.

Malinowski, Bronislaw: *A Scientific Theory of Culture,* University of North Carolina Press, Chapel Hill, 1944; Oxford University Press, paperback ed., New York, 1960.

Mangin, William: "Squatter Settlements," *Scientific American,* vol. 217, no. 4, October, 1967.

Manheim, Marvin L.: *Hierarchical Structure: A Model of Design and Planning Processes,* M.I.T., Cambridge, Mass., 1966.

————: "Problem-solving Processes in Planning and Design," *Design Quarterly 66/67,* 1966.

Manuel, Frank E.: *Utopias and Utopian Thought,* Houghton Mifflin, Boston, 1967; Beacon Press, paperback ed., Boston.

McLuhan, Marshall: *The Gutenberg Galaxy,* University of Toronto Press, Toronto, 1962.

————: "Inside the Five Sense Sensorium," *The Canadian Architect,* June, 1961, pp. 49-54.

————: "The Invisible Environment," *The Canadian Architect,* May and June (2 parts), 1966.

————: *Understanding Media,* McGraw-Hill, New York, 1964.

Mead, Margaret: *Continuities in Cultural Evolution,* Yale, New Haven, Conn., 1964.

Meier, Richard L.: *A Communications Theory of Urban Growth,* M.I.T., Cambridge, Mass., 1962.

————: *Science and Economic Development,* M.I.T., Cambridge, Mass., 1956; paperback ed., 1966.

Meier, Richard L., and Richard D. Duke: "Gaming Simulation for Urban Planning," *Journal of the American Institute of Planners,* vol. 32, January, 1966.

Mills, C. Wright: *The Power Elite*, Oxford University Press, New York, 1956; Galaxy Books paperback ed., 1959.

Mills, C. Wright: *Power, Politics and People*, Oxford University Press, New York, 1963.

——: *White Collar*, Oxford University Press, New York, 1951; Galaxy Books paperback ed., 1956.

Minsky, Marvin L.: "Artificial Intelligence," *Scientific American*, vol. 215, no. 3, September, 1966.

Morison, Elting E.: *Men, Machines, and Modern Times*, M.I.T., Cambridge, Mass., 1966.

Morse, P. M., and L. W. Bacon (eds.): *Operations Research for Public Systems*, M.I.T., Cambridge, Mass., 1967.

Mumford, Lewis: *The City in History*, Harcourt, Brace & World, New York, 1961.

——: *The Myth of the Machine*, Harcourt, Brace & World, New York, 1967.

——: *Techniques and Civilization*, Harcourt, Brace & World, New York, 1934; Harbinger Books paperback ed., 1963.

Von Neumann, John: *The Computer and the Brain*, Yale, New Haven, Conn., 1958; paperback ed., 1963.

——: *Theory of Games and Economic Behaviour*, Princeton, Princeton, N.J., 1944; Wiley, Science Editions, New York, 1964.

Neutra, Richard: *Survival through Design*, Oxford University Press, New York, 1954.

Newman, James R. (ed.): *The World of Mathematics*, vols. III and IV, Simon & Schuster, New York, 1956.

Noll, A. Michael: "Computers and the Visual Arts," *Design Quarterly 66/67*, 1966.

Oettinger, Anthony G.: "The Uses of Computers in Science," *Scientific American*, vol. 215, no. 3, September, 1966.

Ortega y Gasset, José: *The Dehumanization of Art*, Princeton, Princeton, N.J., 1948; Doubleday, Anchor Books, Garden City, N.Y., 1956.

Owen, Wilfred: *The Metropolitan Transportation Problem*, Brookings, Washington, 1956.

Passoneau, Joseph R., and Richard Wurman: *Metropolitan Atlas: 20 American Cities*, M.I.T., Cambridge, Mass., 1966.

Peckham, Morse: *Man's Rage for Chaos*, Chilton, Philadelphia, 1965.

Perloff, Harvey S., and Lowdon Wingo, Jr.: *Issues in Urban Economics*, Johns Hopkins, Baltimore, 1968.

Pierce, J. R.: *Symbols, Signals, and Noise*, Harper & Row, New York, 1961.

The Planning of a New Town: Greater London Council, London, 1961.

Polanyi, Michael: *Personal Knowledge*, University of Chicago Press, Chicago, 1958.

Raisbeck, Gordon: *Information Theory*, M.I.T., Cambridge, Mass., 1964.

Rapoport, Amos, and Robert E. Kantor: "Complexity and Ambiguity in Environmental Design," *Journal of the American Institute of Planners*, vol. 33, July, 1967.

Rasmussen, Steen Eiler: *Experiencing Architecture*, Wiley, New York, 1959.

——: *Towns and Buildings*, Harvard, Cambridge, Mass., 1951.

Report of the National Advisory Commission on Civil Disorders: Dutton, New York, 1968.

Reps, John W.: *The Making of Urban America: A History of City Planning in the United States*, Princeton, Princeton, N.J., 1964.

Ricci, Leonardo: *Anonymous (20th Century)*, George Braziller, New York, 1962.

Riesman, David: *Abundance for What?* Doubleday, Garden City, N.Y., 1964.

——: *The Lonely Crowd*, Yale, New Haven, Conn., 1950; paperback ed., 1961.

Rodwin, Lloyd: *The Future Metropolis*, George Braziller, New York, 1961.

Rudofsky, Bernard: *Architecture without Architects*, Museum of Modern Art, New York, 1964.

Santayana, George: *Reason in Art*, vol. 4 of *The Life of Reason*, Collier Books, 1962.

Sekler, Edward F.: "The Visual Environment," in *The Fine Arts and the University*, Macmillan, Toronto, 1965.

Selye, Hans: *The Stress of Life*, McGraw-Hill, New York, 1956.

Sitte, Camillo: *City Planning*, Random House, New York, 1965.

Sjoberg, Gideon: *The Preindustrial City: Past and Present*, Free Press, New York, 1960.

Smailes, Arthur E.: *The Geography of Towns*, Hutchinson, London, 1957.

Smithson, Alison (ed.): *Team 10 Primer 1953–1962*, special issue of *Architectural Design*, vol. 32, no. 12, December, 1962.

Srole, L., T. S. Langner, S. T. Michael, M. K. Opler, and T. A. C. Rennie: *Mental Health in the Metropolis*, vol. I of The Midtown Manhattan Study, McGraw-Hill, 1962.

Storr, Anthony: *Human Aggression*, Atheneum, New York, 1968.

Sutherland, Ivan E.: "Computer Inputs and Outputs," *Scientific American*, vol. 215, no. 3, September, 1966.

Taube, Mortimer: *Computers and Common Sense*, Columbia, New York, 1961.

Theobald, Robert: *The Challenge of Abundance*, Potter, New York, 1961; Mentor Books paperback ed., New York, 1962.

Tomlinson, R. F.: "A Geographic Information System for Regional Planning," in G. A. Stewart (ed.), *Land Evaluation*, Macmillan (Australia), 1968, pp. 200–210.

Tönnies, Ferdinand: *Community and Society*, Harper & Row, Torchbooks, New York, 1963.

Toynbee, Arnold J.: *A Study of History*, 12 vols., Oxford University Press, London, 1934–1961.

Turner, John C.: "Dwelling Resources in South America" (special issue), *Architectural Design,* vol. 33, no. 8, August, 1963.

Tyrwhitt, J., J. L. Sert, E. N. Rogers (eds.): *CIAM 8: The Heart of the City,* Pellegrini & Cudahy, New York, 1952.

Vernon, M. D.: *The Psychology of Perception,* Penguin, Baltimore, 1962.

Wachsman, Konrad: *Wendepunkt im Bauen,* Krausskopf-Verlag, Wiesbaden, 1959.

Walmsley, Anthony: "Planning the Landscape of Pakistan's Capital," *Landscape Architecture,* October, 1965.

Ward, Barbara: *Spaceship Earth,* Columbia, New York, 1966.

Warner, Sam Bass, Jr. (ed.): *Planning for a Nation of Cities,* M.I.T., paperback ed., Cambridge, Mass., 1966.

Weber, Max: *The City,* original German ed., 1921; Free Press, New York, 1958; Collier Books paperback ed., New York, 1962.

Wells, Malcolm B.: "Nowhere to Go but Down," *Progressive Architecture,* February, 1965.

White, Morton and Lucia: *The Intellectual Versus the City,* Joint Center for Urban Studies, Cambridge, Mass., 1962; Mentor Books paperback ed., New York, 1964.

Wiener, Norbert: *Cybernetics,* M.I.T., Cambridge, Mass., 1961; paperback ed., 1965.

———: *The Human Use of Human Beings,* Houghton Mifflin, Boston, 1950; Doubleday, Anchor Books, Garden City, N.Y., 1954.

Wind, Edgar: *Art and Anarchy,* Faber, London, 1963.

Wolfe, Roy: *Transportation and Politics,* Van Nostrand, Princeton, N.J., 1963.

Wright, Frank Lloyd: *The Living City,* Horizon Press, New York, 1958.

Wurster, Catherine Bauer: "Can Cities Compete with Suburbia for Family Living?" *Architectural Record,* vol. 136, December, 1964.

Wyburn, G. M. (ed.): *Human Senses and Perception,* University of Toronto Press, Toronto, 1964.

Zucker, Paul: *Town and Square,* Columbia, New York, 1959.

ILLUSTRATIONS

Sources are credited in parenthesis.

1. Painting of Nürnberg, 1515. (Germanisches Nationalmuseum, Nürnberg.)
2. Cable car from outskirts of Lucerne to nearby Mount Pilatus in Switzerland. (Swiss National Tourist Office.)
3. View of Avila, Spain. (Spanish National Tourist Office, Toronto.)
5. Dinkelsbühl, Germany. (Consulate General of Germany, Toronto. Copyright: German Features.)
6. Photograph courtesy of Witco Chemical Corporation.
7. South side of Gotthard pass in the Swiss Alps. (Swiss National Tourist Office.)
9. View of central Tokyo at night. (Consulate General of Japan, Toronto.)
11. *Landsgemeinde* in session in Glarus, Switzerland. (Swiss National Tourist Office.)
12. Aerial view of New York City. (United States Information Service.)
13. Pedestrian street in Halen near Bern, Switzerland. *Photographer:* Leonardo Bezzola, Baetterkinden.
14. Typical street in Jijona, Spain. (Spanish National Tourist Office, Toronto.)
15. Marina City in Chicago. *Architects:* Bertram Goldberg Associates. *Photographer:* Hedrich-Blessing.
16. City hall and market square in Tübingen, Germany. (Consulate General of Germany, Toronto.)
17. Copyright: George Banz.
18. Yorkville district in Toronto. *Photographer:* Boris Spremo.
19. Habitat 67 housing complex in Montreal. (Central Mortgage and Housing Corporation.)
20. Traditional "shopping center" in Lugano, Switzerland. (Swiss National Tourist Office.)
21. Copyright: George Banz.
22. Part of a theoretical study for a subarctic town by Ralph Erskine. Copyright: Ralph Erskine, Drottnignholm, Sweden.

23. Downtown Lower Manhattan Plan. *Architects and planners:* Wallace, McHarg, Roberts, & Todd. *Architects and planners:* Conklin & Rossant. *Transportation and planning consultants:* Alan M. Voorhees & Associates, Inc. (New York City Planning Commission.)

24. *Photographer:* Peter Christopher, Toronto.

25. View of Dubrovnik, a fashionable resort outwardly little changed since the Middle Ages. (Consulate General of Yugoslavia, Toronto.)

26. Urban renewal in antiquity. From Paul Zucker, *Town and Square,* Columbia, New York, 1959, p. 38.

27. *Photographer:* Boris Spremo, Toronto.

29. Manhattan. *Photographer:* Caru Studios, Inc.

30. William Penn's plan for Philadelphia, 1683.

31. The old town of Lucerne in Switzerland. (Swiss National Tourist Office.)

32. Photograph by courtesy of Honeywell, Inc.

33. Project *Zum Bauhof* in Zürich, Switzerland. *Architect:* Werner Gantenbein. *Photographer:* Hansruedi Jutzi, Zürich.

34. *Architects:* Affleck, Desbarats, Dimakopoulos, Lebensold, Sise.

35. Peabody Terrace—married student housing for Harvard University. *Architects:* Sert, Jackson, and Associates.

36. Zürich, Switzerland. (Swiss National Tourist Office.)

37. Photograph by courtesy of the Hertz Corporation.

38. View of San Juan in Puerto Rico. (Puerto Rico Information Service.)

39. Street in Appenzell, Switzerland. (Swiss National Tourist Office.)

40. Photograph by courtesy of United Nations.

41. Toronto-Dominion Center in Toronto, designed by Mies van der Rohe. *Photographer:* Michael Brook.

42. Apartment buildings in Denmark, based on the Jespersen System of prefabrication and assembly. (A. Jespersen & Son, International A/S. Copyright: Palle Hestbech, Kopenhagen.)

43. *Architects:* Affleck, Desbarats, Dimakopoulos, Lebensold, Sise. *Photographer:* Michael Drummond, Montreal.

44. *Photographer:* Marcel Corbeau, Pierrefonds, Quebec. (Francon Ltée., Montreal.)

45. Photograph by courtesy of the Federal Government Department of Public Printing and Stationery, Ottawa.

46. Charles Theater in Baltimore. *Architect:* John M. Johansen.

47. Housing development *Halen* near Bern, Switzerland. *Photographer:* Albert Winkler, Bern.

48. John Hancock Center in Chicago. *Photographer:* Newmann-Schmidt Studios, Pittsburgh. (Aluminum Company of America.)

49. Photograph by courtesy of the Ontario Department of Highways.

50. Place Ville-Marie in Montreal. *Associated architects:* I. M. Pei & Associates and Affleck, Desbarats, Dimakopoulos, Lebensold, Michaud, Sise.

51. Matthäus Merian, Lübeck in the seventeenth century. (Germanisches Nationalmuseum, Nürnberg.)

52. York Square in Toronto. *Architects:* A. J. Diamond and Barton Myers. *Photographer:* Ian Samson.

53. Whitehall in London seen from Trafalgar Square. (British Travel Association.)

54. Brugge in Belgium; view toward the Belfry. (Consulate General of Belgium in Toronto.)

56. Aerial view of the old part of Bern, Switzerland. (Swiss National Tourist Office, New York.)

57. Viljo Revell and John B. Parkin Associates, Associated Architects and Engineers. (Photographs: (a) Boris Spremo, (b) City of Toronto, (c) Panda Associates.)

58. Society Hill Towers in Philadelphia. (*Architects:* I. M. Pei & Partners.)

59. Habitat 67 in Montreal. (*The New York Times.*)

60. Scarborough College, Toronto. (University of Toronto.)

61. Photograph by courtesy of Harvard University.

62. Olten in Switzerland. (Swiss National Tourist Office.)

63. Marseille in France. (Wilhelm Gail'sche Tonwerke, Giessen.)

64. Peggy's Cove in Nova Scotia. (Nova Scotia Information Service.)

65. Historic buildings in Munich, Germany. (Consulate General of Germany in Toronto. Copyright: German Features.)

66. Place de la Concorde in Paris. *Photographer:* Josette Banz.

67. Champs-Élysées in Paris. (French Government Tourist Office in Montreal.)

68. The Royal Crescent in Bath. (Professor James Acland.)

69. Photograph by courtesy of R. Buckminster Fuller.
70. Alameda Park in Mexico City. (Mexican Government Tourist Department.)
71. Jean Tinguely, *Homage à New York*. (David Gahr, New York.)
72. Proposal for an urban nature conservation project by the architect Malcolm B. Wells.
73. Resort hotel at Borga in northern Sweden, its main roof serving as ski slope. *Architect:* Ralph Erskine.
74. Sea city designed for 30,000 inhabitants. (Pilkington Glass Age Development Committee.)
75. Traditional houseboats near Shanghai in China. Copyright: National Geographic Society.
76. Photograph by courtesy of Rohm & Haas.
77. The Post Office Tower in London. *Photographers:* London News Agency Photos, Ltd. (British Information Services.)
78. Nineteenth-century print. (Dudas Kuypers Rowan, Ltd., Industrial Designers, Toronto.)
79. Photograph by courtesy of Professor James Acland.
80. (a) Drawing by courtesy of the Cumbernauld Development Corporation. (b) Photograph by courtesy of A. D. Margison and Associates, Ltd., Toronto.

INDEX

The superscript number indicates that the name does not appear on that page in the text but may be found in the bibliographical References, by chapter, at the end of the book.

Adaptation energy, 25-26, 48
Advertising, 21, 174
Activity:
  channeling of, 142
  crowding, 26, 66
  density of, 17, 54-55, 142
  distribution of, 158
  integration of, 144-146
  patterns of, 149
  zones of, 151
Africa, 137-138
Agriculture, 65, 70
Alexander, Christopher, 142[15]
Alienation, 18, 96
Analysis:
  cost, 133
  feedback, 156, 157
  of urban interaction, 150
  of urban processes, 154
Anonymity in hive, 41
Anthropology, 22
Architecture:
  as art, 168
  character of, 79
  function of, 53
  idealizing, 123
  interest in, 151
  as medium of communication, 20, 95, 117, 132
  modern, 61, 122

Architecture (*cont.*)
  official, 111
  of total involvement, 40
Ariès, Philippe, 26[3], 28[4,5]
Art:
  as anti-environment, 53, 129
  architecture as, 168
  escape through, 54
  as medium of communication, 20, 95, 117
  need for, 38-40
  symbolic meaning of, 91
Ataxia, communal, 21
Automation:
  abundance through, 63
  of building production, 78
  of design, 78, 170, 174
  of design process, 162-175
  effect on global trends, 119
  effects on communal life, 17
  potential of, 31, 82
  of routine human functions, 12
Autonomy, individual, 141

Bacon, Edmund N., 117[7]
Banham, Reyner, 92[4]
Bath, Crescents of, 122
Behaviour, deviant, 22
Bias of Communications, The, 20
Blumenfeld, Hans, 10[9], 31[10], 69[4], 117

Boulding, Kenneth E., 127
Boundaries:
  communications, 19
  community, 58, 104
  conflict at, 45
  definition of, 35
  of dwellings, 33
  legal, 35
  local, 131, 136
  political, 65, 161
  of private space, 36, 37
  of project space, 164
  of urban space, 13, 49, 96, 100, 140-141
Brasilia, 98, 117
Breese, Gerald, 137
Brown, Norman O., 91, 118, 127
Bruner, Jerome S., 142[16], 151[1]
Bureaucracy, 61, 81, 84, 123-124, 136
Business:
  bureaucracies of, 61, 136
  community, 58
  management, 142
  megamachines of, 150
  (*See also* Central business districts)

Cantrill, Hadley, 38
Capital:
  accumulation of, 84-85
  assets, 123

Capital (*cont.*)
  costs, 169
  investment, 72, 81, 122, 134, 153, 164
  lack of, 137
  requirements, 162
Cars:
  in city, 123
  confinement in, 143
  escape by, 14
  parking, 167, 171
  status display through, 41
Centers:
  of activity, 118
  cultural, 121
  decay of, 130-131, 140-141
  evolution of, 18
  location of, 80
  population, 138
  shopping, 160, 163
  urban, 3, 9, 149
Central business districts:
  decay of, 80
  population densities in, 65
  revitalization of, 123
  subcommunities in, 48
  as urban component, 9
  as urban core, 68
Chandigarh, 117
Chaos:
  rage for, 38
  visual, 41
Chicago, Columbian Exposition in, 92
Choice:
  individual autonomy as, 141
  in optimum environment, 37
  of products, 103
  of residential location, 104
  in urban living, 31
  (*See also* Options)
Cities:
  ancient, 166
  center, 130
  as communications system, 80
  congestion in, 64
  as container, 51
  European, 137
  Greek, 117
  image of, 50, 63, 64, 100
  living, 119
  as mass medium, 117
  medieval, 36, 46, 52, 99, 144
  as megamachine, 18, 40
  modern: communications in, 80
    life in, 149-150
    as metropolitan core, 118
    roots in, 113
    in underdeveloped countries, 138
  at night, 23
  North American: central business district
    in, 80, 123
    financial situation of, 67
    formative period of, 68
    formlessness of, 96
    as model, 137
  opportunities in, 74
  regional, 65

Cities (*cont.*)
  traditional: communications in, 22
    forms, 15, 94, 141
    individual in, 94, 113
    order in, 58
    as public space, 28
    social homogeneity in, 56
    subcommunities in, 10
    as work of art, 53
  walls of, 3, 4, 8, 36, 140-141
  as work of art, 53
Climate:
  control, 6
  effect on land values, 66
  effect on needs, 37
  information on, 131
  modification of, 64
  protection from, 3
  as resource, 80
Clusters:
  of buildings, 164
  evolutionary, 30
  of rooms, 171
  of spaces, 139
  of subcommunities, 56
Codes:
  in automated design process, 167
  as constraints, 58-61
  control through, 22
Cohesion, social, 100
Communications:
  adaptation of process, 11
  channels of, 142, 153
  commercial use of, 132
  control, 21
  electronic, 9, 16-17
  through form, 10
  global, 114, 134, 140
  in homeostatic process, 22
  kinetic, 101
  load, 34
  needs, 26, 35
  network, 56
  overload, 21, 46-48, 133
  patterns of, 33
  problems, 159
  random, 21, 56
  through secondary contacts, 8
  within subcommunities, 19
  techniques of, 15, 23, 119
  withdrawal from, 34
  (*See also* Media of communications)
Communications systems:
  basic, 19
  city as, 80
  design of, 164
  function of mass media in, 56
  self-feeding, 81
  in traditional city, 15
Communities:
  boundaries of, 58, 141
  business, 58
  closed, 8, 14, 113
  and privacy, 32
  pseudovillage, 13
  residential, 140

Communities (*cont.*)
  rifts in, 132
  size of, 10
  stability of, 58
  structure of, 21, 142
  traditional, 8
  village, 12, 87-88
  (*See also* Multicommunities; Subcommunities)
Community, world:
  basis of, 13
  concept of space in, 36
  emerging, 32, 131
  plug-in character of, 17
  values in, 56
Compartments, urban, 23
Component form, 89, 94, 171
Computer(s):
  application to design, 161-175
  control function of, 136, 153
  in problem solving processes, 151, 152
  systems, 123-124
  uses, 160
Computer-aided processes, 146
Conflicts:
  in establishments, 51
  in multicommunities, 49
  need, 43-48, 84, 135, 162
  need for, 61
  of objectives, 154
  potential for, 164
  projection of, 158-159
Constraints:
  artifacts as, 51-53
  conventional wisdom as, 58-61
  in design process, 165
  establishments as, 50-51
  fiscal, 131-132
  as guides, 61
  institutions as, 88
  on movement, 60
  physical, 63, 169
  on population densities, 54
  shifting, 73
  as stabilizers, 56-58
  of tradition, 112
  on urban design, 61
  on urban development, 81, 133-135, 157
Control:
  of automatic processes, 161
  of building process, 74, 75
  centralized, 72
  communal, 22
  of demand, 142
  through design, 23
  environmental: danger of loss of, 84
    in early city, 5-7
    exercise of, 58, 96
    global, 83
    improvement of, 156
    need for, 26
  over form, 81, 103
  functions, human, 162
  over land values, 67
  policy, 170
  systems, 155

Control (*cont.*)
  theory, 153
  traffic, 83, 162
  of urban development, 132
  of urban processes, 144, 154
  (*See also* Design control)
Core, urban:
   activity in, 17
   city as, 118
   as transportation center, 64
Corruption, 130
Crime, 130
Crowding:
  activity, 26, 66
  causing conflict, 44
  escape from, 72
  for security, 5
Culture as medium, 30
Cumbernauld, 146
Cybernetics, urban, 19-23

Data bank, urban, 156, 162, 169
Decay:
  social, 46
  urban, 94-95, 130
Demand:
  control of, 142
  as reflection of needs, 51
  stimulation of, 174
  for stimulation, 44
  transfer of, 104
Densities:
  activity, 17, 54-55, 142
  building, 65-66, 135
  high, 34, 146
  maximum, 169
  population, 54, 65-66, 69-70
Design:
  application of systems approach to, 154
  automation, 170, 174
  complexity of, 136
  concept, 172
  criteria, 167
  housing, 166, 171, 174
  industrial, 103
  invention in, 144
  as realization of dream, 125
  tools, 35
  urban: application of computer to, 174
   constraints on, 61
   problem of, 33
   success or failure of, 122-123
   systems approach to, 171
Design approach, conventional:
  basis of, 23
  failure of, 146
  inadequacy of, 141
  limitations of, 150
  path-place dichotomy in, 143
  simplifications inherent in, 171
  simulation of, 163
Design control, human, 169, 171
Design process:
  automated, 162, 166-173
  control over, 81

Design process (*cont.*)
  as intermediary, 144
  rationalization of, 175
Design units, 166-173
Disease, 48
Distribution:
  of activity, 158
  of information, 16
  pattern, 164
  of people in project space, 165, 169
  of population, 158
  systems, 149-150
Doxiadis, C.A., 11
Drug addiction, 130
Dwelling:
  boundaries of, 33
  as container, 51
  custom-built, 103
  as design unit, 166
  form, 32, 94
  as house or home, 32
  location of, 104
  modern, 139
  optimum, 33
  as place of work, 72-73
  relationship to street, 33
  safety in, 140
  space, 27, 33
  squatter, 74
  as status symbol, 27
  in subcommunities, 58
  traditional: needs satisfied in, 32
   obsolescence of, 120
   standardized form of, 73
  types, 33, 174
  in *unité d'habitation,* 144
  units, 171

Ecology:
  of nature, 65
  urban, 164
Education, 80, 113, 151
Ellul, Jacques, 103, 124[20], 125
Energy:
  adaptation, 25-26, 48
  atomic, 80
  transportation of, 80
Escape:
  blocked, 61
  by car, 14
  from crowding, 72
  from effects of technology, 31
  from tradition, 54
Establishments, 50-51
Europe, 137-138
  medieval, 139
Expressways:
  aesthetics of, 72, 92
  as boundaries, 96
  scale of, 135
  (*See also* Highways)
Evolution:
  cultural, 30, 40
  of urban centers, 18
  of urban habitat, 174
  (*See also* Clusters, evolutionary)

Family:
  extended, 138
  in history, 26
  as institution, 46
  security in, 69
  structure, 27, 32
Feedback:
  analysis, 156
  in automatic design process, 162
  environmental, 19-23
  form-function, 98
  lack of, 132
  process, 153-154
  use of, 158-159
Fitch, James Marston, 92[5]
Food:
  local supplies, 54
  production, 65, 87
Form:
  attitudes to, 98
  closed, 100
  coherence of, 98
  collective: as component, 94
   concept of, 104-109
   evolution of, 118
   scale of, 170-171
  compositional, 101
  continuity of, 104
  definition of, 122
  empty, 53, 112
  fitness of, 92
  monumental, 123
  random, 89
  response to, 165
  specialized, 121
  (*See also* Component form; Group form;
   Megaform; Unit form; Will to form)
Form determinants:
  bearing structure as, 172
  dominant, 118-119, 164
  forces, 92, 159
  interaction of, 150
  systems as, 154, 162
  technology as, 103
Fuller, R. Buckminster, 127
Function:
  of artifacts, 112, 120-121
  form giving, 170
  and form, 88-91, 94, 98
  integrated, 136, 146
  productive, 124
  of urban habitat, 173

Galbraith, John Kenneth, 46[5], 58
Gans, Herbert J., 10[8], 65[2]
Geometry, 116, 173
Germany, Nazi, 111
Ghetto, 35, 48, 138, 141
Giedion, Sigfried, 31, 124
Glazer, Nathan, 46[3]
Goedel's incompleteness theorem, 174
Gombrich, E. H., 117
Great Britain, 146
Gross national product, 131
Group form, 109, 171

Habitat 67 housing project in Montreal, 172
Hall, Edward T., 102
Hamburg, 70
Health:
  of community, 31
  and environment, 144, 156
  mental, 130, 156
Highways:
  as boundaries, 140
  effects of, 156
  and land use, 156
  location of, 64
  potential of, 20
  as public space, 36
  widening, 152
Hilberseimer, L., 44[1], 94, 118[14]
Hive:
  animal, 40
  anonymity in, 41
  as model, 30-31, 144
  trends toward, 124
Hoffer, Eric, 3
Homeostasis:
  organic, 25
  social, 22
Homogeneity:
  of communities, 141
  of populations, 141
Homogenization, social, 44
Hong Kong, 114
Hook, project for new town, 117
Housing:
  design, 81, 166, 171, 174
  developments, 131, 142
  mass produced, 103
  needs, 162, 174
  policy, 162
  public, 121, 123, 160
  production, 73-74, 138
  row, 163
  (See also Dwelling; Shelter)
Housing units, 171, 172
  mobile, 33, 139

Identification:
  with institutions, 46
  with places, 140
Identity:
  expression of, 141
  lack of, 150
  within subcommunities, 8
  of urban environment, 53
Illumination, artificial, 17
Image:
  anti-environmental, 129
  in automated design process, 163
  building, 153
  of cities, 58, 63, 64, 100, 112
  environmental, 101
  historical, 118
  as medium of communications, 125
  of progress, 138
Industrialization of building, 76-79
Industry:
  building, 174

Industry (cont.)
  control processes in, 153
  mobility of, 119
  potential of, 131, 134
  relocation of, 64
  requirements of, 139
Information:
  channels of, 162
  distribution of, 16
  encodement of, 60
  feedback, 153, 162
  in form content of urban artifacts, 160
  inadequacy of environmental, 131
  input, 168
  sensory, transmission of, 12
  storage and retrieval, 61
Innes, Harold A., 9, 20
Institutions:
  as constraints, 88
  dying, 130
  family as, 46
  identification with, 46
  traditional, 51
  urban, 21, 146, 150
Integration:
  forced, 141
  through form, 144-146
  social, 45
Intelligence:
  artificial, 78, 134, 151, 166
  and expertise, 83-84
Intervention:
  through design, 144
  in design process, 166
  in environment, 23, 25, 67, 81-82, 171
  in nature, 51
Involvement:
  architecture of, 40
  in art, 54
  in environment, 18, 44, 96, 100, 112-113
  in mechanized processes, 31
  sense of, 117
  (See also Noninvolvement)
Islamabad, 117
Isolation:
  experience of, 32
  of groups, 28, 56
  of individuals, 28, 34, 37, 56, 69

Jacobs, Jane, 46[4], 65[2]

Kahn, Louis I., 126, 144[17]
Keynes, John Maynard (Lord), 58

Labor, megamachines of, 150
Labor unions, 46, 81, 82
Land:
  allocation of, 138
  competition for, 63-73
  cost of, 169
  needs, 66
  ownership of, 50, 135

Land (cont.)
  as real estate, 63
  surplus, 136
  values, 66-68
Land use:
  agricultural, 70
  constraints on, 131
  effect of need conflicts on, 46
  extractive, 68
  legislation, 60
  patterns of, 135, 161
  policy, 162
  processes of, 153
Landscape:
  artificial, 67
  intimate, 140
  shaping of, 134
Langer, Susanne, 30
Laws, 150, 157
  control through, 22
Le Corbusier, 12, 68, 98, 118[14], 142,
  144-146, 173
Legislation:
  land use, 60
  zoning, 66-67
Leisure, 36, 80, 118, 125
Life-style, 32, 139, 149
Links:
  between communities, 7
  between individuals, 17
  between organizations, 81
  perceptual, 165-166, 169
  between subcommunities, 18, 132
London, 100, 102
London County Council, 92
Lynch, Kevin, 112

McLuhan, Marshall, 9, 18, 20, 23, 27
Macrosystem, urban, 157, 160-162
  concept of, 155-156
Manhattan, 56-58, 65, 69-70, 100
  (See also New York)
Market, traditional, 20, 36
Marseille, 144
Materials:
  building, 73-74, 79, 138, 178
  handling, 76, 82, 133-134
  industrial, 74
  raw, 125
Mathematics, 116
Mead, Margaret, 30
Mechanization, 31, 82, 100, 150, 175
Media of communications:
  access to, 41
  architecture as, 20
  art as, 20, 95
  bias of, 72, 119
  choice of, 171
  determining nature of community, 10
  image as, 126
  mass, 21, 56, 117
  modern, 132, 136
  natural, 153
  suitability of, 133
Megaform, 109, 171

Megalopolis, 9, 100
    image of, 14
Megamachine, 7, 12, 81, 123, 141, 150
    city as, 18, 40
Megastructure:
    organizational, 136
    urban, 33
Melting pot, 55-56
Merchandizing, 76
    (*See also* Advertising)
Merton, Robert K., 44[2]
Metropolis:
    design of, 164
    form of, 94, 100, 114, 123
    lack of unity in, 152, 153
    multiples in, 166
    scale in, 101
    as suburb, 140
    tradition in, 119
    values in, 44
Mies van der Rohe, Ludwig, 95[9]
Migration, global, 119, 139
Miletus, 117
Mobility:
    global, 32, 72, 113, 139
    social, 141
    urban, 9
Model:
    animal hive as, 30, 144
    conjectural, 156
    master plan as, 153
    mathematical, 164
    traditional city as, 137
Modularity, mindless, 76, 134
Modules:
    space, 166, 169, 179
    structural, 166
Modulor, 173
Montreal, 172
Monuments, 41, 91, 125, 152
More, Sir Thomas, 127
Moscow, 114, 117
Movement:
    channeling of, 142
    to city, 114, 138
    constraints on, 60
    encapsuled, 14, 18, 28
    patterns of, 33, 164
    pedestrian, 101, 109, 146
    vehicular, 146
Movement system:
    as amenities, 144
    planning and design of, 164
    in project space, 167
    simultaneous, 100
    urban, 124
    urban habitat as, 143
Moynihan, Daniel P., 46[3]
Multicommunities:
    concept of, 8-10
    conflict in, 49
    limiting size of, 12
    priorities in, 83
    traditional artifacts in, 118
Multiples in urban environment, 165
Mumford, Lewis, 6[1,2], 7, 10, 12, 123

Nature:
    as anti-environment, 53
    as development constraint, 150
    ecology of, 65
    intervention in, 51
    links to, 164
    mastery over, 5-7
    orientation in, 116-117
    relation to private space, 37
    as resource, 7, 80, 124
    as threat, 3-5
    variety of, 129
Needs:
    accumulation of, 49
    basic: as basis for design process, 164
        constancy of, 91
        of constituents, 52
        independent of environment, 111
        at subsistence level, 43-44
    as basis for design process, 169-170
    changing, 144
    conflict of, 43-48, 84, 135
    for conflict, 61
    disregard for, 124
    for high densities, 34
    for orientation and security, 140
    priorities of, 50
    for privacy, 35
    projection of, 158-159
    for stimulation, 38-41
    transitory, 49, 88, 89, 120, 132
    unsatisfied, 131
    (*See also* Communications, needs; Shelter,
        needs; Space, needs)
Neighborhood, 8, 83, 100, 141, 151
Network:
    communications, 56, 136
    electronic, 9
    transportation, 13, 15, 54, 80, 84, 133, 155
New York, 114
    (*See also* Manhattan)
Noise, 48, 131, 156, 168
Noninvolvement:
    spaces of, 36
    strategies of, 54
Nonspace, urban, 28
North America, 137-138
    (*See also* Cities, North American; Suburbs,
        North American)

Obsolescence, urban, 94, 120-123
Office buildings, 50, 68, 81, 123, 138, 143,
    163, 166
Optimization of design, 164
Options:
    in communications, 17
    in multicommunity, 8
    in traditional city, 54
    of withdrawal, 25, 34
    (*See also* Choice)
Order:
    abstract, 116-117
    hierarchical, 142, 161
    organic, 58, 116-117
    visual, 56-58

Organizations:
    of building interiors, 143
    existing, 162
    functional, 142
    interaction of, 150
Orientation:
    building, 169
    toward centers, 64
    global, 138
    need for, 140
    process of, 153
    in space, 112-118
    in time, 114-118

Paris, 68, 114, 117, 122
    boulevards of, 102
    18th-century, 100
Patterns:
    of activity, 149
    circulation, 153
    of communications, 33
    distribution, 164
    geometric, 117, 173
    of human relations, 55
    land use, 135, 142
    linkage, 157, 164
    of movement, 33, 164
    of social life, 138-139
    of subcommunities, 113
    traffic, 142, 161, 167
    visual, in environment, 153
Peckham, Morse, 38[14], 40
Pedestrian:
    neglect of, 123
    movement, 101, 109, 146
    in project space, 165
    traffic, 167
Penn, William, 56
Perception:
    of form, 101
    of reality, 151
    of space, 14, 35
Philadelphia, 58
Place:
    confinement in, 104
    meeting, 31
    roots in, 113
    sense of, 118, 140
    in territory, 138-139
Place Vendôme, 122
Planning:
    control over, 81
    and design, 144
    expertise, 160-161
    as expression of will to form, 125
    process, 162-172
    scale of, 135-136
Planning approach, conventional:
    basis of, 23
    consequence of, 70
    constraints of, 152
    inadequacy of, 138, 141, 142
    limitations of, 150
    path-place dichotomy in, 143
Plato, 127

Polanyi, Michael, 38[14]
Police, 21
Pollution:
    air, 83, 131
    environmental, 124, 130, 156
    water, 131
Population:
    counts, 160
    density, 54, 65-66, 69-70, 135
    explosion, 69
    fragmentation of, 144
    growth, 124, 132, 138, 150, 162
    homogeneous, 131
    mobility of, 139
    pressures, 55, 136
    projections, 158-159
Power elite, 58
Power structure, 9
Prefabrication of building components, 79,
    82, 139, 166
Priorities of needs, 50
Privacy:
    design for, 26
    in medieval cities, 36
    in modern cities, 37
    need for, 35
    as option, 34
    within project space, 168-169
    in traditional cities, 22, 28
Process, social delamination, 132
Project space, 164-169
Proportions, 172, 173
Pseudovillages, community, 13

Quality, architectural, 172

Real estate:
    investments, 72, 132
    profit, 83
    transfers, 161
    value of, 63
Regions:
    economic growth of, 118
    interlinked, 54
    merging of, 114
    metropolitan cores in, 44
    shelter needs in, 174
Renewal, urban, 52, 74, 131
Research, motivational, 174
Resources:
    allocation of, 170
    availability of, 154
    capital, 134
    extraction of, 7, 124
    lack of, 84
    natural, 80
    waste of, 65, 134
Ricci, Leonardo, 127
Riesman, David, 18, 22, 26, 55
Rio de Janeiro, 114
Rome, Imperial, 117
Ruskin, John, 95
Russia, Stalinist, 111

Scale:
    of capsule, 14
    extrahuman, 101
    global, 6, 14
    hierarchy of, 112
    human, 94, 96, 102, 103, 173
    intimate, 102, 140, 173
    mega-, 99, 102
    personal, 101, 165, 168, 173
    public, 102, 165, 171, 173
    of urban development, 136
Science:
    engineering, 134
    life, 124
Security:
    individual, 36-37, 69
    job, 81
    need for, 140-141
    of traditions, 53
Selye, Hans, 25
Services, municipal, 138, 162
Shelter:
    basic, 25, 138
    needs, 25-35, 162, 174
    optimum, 31-37
    traditional urban, 73
    (See also Dwelling; Housing)
Slums, 10, 23, 65, 113
    clearance, 135
    scale of, 102
Sociology, 22
South America, 117, 137-138
Space:
    communal, 36
    competition for, 146
    continuity of, 109
    dwelling, 27
    fragmented, 22
    global, 14-16
    hierarchy of, 35-36
    needs, 35-41, 44
    neutral, 34
    orientation on, 112, 114-118
    perception of, 14, 23, 35, 116-117
    private: clusters of, 139
        containment in, 165
        extended, 36
        integrated with public space, 136
        replacing public space, 48
        in residential subdivisions, 28
        security in, 36-37
    public: containment in, 170
        creation of, 170
        formation of, 28
        as related to private space, 35-36, 48,
            136
    social, 13
    subdivision of, 35, 141
    (See also Nonspace, urban; Project space)
Specialization:
    of form and function, 121-123
    of individual function, 88
    of knowledge, 127
    of skills, 73
Sports, 37
Sprawl, urban, 119

Square:
    communications function of, 15, 20
    as public space, 36
    Renaissance, scale of, 102
Squatter dwellings, 74
Squatter settlements, 117
Stability:
    of communities, 58
    experience of, 32
    of subcommunities, 22, 55
Stabilizers, social, 56-58
Standard of living, 69, 81, 85, 131, 136, 149
Standardization of building components,
    76-78
Statistics, social, 22
Status:
    in community, 40-41
    display, 27, 41
    effect on perception, 100
Status quo, 56, 161
Stimulation:
    of demand, 174
    need for, 38-41, 44
    sensory, 36, 109
    visual, 165
Stockholm, 114
Storr, Anthony, 31[12]
Stratification, social, 44
Street(s):
    functions, 11, 15, 28
    life in, 18
    medieval, 7, 36, 166
    as part of urban habitat, 33, 163
    as public space, 36
    suburban, 104
    system, 123, 143
    width, 83, 150
Stress of life, 25, 48-49
Structures, multiple-use, 73, 136
Subcommunities:
    boundaries of, 35
    closed, 48
    communications within, 19
    concept of, 8-13
    identity within, 8
    interaction of, 16, 31, 58
    interrelationship between, 50, 141
    needs of, 130-131
    postliterate, 113
    roots of, 112
    social function of, 46
    special interests of, 28, 160
    stability of, 22, 55
    in underdeveloped countries, 138
    in urban space, 27-28
    values in, 53, 63
Subdivision:
    residential, 28, 48
    of urban space, 35, 141
Subsystems, urban, 22, 84, 154, 155, 161, 174
Suburbs, 44, 65
    metropolis as, 140
    North American, 117
Subways:
    orientation of, 64
    potential of, 20

Symbiosis, man-machine, 161–162, 168
Symbol:
    dwelling as, 32
    manipulation by computer, 161
    status, 27
    urban form as, 141
Symbolism of form, 95, 111–113
Systems:
    bias, 155, 157
    control, 155
    definition of, 154
    environment, 156, 164
    formulation phase, 156, 157
    fragmentation, 160
    hierarchy of, 154–155
    planning phase, 156, 157
    study phase, 156–157, 168
    urban micro-, 155
    (*See also* Communications systems;
        Macrosystem, urban; Movement
        system; Subsystems, urban)
Systems approach, 154–159, 161

Taste, ruling, 50
Taxation policies, 132, 136
Techniques:
    building, 121, 134, 172
    of communication, 15, 23, 119
    control, 153
    management, 134, 136
    measuring, 131–132
    of transportation, 15, 119
Technology:
    basis of, 13
    battle against, 175
    boundaries created by, 139–140
    characteristics of, 124–125
    constraints of, 103, 151
    electronic, 61, 127, 132
    lack of direction of, 23
    and obsolescence, 120
    potential of, 134
    side effects of, 26
    values of, 130
    withdrawal from, 31
Territory, 22, 138–139, 141
Theory:
    aesthetic, 120
    architectural, 173
    control, 153
    need for, 142

Time:
    distribution in, 164
    orientation in, 114–118
Tönnies, Ferdinand, 7[4]
Topography, urban, 66
Toronto, 70
Toynbee, Arnold J., 8
Tradition:
    as basis for control, 22, 153
    constraints of, 112, 138
    in dwelling construction, 87
    intellectual, 117
    in metropolis, 119
    overlay of, 114
    role of, 53–56
Traffic:
    automotive, 48, 53, 120, 153, 155
    flow, 151
    high-speed, 165
    in office building, 123
    patterns, 142, 161, 167
    pedestrian, 167
    volume of, 154
Transportation:
    air, 100
    by car, 14
    effects on production, 79
    facilities, 171
    land needs of, 66
    network, 54, 80, 84
    problem, 139
    system, 13, 20, 64, 65, 133, 154
    techniques of, 15, 119
    underground, 133
Trends:
    determination of, 142
    extrapolation of, 69–70
    of urban development, 119–125

Unions (see Labor unions)
Unit form, 102–104, 171
Urbanization:
    global, 69, 151
    process of, 36
    subsistence, 137
Utopia, 128–129

Value(s):
    in architecture, 168, 171
    bias, 48–50, 60, 63, 95

Value(s) (*cont.*)
    collective, 112, 130–132
    communal, 22, 56, 72, 83, 124, 140
    and form, 8, 88
    human, 175
    imposed, 123
    judgements, 120, 155, 160
    in metropolis, 44, 114
    and order, 58
    of perceptual links, 165
    of real estate, 63, 66–68
    social, 45
    in subcommunities, 53
    systems of, 83
    traditional, 53
    use, 119, 135
Venice, 117
Villages:
    agricultural, 7, 87
    communications within, 19
    community, 12, 88
    roots in, 113
    size of, 10
    (*See also* Pseudovillages)

Washington, D.C., 111
Wiener, Norbert, 21, 23
Will to form:
    in automated design process, 162–175
    expression of, 104
    as expression of basic drives, 91
    in feedback relationship, 96
    in planning, 125
    in systems approach, 159
    as will to dominate, 111
Withdrawal, individual:
    effect of, 34
    in face of technology, 31
    opportunity for, 17, 22
Work:
    as escape, 54
    hours of, 17, 21, 65, 74, 119, 142
    places of, 58, 72–73, 118, 142, 174
    value of, 130
Wright, Frank Lloyd, 44[1]

Zoning legislation, 66–67
Zoning practices, 72–73
Zoning regulations, 35
Zurich, 114